MW00996022

HOMEOWNER'S MANUAL

ADVICE ON MAINTAINING YOUR HOME
FROM TOM SILVA, RICHARD TRETHEWEY, AND STEVE THOMAS

FOREWORD

<< After working with Richard, Tom, and Steve all these years at *This Old House*, I can say that what you see on the show is only a fraction of their knowledge and common sense. In house after house, I've seen Tom and Richard solve problems that would stump less experienced craftsmen. Both of them apprenticed with their fathers, as I did, which gives them a house sense that's quite rare these days. In fact, I'd almost bet that Richard was born with a wrench in his hand, and Tom with a hammer. Steve, as the show's host, brings another perspective to this book: the sensibility of the homeowner. While Tom and Richard focus on the fine technical details of building and maintaining houses, Steve reminds us that by taking care of a house, we create a safe and comfortable home. I think you'll see in this book what I've seen in the guys behind it. It will let you look over their shoulders and soak up some of the wisdom they've accumulated while solving the repair and maintenance problems we all face. >> — NORM ABRAM

CONTENTS

INTRODUCTION

MANY OF YOU KNOW US—AFTER ALL, YOU'VE BEEN INVITING *This Old House* into your homes for over 20 years. But we also know you. All three of us travel frequently to home shows and other events, and when you aim your house questions our way, we learn what especially interests you. This book is our way of answering the most common questions we receive, for all the homeowners we haven't yet met. This isn't an encyclopedia of home repair, however. Instead, we wanted to explain how to handle the problems that can affect almost any house, regardless of its style or size. We imagined the book as a primer, a basic guide: an owner's manual. In fact, if a house had a glove compartment, we wanted this to be the book you'd expect to find inside. *** On *This Old House* projects we work on other people's houses. But we're also homeowners, and we face the same maintenance chores you do. (If you think that our gutters stay clean just because we're on television, you haven't faced New England leaves.) In many of the following pages you'll see us working on our own homes, sometimes doing things for ourselves that another professional would do on the show. But we're doing that to emphasize one very important concept: You don't have to be an electrician to replace a dead light switch, you don't have to call the plumber every time a sink backs up, and you don't have to hire a carpenter to fix a sticking door. *** Stewardship is the concept we try hardest to encourage at *This Old House*. When you care enough about a house to maintain it, you join with others who cared for it before and prepare the way for those who will come after. We hope this book will give you enough information and encouragement to care for your house, new or old, and to enjoy the sense of well-being that a well-maintained house affords.
— STEVE THOMAS, RICHARD TRETHEWEY, AND TOM SILVA

section

1

maximizing your home investment

financial considerations / defending your home / safety and security / working with contractors / the homeowner's toolbox / making your home user-friendly / the efficient home

chapter 1

FINANCIAL CONSIDERATIONS

For most people, a home ranks as the single greatest expense they'll ever face. Yet it may also be the most exasperating object they'll ever own. "Our homes are susceptible to so many problems, from water damage to insects, that they sometimes make even the riskiest stock investment seem safe," says Steve. But it's possible to take control of maintenance and repair issues and end up with a house that's not only a sound investment, but also a deeply satisfying place to call home. That combination is just about perfect.

A decade or so ago, people often looked at houses not only as places to raise a family, but also as lucrative investment vehicles capable of generating considerable short-term financial gain. A house would be purchased with the goal of selling it in a year or two, in hopes of trading up to something bigger and possibly even repeating the process. It's a strategy that's often successful in super-heated real estate markets, but sooner or later the market cools. And as many have discovered, the perils of buying near the top of the market are considerable.

"Fortunately we're moving away from that particular cycle toward longer commitments to the same house," Richard explains, which he believes is for the best. A house, after all, is a symbol of the family and a part of the neighborhood, and allows for a singular form of individual expression. "People should look at a home as a work in progress, a canvas," says Richard, "rather than simply as an investment. Through our homes, we show the world what's important to us."

But whether you live in a new house or an old one, the house of your dreams or just a house for the next few years, there are plenty of improvements that can be made. "Everybody has some change they want to make—be it a coat of paint or a brand-new kitchen or a bedroom wing. That's what makes owning a house so much fun," says Steve. "But most people will not be able to do them all at once, the way we do on *This Old House*. Instead, changes may have to be phased in over the years as budget and patience allow."

Before being swept away by the romance of renovating a house, open your eyes. "Take a look at what the house costs, and what the improved version of your house would bring in the neighborhood—and let that guide you in how much you spend on improvements," Steve advises. "It's unwise to overspend, even if you think you'll never want to move." Take a look at the neighborhood itself as well: Just about anything is possible when it comes to improving a house, but no amount of remodeling will change the neighborhood. If the surrounding area makes you unhappy, you'll be just as unhappy after remodeling your house.

> « People should look at a home as a work in progress, a canvas. Through our homes, we show the world what's important to us. » —RICHARD TRETHEWEY

And if your plans include something not found in your neighborhood—an indoor swimming pool, say, or a huge master suite—"then maybe it's time to reevaluate your plan and search for a neighborhood suitable for that level of spending," adds Steve.

Whatever you decide about remodeling, remember that you'll have to maintain the house as well as improve it. "People can figure out and budget for their monthly expenses in terms of electricity and water, but they rarely seem to set aside money for routine maintenance," notes Tom.

Furnaces and boilers should be tuned up regularly (see p. 110), houses should be repainted every 5 to 10 years, and water heaters require replacement every decade or so. The life of an asphalt-shingle roof varies with its exposure. "I've seen them go 25 years before needing replacement, but I've also seen them fail as early as 15 years," says Tom. Neglecting repairs can jeopardize the value of a home. "People should spend money on projects that allow them to live in the house economically and comfortably, and that includes things like good insulation, windows that work, and tight weatherstripping," says Tom. "These things will go farther toward your comfort than will luxuries like granite countertops and walnut cabinets."

When homeowners go to Tom with their plans, they often have bigger dreams than they can afford and end up looking for ways to reduce the cost. "I look at their proposal and give them a price for the job the way it reads on their plans," says Tom. "But I also figure a second estimate to do the job the way I think it should be built—which might mean making portions of the structure sturdier. I always recommend the best insulation and the best heating and cooling systems available. You'll be miserable in the long run if the floors bounce, the windows don't work right, and the heating system is noisy," says Tom. "Instead, spend your money on these things and save the decorative upgrades for later."

Another place not to scrimp is at the hardware store. "No matter what you're buying—from a wrench to a light switch—you'll find it in basic, better, and best quality," says Richard. "And beware of 'basic,' because the entry-level products in the market are usually poor." A contractor buying in bulk might benefit from the savings of using the cheapest light switch, but there's no such advantage to a homeowner who buys a few and has to replace them again in a few years. "You should get the 'better' or 'best' things in all cases," advises Richard, "because the purchase cost is just a fraction of the installation cost."

Whether it's a renovation or a large repair project, prepare for cost overruns of at least 20 percent—and budget it into your plans. "So if you have $50,000 to spend, see if you can get your project done for $40,000," says Tom. "Then you'll have a cushion of $10,000 when you want to add that skylight in the bedroom, or when the contractor discovers that all your sills are rotten." With a 20 percent safety net, "you'll be immune to surprises, and much, much happier for it."

« **Everyone has some** change they want to make. But changes may have to be phased in over the years as budget and patience allow. » —STEVE THOMAS

keeping records

WHAT TO KEEP	DESCRIPTION	NOTES	LOCATION
MATERIAL SAMPLES	Products used in the home, such as tile, vinyl flooring, carpet; also roof shingles and short lengths of vinyl siding.	This is the only way to ensure a perfect match when repairs are required. Also, samples are helpful when color-coordinating subsequent products.	Cardboard box in attic or basement.
KEYS	Spare keys to door locks and deadbolts (also padlocks, luggage, cars, etc.).	Everyone loses keys.	Small metal or plastic box in a part of the house guests don't visit.
MANUALS	Instruction manuals that come with tools, appliances, fans, etc. As a matter of habit, keep every manual you receive.	Manuals offer invaluable information on maintenance, operation, safety, and the location of parts suppliers. Write the date of purchase on the manual to aid in making warranty claims or ordering parts.	In a file cabinet or a large pocket folder.
EMERGENCY CONTACTS	The business card, including emergency phone number, for a plumber, an electrician, a general contractor, and your insurance agent (also poison control and the family doctors).	These should be people who have proven their skill and trustworthiness in prior dealings with you. When disaster strikes, you won't have time to interview a stranger.	On the refrigerator door, on a bulletin board near the phone, or on the inside of a kitchen cabinet door.
PLANS	Original plans for the house, if available. Plans from any remodeling work. Sketches showing the location of septic tank, oil tank filler tube, and well.	Plans identify structural features contractors might need to know about. They make it easy to figure the square footage for painting, floor covering, even air-conditioning estimates.	In a mailing tube to prevent damage.
INSURANCE RECORDS	Homeowner's policy, including updates and coverage change notices. Title insurance policy. Inspection records. Make a yearly voice-annotated videotape of house exterior and every room, including closets; it's the best way to document the condition of the house and its contents.	Because disaster can strike anytime.	Keep tape in safe-deposit box; keep paper records in fire- and water-resistant box at home for easy access.
TAX RECORDS	Mortgage/interest payments; property tax records; utility and maintenance costs (for home office deduction); home improvement receipts (see below). Property purchase records, including closing costs.	Needed for tax returns.	File folder.
HOME IMPROVEMENT RECEIPTS	Receipts for new siding, paint/wallpaper/tile/carpet, additions, major appliances, new furnace, permanently installed cabinets...anything that is permanently attached to the house.	Crucial for figuring tax deductions on sale of house; also good for comparing original costs to replacement costs, and documenting warranty claims.	In readily accessible folders or envelopes, organized by year.

Keeping records goes with owning a house, but that entails more than saving receipts. Some suggestions for what to save and how to save it are found here, but use the chart as a guideline only: Whatever record-keeping system works for you is the best one to use.

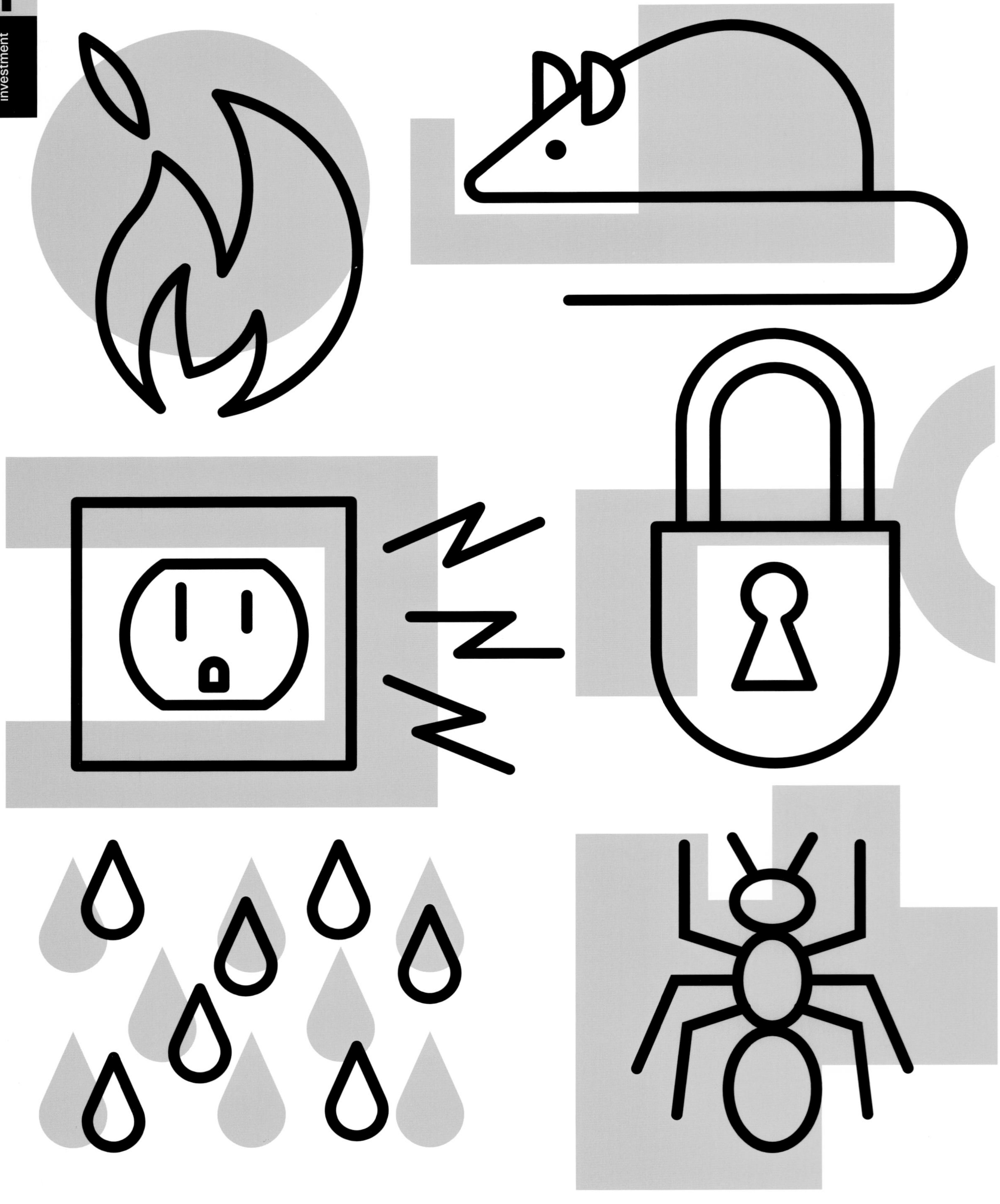

DEFENDING YOUR HOME

A house is part of the environment, and as such is besieged by everything from mildew and mold to termites and carpenter ants. "One of the worst things I ever saw happen to a house was an invasion by a single squirrel," Tom says. Entering through the attic, it somehow found its way into the living area when no one was home, and then vainly tried to get out by tearing and gnawing at every window it could find. "That little squirrel knocked the curtains off the wall, ate at the sash, and ruined the muntins of about 14 windows," says Tom.

Keeping control of the things that can destroy a house is a matter of creating an environment that discourages, rather than actively kills, unwanted invaders. Instead of sprinkling pesticides and rodenticides, for example, take a close look at the outside of the house. If soil rises too close to the wall, it offers an invitation for insects and mice. If gutters are clogged or not connected properly to downspouts, the stagnant pools and constant dripping that result will breed mold and mildew, and the fascia boards will rot. "Overhanging trees are the worst offenders of all," says Tom. "They may look attractive—a sort of cabin-in-the-woods effect—but they are a bridge to your house for everything from squirrels to carpenter ants." And the swaying branches can destroy roof shingles, rip gutters apart, and encourage mold and mildew by leaving the roof in constant shade. "You don't want trees or shrubs pressing against the roof or siding," says Tom. "If they are, you're asking—no, make that begging—for trouble."

Another important step is to seal up all the small holes in the exterior in order to keep out everything from marauding mice to invading wasps. "Look at your house with a critical eye, the way a raccoon might," says Richard. "If somebody removed the oil fill pipe 2 years ago and there's still a hole where the pipe was, it's like a front door for any bug invaders and small mammals." Unbaffled dryer vents are another source of invasion, as are chimneys—especially for raccoons. "There are probably more lurking there than you want to imagine," says Richard, who was surprised once when he disconnected the flue pipe while changing a water heater and found two eyes staring back at him when he peered into the flue. These visits from the animal kingdom aren't always benign. Raccoons, for instance, have been known to climb into the furnace exhaust pipe and plug it up, sending deadly carbon monoxide fumes back into the house. "None of this," says Richard, "is cute."

Sometimes a home has to be defended from its owner. "I've replaced a whole lot of porches, deck stairs, even siding," says Tom, "just because people let their lawn sprinklers spray against the house year after year." If only every problem had such an easy fix.

« **You don't want** trees or shrubs pressing against the roof or siding. If they are, you're asking —no, make that begging—for trouble. » —TOM SILVA

SAFETY + SECURITY

Unless a house is safe, it isn't really a home. Safety comes from good design—properly designed stairs, for example—but also from devices that warn of danger. Among these, fire and smoke detectors are the best known. "These should be hard-wired to the electrical system, which frees you from having to remember about batteries," says Richard.

But one type of alarm too many people overlook could be the most important of all: one that detects accumulations of carbon monoxide, a deadly gas produced by burning heating fuels, including oil, gas, and wood. "When we use insulation, housewrap, and caulking, we create tightly sealed houses," says Richard. "That's why a little bit of carbon monoxide creates a really big problem—especially because it's odorless and colorless." Smoke from a fireplace or woodstove contains carbon monoxide, but it can usually be

smelled before it creates a problem. The real danger, says Richard, comes from basement furnaces and boilers. Gas-fired units, in particular, give off virtually no detectable odor, so a house can fill up with carbon monoxide without anyone knowing it. "Everyone should have a carbon monoxide detector installed right at the head of the basement stairs," says Richard. "And if you hear that one go off, get out of the house!"

Safety threats can also come from outside. Many people regard a burglar alarm as the moat around their castle, but studies show that most alarms are actually false. "Security systems have become like car alarms; people just ignore them because of all the false alarms," says Tom. For protection, he believes, there are more cost-effective things to install than a full-fledged security system, such as burglar-resistant locksets and dead-

bolts (see p. 76). "That's the kind of protection I want—and it doesn't cost me $20 a month."

Steve, however, is a firm believer in alarms, particularly because a house can be fitted at the same time with a low-temperature sensor to warn of pipe-freezing temperatures, and water alarms that can signal a monitoring service to have someone check the basement if you're gone.

Common sense can also protect your house. "Don't let mail or newspapers accumulate when you're absent," says Tom. "Tell the neighbors when you'll be away, and use lighting timers so that the house isn't completely dark—or worse, left with lights on 24 hours a day."

Still, security alarms do offer peace of mind, especially for the elderly. "My mother has one, and it gives her a sense that there's some way to notify the world if she needs help," says Richard. For those who feel particularly vulnerable to break-ins, Richard recommends hiring a security consultant to develop a balanced security plan rather than relying on a single system that could let you down.

« Everyone should have a carbon monoxide detector. And if you hear that one go off, get out of the house! » —RICHARD TRETHEWEY

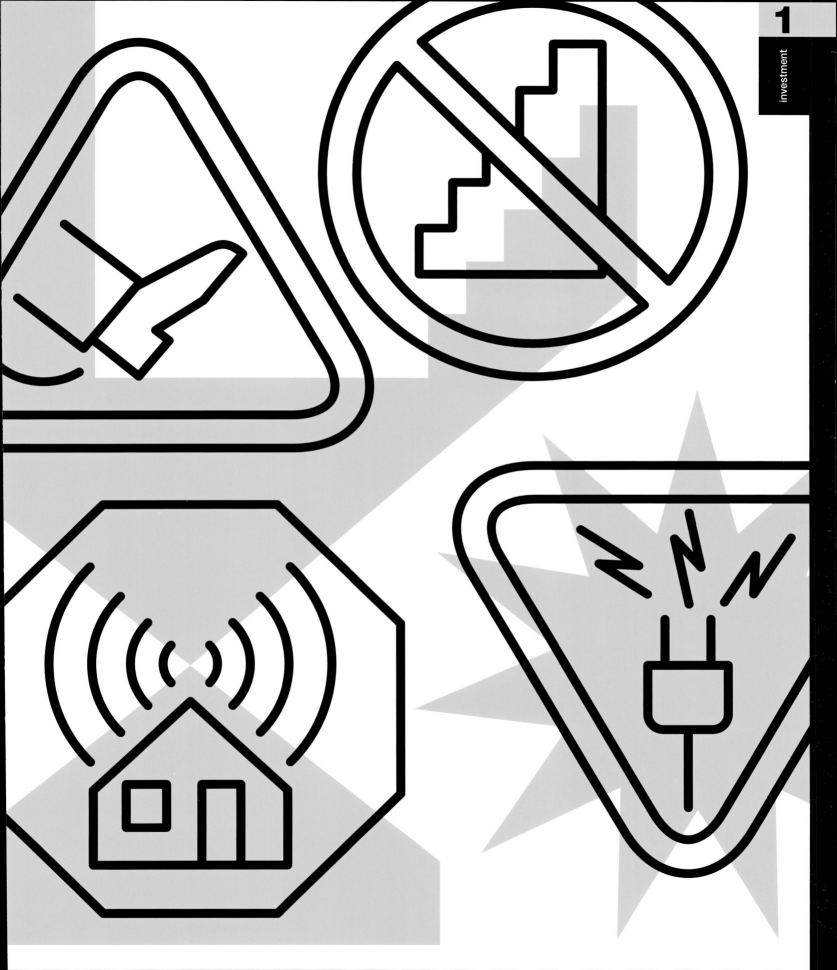

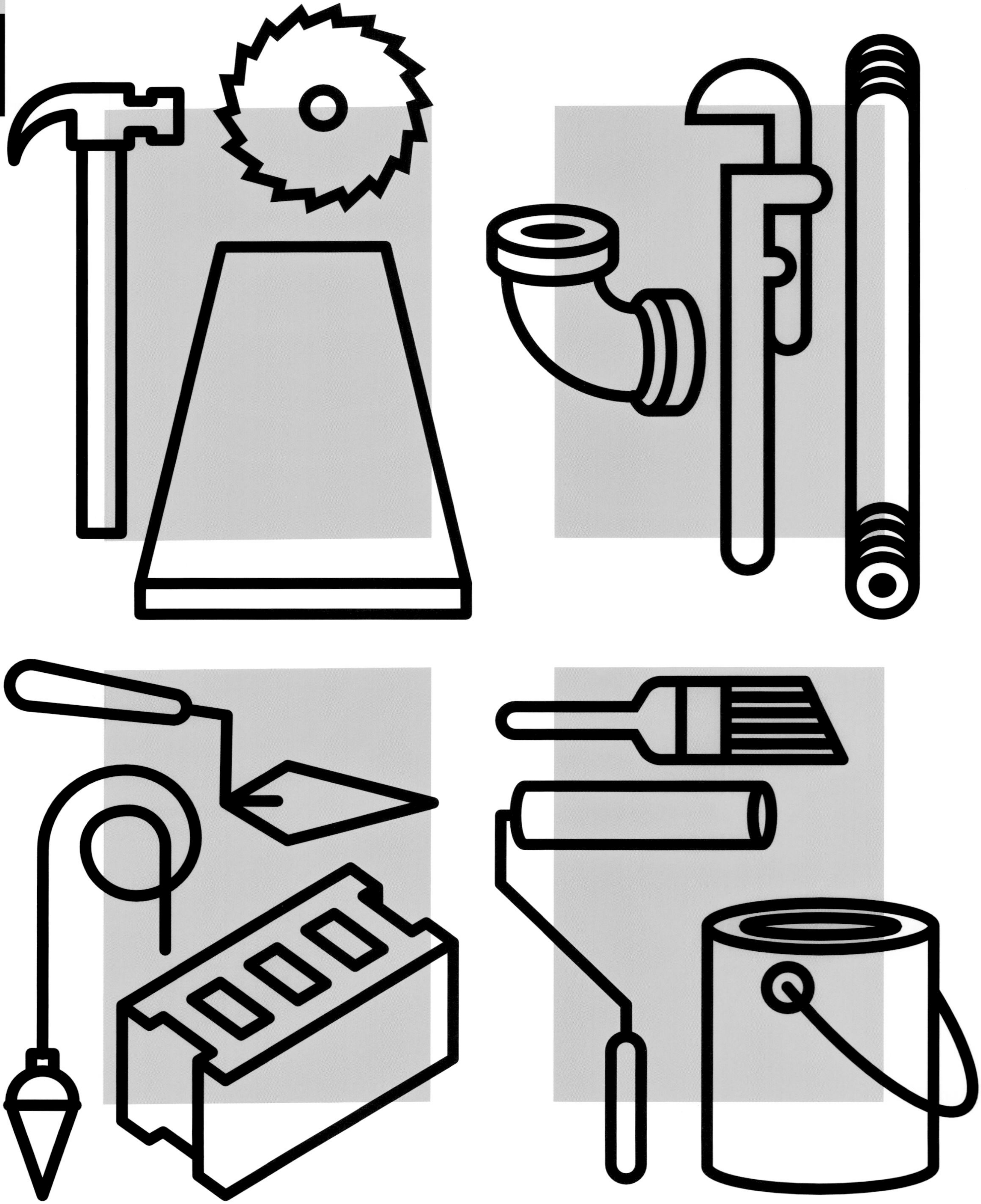

WORKING WITH CONTRACTORS

Few homeowners can, or want, to tackle every repair or renovation a house requires. But choosing a dependable contractor ranks as one of the major aggravations of home ownership. "If you watch only the news, you'd think that every contractor is always one step away from criminal behavior, but that couldn't be further from the truth," says Richard. "The real problems come when homeowners try to get a bargain. If you choose your contractor simply by taking the lowest bid, you become a co-conspirator when the project never gets finished, or when you hate the way it turns out."

When choosing a contractor, Richard suggests beginning the process by throwing out the low bid, however tantalizing it might seem. "I always take the middle bid, and sometimes even the high bid," he says. "I know that sounds self-serving coming from a contractor, but the best doctors and lawyers in town are probably the most expensive—and there's a reason for that." But price alone can't be the deciding factor: Take a look at the credentials of the person you're about to hire.

This can be awkward, but it's vital, says Tom. "Say to the person, 'Give me a couple of examples of projects you've done like mine,' and then go see them." Look beyond the finished decor to see if walls are straight and plumb. Check for peeling paint indoors and stained ceilings—sure signs of leakage, particularly near chimneys and skylights. "Ask the homeowner if he or she was happy with the contractor," Tom advises. "Did the person show up on time? Were problems solved promptly? Were phone calls returned?"

A lack of specificity in a contract, says Steve, can let the contractor use cheaper materials. But the biggest risk in any project is a contractor who takes the money but fails to complete the job. State laws that require contractors to be licensed and bonded provide some protection, but they don't eliminate fraud. To further protect yourself, agree in advance on a specific payment schedule and stick to it, says Tom. "If you have to pay for things in advance, such as custom cabinets, ask to see receipts as proof that they've actually been ordered," he says. "You want your money to go toward finishing your job, not another one. And ask for a regular accounting of costs so you know where you stand."

Successful projects involve a measure of trust between the homeowner and the contractor. You're the employer, after all, and you have a right to ask questions and understand what's going on. "You'll be involved with these people in the most intimate of settings—your home," says Richard. Start the relationship right. "Get to know them, and ask yourself, 'Do I trust this person?'" he adds. "I know that sounds really weird, but you're not just buying a project—you're also buying the person who's building it."

« If you choose your contractor simply by taking the lowest bid, you become a co-conspirator when you hate the way it turns out. » —RICHARD TRETHEWEY

THE TOOLBOX

SCREWDRIVERS You'll need two different types—slotted head and Phillips head—and three sizes of each: small, medium, and large. Plastic handles are best; they're durable and provide a level of electrical insulation.

CORDLESS DRILL Tom thinks a 9.6- or 12-volt cordless drill is better suited to the average homeowner than a corded drill, but either will work. A ⅜-inch chuck handles the bits and accessories most homeowners need.

DRILL BITS Get a set of twist bits ranging from ¹⁄₁₆ inch to ½ inch and a set of spade bits from ¼ inch to 1 inch (see appendix).

CIRCULAR SAW Yes, a handsaw will suffice for many jobs, but a 7¼-inch power saw is faster, more accurate, and more versatile. A carbide-toothed blade is best for general use.

JIGSAW This easy-to-use power tool is indispensible for cutting curves and irregular shapes in almost any material. Get a selection of wood- and metal-cutting blades.

BLOCK PLANE This is what Tom reaches for when he has to shave off small amounts of wood or bevel an edge.

WOOD RASP Rows of metal teeth make short work of shaping wood.

METAL FILES To shape metal and sharpen the edges of shop and yard tools, get fine and coarse grades of the following types: flat, triangular, and round.

LEVEL A 2-foot carpenter's level will handle most tasks around the house.

HAMMER For general use around the house, Tom recommends a wood-handled claw hammer with a 16-ounce head.

HACKSAW Ideal for cutting pipes and bolts.

NAIL SET Struck with a hammer, a nail set drives nailheads beneath the finished surface to conceal them. Get a 3-piece set.

CENTER PUNCH Used with a hammer to mark a center point prior to drilling metal.

UTILITY KNIFE As befits its name, this razor-sharp tool cuts and shapes a variety of materials. Keep plenty of blades on hand.

TAPE MEASURE A 16-foot metal tape with a sturdy hook is Tom's most used tool.

SAFETY GEAR Don't risk your safety doing home work. Get a pair of impact-resistant safety goggles, some disposable foam earplugs and dust masks, and leather work gloves.

STEPLADDER A 4-foot wood or fiberglass ladder is portable enough to suit many jobs. Get a commercial grade: "Your life is on that ladder," says Tom, "so make it a good one."

ADJUSTABLE WRENCH An 8-inch model is the basic tool for working on nuts and bolts.
GROOVE-JOINT PLIERS With big jaws and a strong grip, these pliers are versatile, and invaluable for plumbing work.
CLAMPS More is better, says Tom, but you'll need at least 6 plastic squeeze clamps and several bar clamps 3 or 4 feet long.
COMBINATION SQUARE Used as a general layout tool; a 12-inch square suits most maintenance and repair needs.
EXTENSION CORD A 25-foot, 12-gauge cord feeds work lights and power saws.
VOLTAGE TESTER The small bulb on this inexpensive two-pronged tool lights up when electricity is reaching a switch or outlet.
CIRCUIT ANALYZER For troubleshooting electrical systems, this three-prong plug uses a

series of tiny lights to identify an outlet's polarity and alert you to missing ground wires.
FLASHLIGHT The best light stands upright; a swiveling head aims light where you need it.
CAULKING GUN Get a good one: "The cheap ones usually break," reports Tom.
LINESMAN'S PLIERS These heavy-duty wire cutters also crimp, twist, and grip.
WORK LIGHT If you can't see what you're doing, how can you do it right? Tom prefers models with a heavy cord, a three-prong plug, and a break-resistant bulb.
WOOD CHISELS Nothing beats a chisel for shaping wood. Get three sizes: ¼, ½, and 1 inch. Just don't use them to open cans.
PLUNGER Also known as a plumber's helper, make it your first response to a clogged drain.
PLUMBING SNAKE If the plunger fails, a

coiled metal snake will root out clogs.
BASIN WRENCH There are two ways to get at faucet nuts, says Richard: "Either bloody your knuckles or use a basin wrench."
TOOLBOX You'll need a large compartment for big tools, and a couple of trays or drawers for the smaller ones.
COMBINATION TOOL Used for wire stripping, crimping terminals, and restoring cross-threaded bolts to health.
PIPE WRENCH "A 14-inch pipe wrench," says Richard, "will persuade most any nut or pipe to loosen." The serrated jaws grip tightly.
NEEDLENOSED PLIERS Nothing beats this tool for working with wire in tight spaces.
POCKETKNIFE A two-bladed knife serves as Tom's default cutter, pryer, and prober. Steve and Richard would rather carry a multi-tool.

controls for your house

ITEM	WHAT IT CONTROLS	HOW TO FIND IT	LOCATION IN YOUR HOUSE
MAIN WATER SHUTOFF	The entire household water supply.	Look for a valve (p. 202) in the basement, near where a water pipe enters from outside.	
MAIN ELECTRICAL SHUTOFF	The entire household electrical system.	Look for a large gray metal box (the service panel) attached to a foundation wall in the basement; it's often on the wall closest to the driveway. Open the panel's door; the main shutoff will be a switch or lever at the top.	
SUBPANEL ELECTRICAL SHUTOFF	The electrical supply to buildings not connected to the house.	Look for a small gray metal box. It could be in the outbuilding or near the main service panel. The shutoff may be a switch inside the panel door, or a large lever alongside.	
SHUTOFF: OUTDOOR SPIGOT #1	An individual spigot on the outside of the house.	Look for a valve in the basement or crawl space, just inside the house foundation from the spigot.	
SHUTOFF: OUTDOOR SPIGOT #2	See above.	See above.	
SHUTOFF: OUTDOOR SPIGOT #3	See above.	See above.	
FURNACE/ BOILER CUTOFF	Shuts off fuel supply to the furnace or boiler.	Look for a switch near the top of the stairs leading to the basement; it may have a red switchplate.	
THERMOSTAT	Shuts off the heating or cooling system.	A house may have several thermostats. Look on interior walls, about 5 feet above the floor.	
GAS SHUT-OFFS	Individual gas appliances, such as a range or water heater.	A shutoff is typically located on the black gas supply pipe leading to the appliance.	
FIXTURE WATER SHUT-OFFS	Shuts off water to an individual fixture such as a faucet or toilet.	Look for a small valve on the supply pipe coming out of a nearby wall. It may be inside a cabinet.	

A car isn't much use unless you can operate the controls, but it's possible to live in a house quite well without doing much more than twisting a thermostat dial now and then—until a problem crops up. If a water pipe bursts or an appliance starts smoking, that's when you'll need to get your hands on the controls of your house, and quickly. Will you know what to do? Take some time now to fill in the last column of this chart, noting the locations of all critical household controls. Gas shutoffs should be used only in an emergency.

MAKING
YOUR HOME USER-FRIENDLY

To many people, a house is more complicated than a spaceship. "From the maintenance needed by the web of plumbing and electrical lines to the simple stuff like keeping door hinges moving freely and windows closing tight against the weather, there's a great deal to keep track of," says Steve. "Getting a grip on it all takes a little effort at first."

To gain control, homeowners should understand the house in terms of things that require maintenance and repair, "even if you'll ultimately hire someone else to do the work," says Steve. Beyond that, there will inevitably be emergencies that require instant attention. "You can't wait for the plumber to show up when a leaking pipe is turning your kitchen into Lake Meade," says Richard. "You have to act." Know the location of every plumbing or electrical shutoff, adds Steve, "so you can describe it over the phone to the babysitter."

The two most important parts of a house, at least from the standpoint of emergency readiness, are the plumbing system and the electrical system. "In both cases," says Richard, "learn how to shut them off." That just might be the most important home-owning skill anyone can master.

For the plumbing system, look for shutoff valves near each faucet and toilet. "Go there right now and find them, and turn each one off and on to see for yourself how they work. . . before you have a problem," advises Richard. Shutoffs are also located in the basement, within a few feet of outdoor faucets—these are the ones you should close every fall in order to drain water out of the faucet so it won't freeze and rupture the pipes.

Another shutoff is also located in the basement or crawl space, and can be found where water enters the house: This is the main shutoff. "This will cut water to the entire house, and it's where you should run when a pipe breaks and starts to geyser, or when the water heater springs a leak," says Richard. "That can spell the difference between a simple mishap and disaster."

The main service panel, sometimes called the circuit box or the service entrance, is the electrical equivalent of a plumbing shutoff. Open the panel door right now and take a look: You'll see rows of circuit-breaker switches (or in the case of older systems, fuses). Each switch controls a small network of outlets, switches, and lights in a particular part of the house, and each such circuit should be labeled so it can be promptly turned off whenever anyone is working on wiring, replacing switches or outlets, or installing new fixtures. "Knowing how to do this will save you the expense of having to call the electrician when a circuit blows, simply to have him turn the circuit back on for you," says Tom. "It's just a flick of the switch—learn how to do it for yourself." For use in a major emergency, there's a main shutoff switch at the top of the service panel that will cut power to

« You can't wait for the plumber to show up when a leaking pipe is turning your kitchen into Lake Meade. You have to act. » —RICHARD TRETHEWEY

everything in the house at once. "Keep a flashlight handy so you can find the breakers in the dark, because that's when you'll most likely be looking for them," says Tom. If there's an outlet nearby, keep an inexpensive emergency light plugged into it—the kind that goes on when the power goes off; it's a great alternative to dead batteries.

Today's houses contain maintenance-hungry items such as water heaters, furnaces, garbage disposals, water softeners, and alarm systems. "There's virtually no device in the house that can be altered or adjusted without the manual," says Steve. "In my own house, I can't even adjust the clock on the stove for daylight savings time without reading the manual." Save them all. For some devices, such as the water heater and the furnace, it's easy enough to put the manual in an envelope and attach it to a nearby wall. Or you can keep them in a folder somewhere. "I have mine in a drawer in the kitchen," says Steve, "so I know right where to go if I need them."

Keeping accurate records also plays a crucial role in making a home user-friendly. Records can help you to schedule routine maintenance tasks, such as changing the furnace air filter, or can help you keep track of when the heating system was last cleaned. Receipts document your household repair and renovation expenses, and those can be valuable when you have to make a warranty claim or when it comes time to sell the house. "Save everything," says Tom. "That way, whenever you sell your house, you'll be able to recoup your investment and handle your taxes much better."

Anticipating repairs and gathering the equipment needed to make them simplifies household maintenance. "Whenever I buy an appliance, I always ask the dealer what parts are most likely to come up for routine replacement, and I order the spares right away," says Steve. Around the house, this can include lightbulbs, washers, spare switches for furnace blowers, even parts for the toilet flushing mechanism. "That way I'm able to make the repair right away, rather than having it turn into a weeks-long odyssey while I order the part, wait for it to arrive, then find the time to fix it."

Purchasing the right cleansers for specific surfaces can also keep a house looking better for longer. "Plan for a stain before it happens, and have the right cleaner on hand to remove it from any surface immediately," says Steve. "Here, speed is everything." The longer dirt stays on a surface, the harder it will be to remove.

Setting aside some space for making minor repairs and storing commonly-used tools (p. 22-23) also helps keep a household functioning smoothly. "Everybody needs some sort of a work space," says Tom. "Once you get organized, you'll be surprised at the number of things you can handle yourself." Steve agrees: "Even a well-organized closet can serve as a work area."

Another way to make a home user-friendly is to find a contractor to make the larger repairs. "It can be difficult to find somebody good that you trust," says Richard. "But it makes all the difference in helping you stay on top of things, rather than constantly falling behind and getting frustrated."

« **Once you get** organized, you'll be quite surprised at the number of things you can handle all by yourself. » —TOM SILVA

household adhesives

NAME	DESCRIPTION	ADVANTAGES	DISADVANTAGES
YELLOW GLUE	Some formulas suited only to interior projects. Type II formula suitable for outdoor use.	Inexpensive, widely available. Sands easier than white glue. Water cleanup. Strong.	May set too quickly for complex assemblies.
WHITE GLUE	Nontoxic formula useful for crafts and wood toys.	Inexpensive. Water cleanup. Invisible glue line. Can be stored for long periods.	Poor water resistance. Clogs sandpaper. Relatively weak.
POLYURETHANE LIQUID	Strong, moisture-curing formula for indoor and outdoor use.	Can be used on wood with relatively high moisture content. Foams during cure to fill gaps. Easy to scrape excess glue away from joints when dry.	Expensive. Foaming action can be difficult to control. Difficult to remove from hands.
POLYURETHANE MASTIC	Marine-grade adhesive-sealant with great strength and gap-filling ability.	Very strong. Waterproof. Excellent for filling gaps.	Expensive. Messy application. Not widely available.
EPOXY	Liquid resin and hardener mix for small repairs, filling holes.	Waterproof. Great strength.	Expensive. Full curing can take several days. Noxious fumes. Cleanup difficult.
CONTACT CEMENT	Used most frequently for bonding plastic laminates and wood veneers to plywood substrates; also useful for strong wood-to-wood bonds.	Instant bond. High water resistance. Economical. Easy to spread quickly over large areas.	Instant bond doesn't allow shifting. Vapors are flammable (some formulations less than others). Requires coating both surfaces.
HOT-MELT GLUE	Thermoplastic adhesive dispensed by electric glue gun. Good for simple, quick repairs.	Instant grab that hardens within seconds, so no clamping required. Easy to use.	Heated glue can burn skin. Extremely short working time. Excess can't be sanded. Requires special gun for application. Gun takes time to heat. Relatively low strength. Does not compress well.
CYANOACRYLATE	Superglue bonds a variety of materials almost instantly. Good for small projects.	Bonds quickly, so joint can be held with finger pressure. Liquid versions can seep into thin joints; gel forms can fill gaps.	Very expensive. Joints must fit precisely. Won't adhere to porous woods. Bonds skin.
MASTIC	Designed to be troweled over large areas when adhering ceramic tile, resilient flooring, and some types of carpet.	Relatively inexpensive and widely available. Allows easy repositioning. Water-resistant.	Fumes require adequate ventilation. Can be messy to apply. Some "all-purpose" formulations aren't suitable for adhering sheet vinyl flooring.
CONSTRUCTION ADHESIVE	Used for bonding plywood and other panel products to framing.	Strong bond, maintains flexibility. Resistant to moisture. Applies quickly to framing.	Usually requires caulk gun for application.

THE EFFICIENT HOME

In the rush to make a home look good, many homeowners neglect to take care of the underlying problems first. "When people think of comfort, they think of soft couches and thick-padded carpeting," says Richard. "But comfort goes far deeper than that—right down to the heating and cooling systems." Not only do these maintain the internal temperature of the house, which is the most obvious measure of comfort, but they also cost the most to run in terms of monthly bills. "Taking care of energy efficiency here can save you a huge amount of money," he says.

Even if it has been well maintained, an old furnace or boiler simply can't match the efficiency of a new one—and the cost of replacing it, despite the heavy initial expense, can often be recouped. "If you've got equipment that's 15 years old or older, it almost certainly pays to make the change," says Tom. Old water heaters, too, tend to operate much less efficiently than new ones, and that makes them good candidates for replacement.

Yet smoothly running heating and cooling appliances are only a part of the efficiency equation. Making the house tight is the other. "You can have the most up-to-date boiler or furnace, but you'll still freeze in the winter if you have a house full of drafty windows, or a big gap beneath the front door," says Tom. In this battle, inexpensive weatherstripping ranks as the ultimate weapon. With careful application, even the oldest windows and doors can be reasonably energy-efficient. And as a result, the entire house will feel warmer.

After weatherstripping windows and doors, the next most effective way to improve the energy efficiency of your house is to add insulation. Just because you have some doesn't mean you have enough. "How much you really need," notes Tom, "depends on where you live." Not only is insulation poorly installed or missing altogether in many houses, but it can also get damp from moisture escaping from the house. "Damp insulation will give you all the thermal protection of a wet blanket," he says.

Across the country, household efficiency has increasingly meant saving water as well as energy. With shortages and rising rates in some areas, expect this to become even more of a priority in the coming years. The response has been, in part, to improve the efficiency of water-guzzling fixtures. "What we've seen so far, with low-flow toilets and showerheads, is just the beginning," says Richard. But a huge amount of water could be saved simply through proper maintenance. "The constantly running toilet and the dripping faucet may seem like isolated problems, but add all of them up and you might be wasting thousands of gallons of water a year," says Richard. "It's good for your conscience to control these things. And, increasingly, it's good for your wallet as well."

« **You can have** the most up-to-date boiler or furnace, but you'll still freeze in the winter if you have a house full of drafty windows. » —TOM SILVA

looking for trouble

what hurts a house / where to find problems / 60-minute inspection guide / planning and prioritizing / building codes / regular maintenance

chapter 2

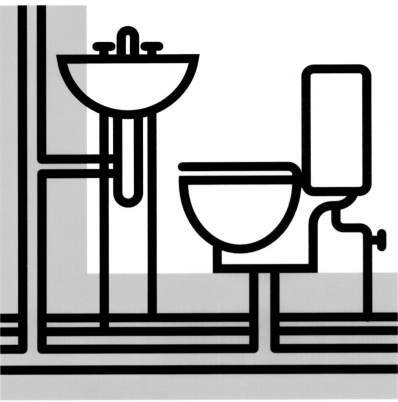
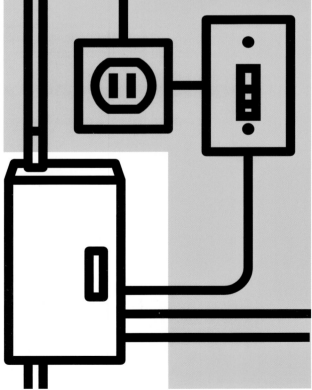
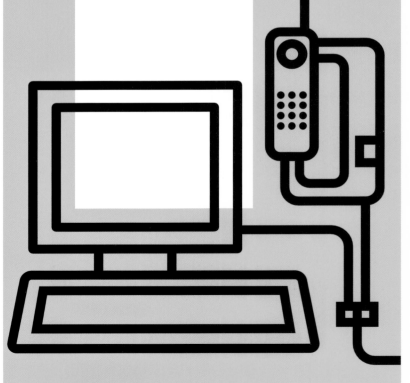

WHAT
HURTS A HOUSE

A house is more than a box that keeps your stuff—and you—from getting rained on. Sometimes it seems almost alive. "People tend to think of a house as some sort of immovable, unchanging bunker, but in reality it's a constantly moving thing," says Richard. Moisture enters it and leaves, wood expands and contracts, and air moves through the rooms. "When we heat and cool a house, we create a lot of moisture-related problems that can rot it—generally from the inside out." Today's homes are sealed to reduce heating and cooling loss, and that means excess moisture isn't able to escape, either. "And moisture is probably the worst enemy your home has to face," notes Steve. Few homeowners understand the destructive forces unleashed by water vapor and condensation: they can damage any system in the house, and not just the ones made of wood. Moisture

comes from the steam of a morning shower, the clouds of vapor released by cooking, even from the simple act of breathing, which can add as much as half a pint of water to the air every hour. Combine that with a basic fact of physics—warm air holds far more moisture than cold air—and you'll begin to recognize a problem just waiting to happen.

In a heated house, warm, moist air gradually moves from the rooms into the walls and ceilings, eventually reaching the relatively cold surfaces near the siding. That's when the air dumps its load of moisture in a process called condensation. "We've stripped off the drywall in bathrooms of fairly new houses," recounts Tom, "and found that every 2x4 and all the sheathing was completely rotted." In a cooled house, the situation is reversed. Either way, condensation deposited in walls will inevitably lead to problems.

The remedy, says Richard, lies in controlled ventilation. This includes exhaust fans in the bathrooms and the kitchen, which whisk away cooking steam and bathroom fog before they can seep into the walls. A plastic vapor barrier laid over the inside surface of the framing keeps any moisture that does seep through the walls from reaching the insulation.

Natural ventilation also helps to preserve a house. As warm air escapes the attic through vents in the gable ends or along the ridge, cooler air is drawn in through soffit vents at the low edge of the roof. The flow keeps the roof cool in hot weather, exhausts moisture, and eliminates ice damming in cold weather. It also extends the life of the roof shingles by preventing the roof from overheating as it bakes in the summer sun. To work properly, however, the airflow needs a clear path to the attic. If the path is blocked by insulation, you'll know it: Upstairs rooms will get especially hot in the summer. The solution is marvelously simple: Inexpensive foam chutes can be placed against the underside of the sheathing to keep the pathway open.

« As we heat and cool a house, we create a lot of moisture-related problems that can rot it— generally from the inside out. » —RICHARD TRETHEWEY

where to find problems

OUTSIDE THE HOUSE	INSIDE THE HOUSE
DOWNSPOUTS: Loose or missing elbows let water splash against the house, causing rot and basement leakage.	**SUBFLOOR:** Poked with a screwdriver from the basement, it should be solid rather than spongy and yielding, which indicates decay. Repair may be difficult.
GUTTERS: Look for clogs that can send water down the side of the house. Check for dripping from seams.	**BASEMENT:** Should be clean-smelling, with no hint of mold or mildew; stains or rust on objects (including posts) that touch the floor indicate moisture seepage or periodic flooding. Insulate cold-water pipes if sweating (condensation) is a problem.
PAINT: Peeling could be a sign of a wet basement or moisture penetrating the walls from inside the house.	**WATER PIPES:** Should be free of corrosion. What appears to be corrosion on hot-water pipes, particularly near hydronic boilers, may actually be residue from a small leak.
CAULK AROUND WINDOWS AND SIDING: If missing or pulling away, the gaps could lead to water infiltration.	**CAST-IRON DRAINPIPES:** "Softness" suggests that corrosion has eaten away the inside of a pipe; you'll hear softness as a dull thud when you tap the pipe with a screwdriver handle.
GRADE AROUND FOUNDATION: Should be at least 8 inches below the siding; should slope away from the house.	**SERVICE PANEL:** Rust indicates serious problems; consult an electrician. DO NOT TOUCH wires or terminals.
ROOF SHINGLES: Broken or missing shingles weaken the weather defense of any house.	**CAULK AROUND THE TUB AND SINK:** Will let water leak into cabinet or subfloor if missing or deteriorating.
ROOFTOP VENTS: Globs of tar around a vent indicate that a leak has been sloppily patched—and will inevitably leak again. Replace the vent's flashing.	**TUB SURROUND:** Cracked tiles or damaged grout can allow water to leak into walls. Loose tiles, particularly in the first row around a tub and around faucets, may signal the presence of a long-standing problem.
CHIMNEYS: Mortar should be intact, with no cracked or broken pieces that would allow water to seep in. Check for lifted step flashing that would also invite water.	**FLOORING AT EDGE OF TUB:** Drips from departing bathers can eventually rot the subfloor. Sponginess is one warning sign; loose tile is another.
	INTERSECTION OF KITCHEN BACKSPLASH AND COUNTER: Imperfect joint could let water drip behind cabinets.
	TOILETS: Summertime condensation dripping off the tank can eventually rot the subfloor.
	WALLS AND CEILINGS: Dark blotchy stains signal mildew, most likely from poor ventilation; irregular brownish rings signal a water leak from either a pipe or the roof.

Houses vary tremendously in style, type, construction technique, and a host of other features; that's why we find them so fascinating. No single guide can identify every problem your house is likely to encounter. This chart, however, lists some of the "likely suspects"—the places where problems are most likely to occur in any older house. On the initial walk-through of every This Old House project, Tom, Steve, and Richard pay particular attention to these locations. The root cause of problems in almost every case: water or water vapor.

60-MINUTE INSPECTION GUIDE

Making a regular visual inspection of a house allows you to catch problems while they're small. Once a year will suffice in warm climates, but where it snows, the inspection should be done twice—just before cold weather sets in, and just after it departs. In an hour or so you'll probably find a handful of small problems to fix. "Maintenance problems," explains Tom, "don't heal themselves. You have to walk around your house and find them—before they turn ugly."

Tom begins an inspection outside, where most of the problems are likely to be found. To examine the roof, he uses binoculars to zoom in on any trouble spots (walking around on the shingles can damage them, and binoculars are a lot easier to carry than a ladder). "Look for loose flashing, particularly along the edges of the roof, around the chimneys, and next to the dormers, and check for

missing or broken shingles," he says. If Tom sees signs of clogged gutters, such as twigs sticking out the top or dirt stains on the siding, he'll climb a ladder later to investigate.

Walking slowly around the outside of the house, Tom checks for foundation plantings or tree limbs that are touching the walls or roof. "That damages siding and roofing, and creates a moist situation where mold and mildew thrive; you definitely want to trim it back," he says. While outside, he also checks for any signs of peeling paint, which could hint at moisture condensation problems within the house. He looks for damaged screens and storm panes, and checks for clogged weep holes on storm-window frames that might trap water against the sill (they can be poked open with a paper clip). Then he examines the caulk around windows, corner boards, and outdoor faucets to make sure it's intact.

He also makes sure that the soil against the foundation is at least 8 inches below any wood and slopes away from the house. Any higher, and insects will get at the siding.

Exterior porches, decks, and stairs are high on the maintenance agenda. Tom looks for torn or loose screens, and loose boards. He taps a screwdriver against areas where decks or stairs have been bolted to the house. "Wood can look solid," he warns, "but if you knock on it and hear a hollow sound, you've got problems."

Indoors, Tom looks for signs of leakage in basement pipes and checks bathroom floors for signs of rot, particularly near tubs and toilets. Richard recommends taking a look at the corners of every bathroom ceiling, too, to check for dark stains—they signal mold and mildew. "If it's there, I would start thinking about ventilation big-time in the bathroom," says Richard.

Part of the purpose of an inspection is to get to know your house inside and out. "That way," says Tom, "you'll learn to distinguish what's normal from what might be a problem waiting to happen."

« Maintenance problems don't heal themselves. You have to walk around your house and find them—before they turn ugly. » —TOM SILVA

PLANNING
AND PRIORITIZING

By maintaining a house regularly, you can help it to last almost forever, or at least long enough for you to outgrow it. Unfortunately, keeping up with a house often seems like a lost cause before you even start. The solution? Chop the big problem into little ones and tackle them on a regular basis over the course of a year. Once you get into the rhythm of repair, knocking off maintenance chores is a little less painful. Tom's approach is to solve problems as soon as he sees them; "Otherwise," he admits, "I may not get to it for quite a while."

Another helpful strategy is to time your work to the seasons. Cleaning the gutters in January is no picnic, but in September it's not that bad.

If you do outgrow your house, remodeling calls for equally thoughtful planning. "The longer you plan to stay in a house, the slower you should proceed," says Steve. "Take the time to live in your house for a while before remodeling it. Then you can figure out how you live and what you really want." And if you don't plan to stay more than a few years, he adds, maybe remodeling isn't suitable at all.

It's often best to start a remodel by improving the mechanical and structural components of a house. "The heating, the wiring, the stuff behind the walls . . . those are by far the most important," says Tom, "and the smartest places to put your money." Instead, many homeowners paint the walls and refinish the floors first. "They'll end up having to wreck the work they've just done," says Tom. "Always work on the systems before you have fun with the finishes."

Even if the systems aren't worn out, Richard recommends upgrading them whenever the budget permits. "With every remodeling project, you'll probably open some walls, and that often offers an opportunity to update the mechanicals," he says. "We see people all the time putting in new sinks and cabinets, then 6 months later pulling the walls apart again to put in new plumbing because the old pipes sprang a leak."

If your budget is tight, focus attention on what Richard calls "the cocoon of the building"—the areas where you spend the most time. "That's where you're going to be during the longest, hottest day of the summer and the coldest, darkest night in winter," says Richard. "Invest in those spaces to make sure you'll be absolutely comfortable."

The key to surviving any remodeling is to stay focused. "The biggest mistake people make is taking on more than they can handle, and then they get overwhelmed. Very quickly they hate the process," says Tom. "The first thing you ought to do, especially if you're doing the work yourself, is to tackle a small room and complete it. Then begin the rest of the work. When you feel burned out—and you will—stand in the completed room and you'll remember what you're working for."

« Take the time to live in your house for a while before remodeling it. Then you can figure out how you live and what you really want. » — STEVE THOMAS

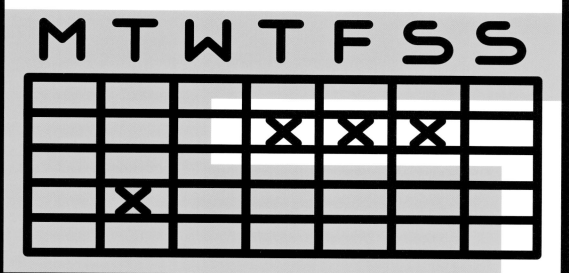

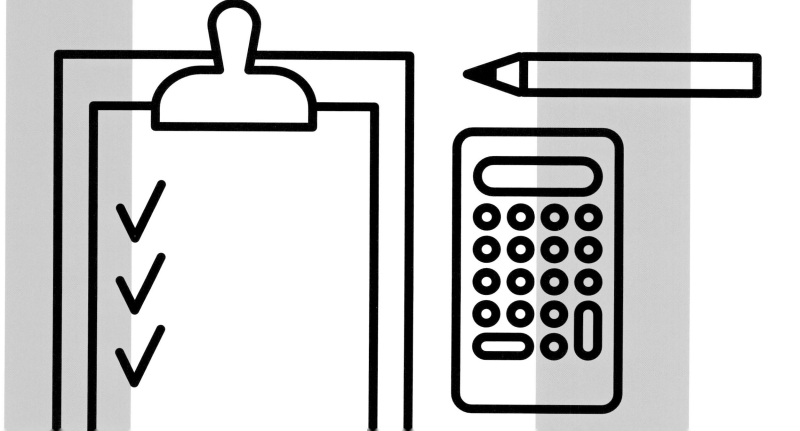

building code sampler

SUBJECT	REQUIREMENT	EXPLANATION
HANDRAILS	Handrails must be provided on at least one side of stairways. They should be no lower than 34 inches and no higher than 38 inches, measured vertically from the nosing (front edge) of the treads.	If you lose your balance, a sturdy handrail will help you to recover it.
SMOKE ALARMS	Smoke alarms must be installed in each bedroom; outside of the bedroom area; and on each story of the house, including basements (but not including crawl spaces and unimproved attics).	If there's a fire, an early warning is your best chance to escape from the house.
STAIRWAY LIGHTING	All indoor and outdoor stairs must be provided with artificial lighting. Interior stairs must have lighting near each landing; exterior stairs must have a light at the top landing.	Adequate lighting improves safety as well as security.
DRYWALL	Screws for attaching drywall to wood framing must penetrate the wood no less than $5/8$ inch.	Enough of the screw's threads must engage the wood to provide a secure hold.
PERMITS	The installation of paint, wallpaper, tile, carpet, cabinetry, countertops, and similar finish work doesn't usually require a permit. Also, a permit is not required for minor electrical repairs and maintenance, including the replacement of household lighting fixtures.	The codes are designed to regulate health and safety issues, not aesthetic issues.
FRAMING	Notches in lumber joists must not exceed one-sixth the depth of the joist, must not be longer than one-third the depth of the joist, and must not be located in the middle third of a joist's span.	This ensures that notches made for plumbing or electrical runs will not weaken the structural integrity of the house framing.
PLUMBING	Burred ends of pipes must be reamed to the full internal dimension of the pipe.	This prevents rough edges from obstructing the water flow.
ELECTRICAL RECEPTACLES	All bathroom receptacles and all kitchen receptacles that serve countertop surfaces must have ground-fault circuit interrupter (GFCI) protection.	The presence of water in these areas makes extra protection essential for safety.
GLAZING	Each pane of glazing in a side-hinged door, sliding door, closet door, or storm door must have an acid-etched, sandblasted, or otherwise permanent manufacturer's or installer's label, designating the type and thickness of glass and the safety glazing standard with which it complies; it must be visible in the final installation. (Some exceptions apply for decorative glass.)	Door glazing is prone to breakage.

Much of the work performed on a house is governed by building codes that protect your safety and health. The codes are usually updated on a 2- or 3-year cycle, and may vary considerably from region to region. Building code manuals cover the details and nuances of codes in great detail, but the chart above lists some of the codes that relate to topics addressed in this book. They are drawn from the "International Residential Code for One- and Two-Family Dwellings" (2000 edition), a publication that is designed to be compatible with the various regional building codes. Use this chart as a general guide only: Your local building department is the best source for the latest code information.

BUILDING CODES

Anyone who begins major home renovations soon discovers they're not alone: Inevitably they will be joined by the local building inspector, who checks to make sure the work is proceeding according to building codes. These regulations don't govern ordinary maintenance such as cleaning a gutter, but they do dictate lots of other things, from stair and railing dimensions to the depth of attic insulation, the location of smoke detectors, and the maximum distance allowed between electrical outlets. "Everybody hates the fact that there's an authority like the building department," says Richard. "But without it, construction quality would drop: There just aren't enough Tommys in the world to guarantee that the job will be done the right way." In addition, building codes and the inspectors who enforce them are the homeowner's best guarantee that a house will be built to last and that contractors follow the plans. "Without a building inspector, I bet a lot of bathrooms would fall into the living room," says Richard.

Several regional organizations develop and publish building codes, based on input from engineers, trade groups, and various industry representatives. Thus codes vary somewhat across the country. States and even individual communities can adopt additional codes that reflect local building realities. California codes, for example, deal with seismic concerns, while Florida codes encourage hurricane-resistant construction. Some rural areas aren't covered by building codes, but as Steve puts it, "Codes reflect good building practices, so why not follow them?"

Zoning laws provide another system of regulations, and control what can be done with a house in terms of expansion. "I've talked with lots of homeowners who've spent a long time planning a big addition," says Richard, "only to discover that they can't build because they'd end up too close to the neighbor's property line." It's better to find out in advance what the restrictions are: Call your city or town offices and ask to speak to a zoning official.

Existing homes usually don't have to be brought into compliance with building regulations that came into effect after the house was built—unless an inspector happens to hear about a safety hazard. "That's why you find houses with steep staircases and old wiring that would never pass modern codes," says Tom.

Though not all projects are subject to building inspection, says Steve, there's no advantage in trying to skirt building codes: "They just make better buildings," he says. And when it comes time to sell a house, the discovery of any non-code additions could nullify the deal. "Get to know your building inspector, and stop by to discuss any projects you're planning—even if it's something as innocuous as reroofing the house," advises Steve. Your house will be a better one for your efforts.

« **Everybody hates the** fact that there's an authority like the building department. But without it, construction quality would drop. » —RICHARD TRETHEWEY

REGULAR MAINTENANCE

Tom has had plenty of clients over the years, but one guy in particular will probably never again deny the importance of regular maintenance. "He wanted us to retile the tub area in a bathroom," recalls Tom, "and it seemed simple enough." That is, until Tom happened to notice that paint on the outside of the bathroom wall was peeling badly. That's when he began to expect problems. "When we opened up the wall, literally the only thing holding it up was the siding and the tile—the studs had completely rotted away." Apparently water had been leaking through the grout and seeping into the walls for quite some time. "Take care of problems while they're small and relatively cheap to repair," says Steve. "If you let them get big, they'll get expensive." Indeed, a small, scrubbable patch of mildew on the siding can turn into an indelible mildew bloom that requires sanding and

repainting. Wood floors ignored until they show unmistakable signs of wear will have to be stripped, sanded, and refinished; periodically screening and recoating the floor is a far easier and less expensive way to keep wood floors looking great. "Clean your carpets regularly, too— they'll last a lot longer that way and give you more for your money," says Steve. Not only that, but regular cleaning also rids the carpet of allergens that can make everybody in the house feel sniffly.

Wherever you find it, water damage must be taken care of right away, or decay will set in. "Probably 75 percent of the houses we've done on *This Old House* have some sort of water damage," says Richard. "You just have to be mean about it. If you see a little drip showing up in your kitchen ceiling, something had to leak long enough for it to finally become noticeable. It's better to go

up and tighten a plumbing connection or recaulk a tub or repair a window than to wait for the whole ceiling to drop in your soup."

There's a lifestyle issue involved with maintaining a house as well, because even the most luxurious house will suffer when little things stop working. "If you have a faucet that drips, or a toilet that won't stop flushing unless you jiggle the handle, your house will be an annoyance," says Richard.

Simple maintenance projects can save money, too ("They're cheaper than repairs," notes Tom). Draining grit and sediment out of the water heater once every year, for instance, will greatly extend its life. Painting one wall of your house each year reduces your annual paint bill to a level that won't induce heart palpitations. And changing the air filters in a forced-air heating system improves its efficiency and, ultimately, your comfort. "You have to learn to love your house as least as much as you love your car," Richard says. "You get cars serviced regularly, don't you? Why would you dream of ignoring your house?"

« **Love your house** at least as much as your car. You get cars serviced regularly; why would you dream of ignoring your house? » —RICHARD TRETHEWEY

section

2

your house's exterior

protecting your roof / reroofing a house / repairing flashing / replacing a three-tab shingle / replacing a wood shingle / washing gutters / replacing gutters / repairing corner trim / reattaching downspouts and leaders / repairing a rake / cleaning out gutters / repairing a fascia / repairing stucco / repairing vinyl siding / repairing clapboard / replacing clapboard / washing siding

chapter 3

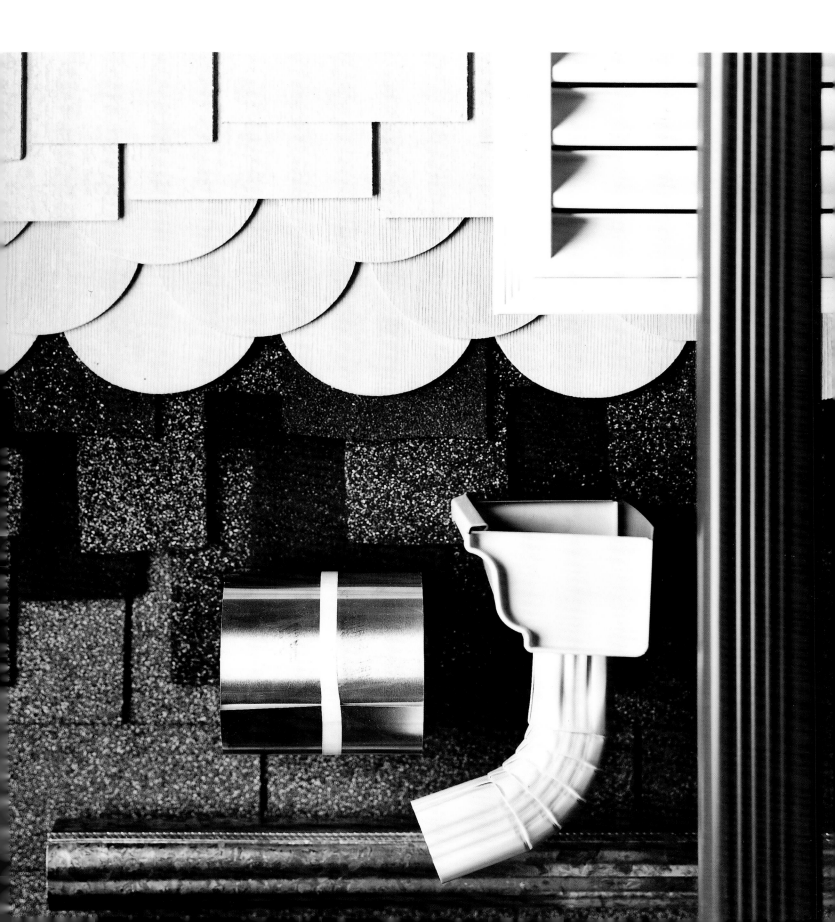

MOISTURE IS THE MOST FORMIDABLE enemy your house faces. Whether it's a gentle rain on a leaky roof, melted snow backing up behind an ice dam, or a storm-driven torrent clawing at the siding, moisture will destroy any house that can be built. Where there's water, mold spores grow, rot gets a good start, and wood-destroying insects set up shop. The Concord Barn, our project in 1989, had a roof that had leaked for years, and we finally had to tear the entire building down and replace it. If you own a home, then, learn this lesson: If water gets in, your house will die young. Keep it out and your house can be immortal. —STEVE

MAINTENANCE **protecting your roof** A roof in good condition performs a not-so-minor miracle: No matter how much rain hits, the shingles direct the water into your gutters. Roofs can withstand a great deal—piles of snow and ice in the winter, baking heat in the summer, and wind at any time of the year. "These sorts of things can make an ordinary driveway crack and heave, but we expect the roof to last 10, 15, 20 years and even longer," says Tom.

That's not entirely unreasonable, as long as basic maintenance tasks aren't neglected. "The main thing to remember is that a roof will last a lot longer if nothing touches it," says Tom; that's why he considers a branch brushing against it as the single greatest danger faced by shingles. "A branch just a couple of inches away from a roof might not look like it's touching," he says. "But on a windy day, as the tree moves back and forth, the branch rakes against the roof." Besides the physical damage, branches also encourage other troublemakers. "Insects drop off the branches and look for wood

Continuously beset by weather, the exterior shell of a house (including siding, roofing, doors, and windows) must be maintained on a continuing basis to prevent decay.

improvements:
exterior doors

An exterior door is an essential part of your house's weatherproof shell. Like siding, it must block every weather event from torrential rain to blistering sun, but it must open, too.

PASSAGE DOORS: Hinged at one side, this is the most common door. Exterior versions typically open inward and press against weatherstripping when closed. Wind blowing against the door, however, can push it away from the weatherstripping. Out-swinging doors are available, but require tamperproof hinges for security. Unless protected by a porch, doors are fully exposed to the weather; the weatherstripping should be inspected each year and replaced as needed (p. 79). Wood thresholds also require maintenance (see p. 83).

FRENCH DOORS: These hinged doors are fully glazed and installed in pairs. "Believe it or not, out-swinging French doors stay shut more tightly than the ones that swing in," says Tom. "The wind just forces them tighter against the weatherstripping." Make sure the doors seal properly where they meet; otherwise they'll leak water and air.

SLIDING DOORS: The large glazed panels of a sliding door are commonly used to provide access to a patio or deck. "They don't swing, so they take up less space during use," says Tom. The lower track in which the doors slide requires maintenance, however. Vacuum it out to remove accumulations of dirt and debris that prevent the door from sliding smoothly. Lubricating the track, says Tom, isn't a good idea because lubricant attracts dirt. If a door doesn't slide smoothly, the rollers on which it glides may have to be adjusted or replaced. Worn weatherstripping that no longer seals the sliding panels to each other should also be replaced.

tom's tip: roof flaws

Homeowners usually wait for a leak to announce that a roof has problems, but signs of potential trouble are visible long before. "A leak usually means the problem has been developing for several years," says Tom. Here's what he looks for when he looks at a roof:

ROOF MOSS: A tiny spreading plant that traps moisture and holds it against the roof, shortening the life of the shingles. "You'll see this first as a greenish tinge on shaded areas of the roof—especially under trees and on the sunless sides of dormers," says Tom.

MISSING SHINGLES: A shingle that's gone can't keep out water. "The damage is easy to spot from the ground with binoculars," says Tom. "And if you see tar paper, you're one step away from big troubles." For repairs, see p. 52.

WORN OR DAMAGED SHINGLES: A shingle with a broken corner can expose the nail beneath, making a leak more likely. Worn asphalt and fiberglass shingles appear darker than surrounding shingles because their protective covering of granules is gone. Cracked or severely curled wood shingles are signs that the wood needs professional attention.

A ROOF WITH PROBLEMS

they can chew through to get into the house," says Tom, and mildew thrives in the shade. The solution is simple: Trim branches so that nothing overhangs the roof.

Moss is another roof destroyer. It often grows on the shaded, damp sides of a house or in the sunless patches beneath an overhanging tree. "No matter what kind of shingles you have," warns Tom, "get the moss off. Before long, the moisture it traps will rot the structure." Moss can be removed with a gentle scrubbing. Tom uses a solution of 1 part chlorine bleach to 3 parts water, which he mixes in a 2-gallon garden sprayer attached to a hose. A dash of dish detergent will encourage the solution to penetrate. "You spray it on, then scrub it off with a soft window-washing brush—but don't scrub asphalt or fiberglass shingles too hard or some of the granular surface will come off," says Tom. He climbs up a ladder and cleans a wide swath of roof, using the brush mounted on a long handle. "Don't walk on a roof when you're washing it. Not only can you damage the shingles, but the roof will be extremely slippery," he warns. Tom washes his roof every 4 or 5 years—or whenever he sees the telltale greenish tinge that signifies the beginning of a moss problem. "If you wait until there's actually a lot of moss up there, more than likely the roofing's shot already—and the sheathing is probably in trouble, too," says Tom.

REPAIR **reroofing a house** "You know you need a new roof if you've got water stains on your ceiling," says Tom. "Even though there may be a leak in only one small area, the chances are good that you're not far from trouble elsewhere." Slate shingles can last 100 years, as can metal roofing. Wood shingles live as long as 50 years, although it could be far less if they were installed improperly or neglected. And three-tab shingles (p. 52), the most popular shingles of all, might last only 15 years but can last much longer. On these shingles, signs that replacement is in order are obvious: "If there are bubbles from the heat, or cracks, or dark spots where the granules have worn off to expose the shingle's core, or if a shingle has blown off the roof and you find when you pick it up that it's very brittle, these are all indications that you might need a new roof," says Tom. "If you've got a 20-year-old

A typical roof system relies on layers of overlapping material to keep water out of the house. The most trouble-prone portions are where shingles meet a vertical surface.

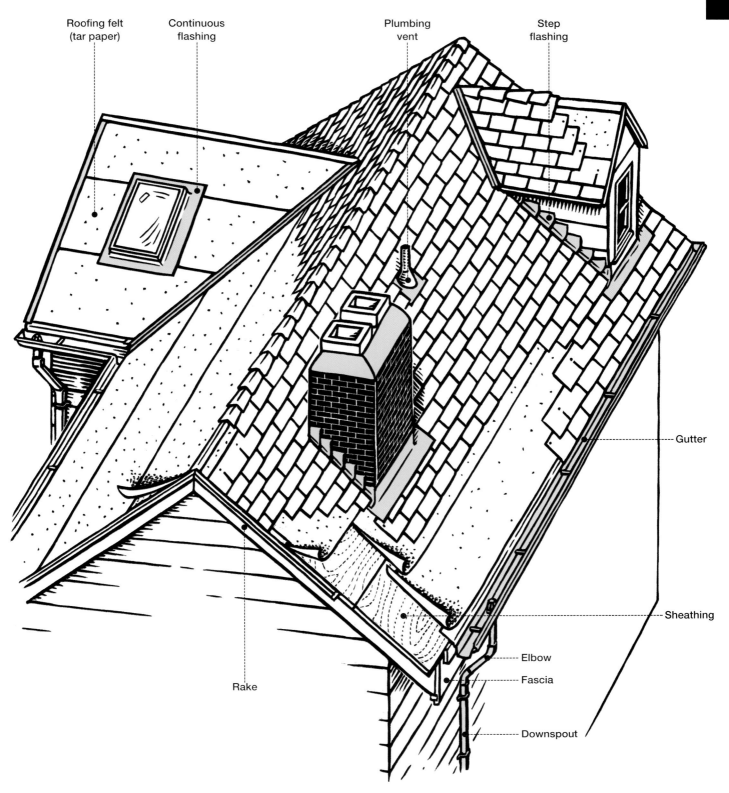

Roofing felt
(tar paper)

Continuous
flashing

Plumbing
vent

Step
flashing

Gutter

Sheathing

Elbow

Fascia

Rake

Downspout

ANATOMY OF A ROOF

asphalt roof, just assume it's on borrowed time." Step up the frequency of maintenance inspections until a new roof is in place.

Before reroofing a house, Tom insists on stripping off the existing shingles instead of adding a second layer over them, even though building codes generally allow a second layer. Tom admits that his approach can cost an extra thousand dollars or more, depending on the size of the roof and the cost of disposing of the old material. "I do this with every roof—whether it's asphalt or wood—for several reasons," says Tom. "First, shingles are heavy; I don't like all that extra weight on a roof. And if part of the existing roof leaks, it will end up being the weakest part of the new roof. But most important, I get a chance to check the condition of the sheathing." Once the roof has been stripped, he replaces damaged or rotted sheathing. Once a solid base is in place, he often applies a flexible, self-adhesive waterproofing sheet made of polymer-modified bitumen around any leak-prone area, including the base of dormers, valleys, and the base of plumbing vents. At the eaves, the same sheets protect against leaks caused by ice dams (ice that builds up on the roof above the eaves, causing water to pool there). "It's like an inexpensive insurance policy," he says.

repairing flashing Flashing works with shingles to keep out water. Typically made of aluminum or copper, it prevents water from seeping into places where the shingles meet other surfaces or different materials. "The flashing basically takes water that comes off a shingle and kicks it away, so it won't be driven back under the shingles," Tom explains. Flashing can sometimes pull away from a house, however, and must be renailed; the nailheads should be covered with roof mastic. Flashing should be completely replaced during a major roof repair.

There are two types of flashing: continuous flashing, which is long strips cut to length; and step flashing, which comes as individual L-shaped pieces that are overlapped somewhat like shingles. Because continuous flashing is so difficult to install correctly, Tom prefers step flashing wherever the roof meets a vertical surface. When he repairs step flashing, he makes sure each new piece slides beneath the piece above it. When installing flashing on a roof, start at the

Moss and mildew are a particular problem where the siding is shaded. Tom sprays the affected area with a water/bleach mix to kill the growth, then rinses the area thoroughly.

safety: working without fear

There's only one way to reach a roof: with an extension ladder. "Buy a commercial-grade aluminum or fiberglass model," says Tom, who once had a cheap ladder buckle beneath him. "Never, ever cut corners with a ladder."

Any ladder can slip if not properly positioned. To keep it standing, Tom plants the ladder's feet one-quarter of its extended length away from the house. "So if it's a 16-foot ladder, you place it 4 feet out," he says. He uses leveling legs to compensate for uneven terrain, and says that a metal support arm known as a standoff will dramatically improve a ladder's stability. Affixed to the top of the ladder, it also protects siding and gutters from damage (ladder cushions protect only siding).

Never carry an extension ladder upright, warns Tom: "You could easily lose control of it and break a window." Worse, you could hit power lines—with fatal results. To move an extension ladder, first lower it, then carry it so its length is parallel to the ground.

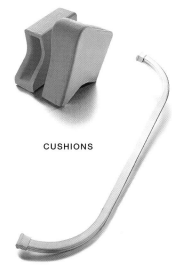

CUSHIONS

STANDOFF

types: three-tab shingles

The traditional wood shingle is expensive and doesn't suit every style of house. That's one reason why three-tab shingles (often called strip shingles) have become the most common residential roofing material of all. Each shingle is slotted to mimic the look of three individual shingles.

The first asphalt-impregnated shingles date to the 1840s. Today the shingles come in two types, depending upon whether the asphalt saturates a cellulose mat (called an organic asphalt shingle) or a fiberglass mat (called a fiberglass shingle). "Fiberglass shingles look the same," says Tom, "but they weigh less and usually come with a slightly longer warranty for a comparable thickness." Either type of shingle comes in 36-inch-long strips.

Architectural (laminated) shingles are made from the same basic materials but have a more pronounced profile. "They're heavier and also slightly more durable, and they hold up better against high winds," says Tom. But they're also more expensive than standard three-tab shingles and may not be as readily available as three-tab shingles.

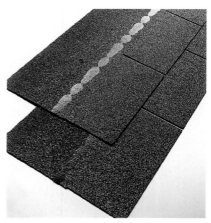

THREE-TAB SHINGLES

bottom and work up, so that the flashing always overlaps the piece beneath it, with a shingle sandwiched between. If it were otherwise, water would be directed under each piece of flashing. Damaged roof flashing can sometimes be repaired, albeit temporarily, by covering the damage with roof mastic.

replacing a three-tab shingle If a relatively new three-tab roof shingle has been damaged by a falling tree branch or by high winds, it can generally be repaired. "You don't have to rip off the whole roof for that," says Tom. "All you need is the right tools and a few extra shingles."

Every shingle is held in place by four nails. "But before you can remove those nails," explains Tom, "you have to take out some nails in the shingle above the one you want to remove." To do this, he slowly works a flat pry bar under the shingle just above the damaged one. "You're trying to break the shingle's seal with one below it," he says. "But the trick is, you don't want to damage that shingle or you'll have to replace it, too." Once the seal has been broken, he probes for nails and pries them up. With enough nails loosened, he can pull out the damaged shingle and remove any remaining nails. Then he slides a new shingle into place, lifts up the shingle above, and secures the newcomer with several roofing nails.

replacing a wood shingle Beautiful as they are, wood shingles—whether installed on the roof or as siding—can split, crack, and occasionally even rot from exposure to the environment. Damaged shingles should be replaced immediately.

When removing a wood shingle, Tom relies on a prying tool with a flat metal bar and a hook on one end, called a shingle ripper. "You slide it up and under the shingle, then probe until you find a nail," says Tom. "Then you hook the tool's end over the nail and bang its handle downward with a hammer, and out comes the nail." The process isn't perfect—adjacent shingles can sometimes be dragged out inadvertently—but it's generally successful. With the old shingle removed, a replacement can be cut to fit the space, allowing a slight gap on either side for expansion. "If you were to

Replacing a three-tab shingle. **1.** *Tom slips a pry bar underneath the damaged shingle to break its seal with the roof, then uses the bar to probe for and remove nails.* **2.** *After removing the shingle, he slips the new one into place and secures it with roofing nails.*

just nail it in place, you'd see the head of the nail. And nobody wants to look at that," says Tom. To avoid this, he uses a disappearing trick worthy of a magician. He slides the new shingle partway into place, leaving it ¼ inch below the row it belongs in. Then he nails the shingle in place with two stainless-steel trim nails, each placed about an inch from the shingle's upper edge. "You have to angle the nails upward, and as close to the bottom edge of the overlapping shingles as possible," Tom says. "Two nails are enough because wood shingles are not very wide." Now comes the trick: Once he's driven the nails in and tapped them flush with a nail set, he holds a wood scrap against the bottom edge of the new shingle and raps it with a hammer to drive it even with the others in its row. As the shingle is driven upward, the nails bend slightly and disappear just underneath the edge of the shingle above.

washing gutters The outside of gutters can develop a grimy film over time, and it's particularly visible on white gutters. To clean it off, Tom heads up the ladder with a rag and a bucket of water mixed with a mild car-wash detergent. As he scrubs off the grime he takes care of another task: inspecting the roof for any signs of damage. "There's no use making all those trips up and down the ladder for nothing," he says. Once the gutters are clean, he hoses off the detergent from the ground.

replacing gutters Positioned along the edge of a roof, gutters are exposed to some difficult conditions. In winter, snow sliding off the roof can bend gutters, particularly if the outer edge of the gutter is above the plane of the roof. Also, falling tree branches seem to reserve their heaviest blows for the troughs. Resting an extension ladder against a gutter is trouble, too, because the combined weight of ladder and home owner is enough to squash the gutter flat (Tom uses standoffs, p. 51, to prevent this). Sooner or later, knowing how to replace a gutter will come in handy.

When Tom replaces a gutter, he first buys a replacement piece that matches the style and material of the existing one as closely as possible. "There are so many varieties that you'll probably have to take an old piece with you to make sure you get the right one," he says.

To replace a wood shingle, Tom slips the new one into place, drives two nails in just beneath the shingle above, then drives the shingle home so the nails will be hidden.

types: roof shingles and shakes

Of all roof coverings available, Tom prefers wood: "On an old house, there's just nothing else that looks as good." Wood shingles and shakes come in a variety of species and styles, though the two noted below are the most common.

Shingles are about ⅜-inch thick at the butt and are typically sawn from the log to produce a relatively smooth surface. Shakes run ⅝ inch thick and are split from the log, giving them a more rustic look. The thicker end-grain edge of shakes tends to soak up more water, says Tom, which makes them deteriorate faster.

Tom uses only products graded Number 1 (Blue Label). They are made from the most rot-resistant part of the tree— heartwood—and feature vertical grain, which lessens the chance of shrinking and cupping.

WESTERN RED CEDAR: More dimensionally stable than white cedar, these shingles age to a silvery gray or a dark brown, depending on the climate.

ALASKAN YELLOW CEDAR: Tight-grained and durable, it weathers to a light gray and has the same durability as red cedar.

SAWN AND SPLIT

types: gutters

Every gutter collects water, but not all gutters are the same. They can be installed in sections or in continuous pieces custom-fitted to the house. "The fewer seams, the less chance of failure," says Tom. Shapes can be box-type or half-round. When attaching gutters, he prefers hanging systems that employ screws rather than nails: "They hold the longest." Materials include:

ALUMINUM: The most common material, it combines stability with decent strength. "Buy the thickest stuff you can," advises Tom, who prefers stock that is .032 inch thick. The standard gutter is about 4 inches deep and 5 inches wide; an unusually large roof might require a larger gutter.

GALVANIZED: Gutters made from steel coated with zinc are sturdier than aluminum, "but they're prone to rust," says Tom. "I usually replace them with aluminum gutters."

COPPER: Although expensive, copper gutters find a use especially in historic houses. "Nothing else looks as good, especially on a brick house," he says. Nor does anything else last as long.

WOOD: Found on old houses, wood gutters have a respectable life span if treated once or twice a year with linseed oil. "That's the key to making them last," says Tom.

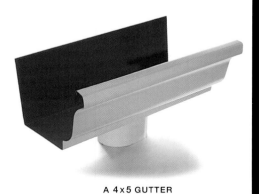

A 4 x 5 GUTTER

Tom then removes the damaged section—all the way to the joints with adjacent pieces. If it's one continuous piece, rather than sections, you can cut a piece out and replace it, but the patch is temporary: "Eventually you'll have to replace the whole gutter," says Tom. He installs the piece exactly as the old one was, using either a bracket system screwed to the roof sheathing or a spike-and-ferrule system that secures the gutter to the fascia. Seal each joint with butyl caulking to prevent leaks. "It's messy stuff to work with," says Tom, "but it stays pliable even when the gutter expands and contracts."

The hardest part about installing a new section of gutter is making sure that it is pitched correctly. "I can't tell you how many gutters I've seen that don't drain—the water just stands there," says Tom. "All that weight can eventually pull the gutter and even the fascia board away from the house." To prevent this, Tom relies on a rule of thumb: A gutter should drop ¾ inch every 15 to 20 running feet. "You can use a level to check the slope or you can do the math," says Tom, "or you can just run water into the gutter to see if it drains away."

repairing corner trim   On many houses, corner trim (often called a corner board) covers the joint where two walls intersect. "Corner boards rot for a number of reasons," says Tom. "Water splashing back up from the ground rots them at the bottom, while water dripping from leaking downspouts or gutters causes rot higher up." The decay is not always visible, so Tom looks for telltale signs of peeling paint or crumbling wood as indications of trouble. Also, the joints or seams can separate, which is another invitation to water infiltration.

If the damage is minor, Tom repairs it with putty as he would siding (p. 69), and if the wood is riddled with damage, he'll remove the entire corner and install a new one. But if neither approach suits the problem, Tom cuts out the damage, particularly if the rot is near the bottom of the board. He cuts through the wood with a circular saw and finishes the cut with a sharp chisel, angling the cut so that the upper section will shed water over the piece he'll put in. Once he cuts the new wood to length and angles it to match its mate, Tom

Repairing the rake. **1.** *Tom cuts through the rake above the damage and pries the trim loose (in this case it did not need replacement).* **2.** *Using the old wood as a template, he cuts new pieces, primes them, and nails them into place. Caulk seals the joints.*

1

2

primes the new wood as well as the cut portion of the old wood. After the primer dries, he butters the mating surfaces with caulk to seal out water, then nails the new piece into place with galvanized finish nails, wiping away any excess caulk that squeezes out.

reattaching downspouts and leaders Downspouts occasionally pull away from their attaching brackets, resulting in a cascade of water that ends up right next to the foundation. "I can't think of a better recipe for a wet basement," says Tom. When this happens, simply reattach the downspout with an aluminum strap and a couple of nails. If part of the downspout is damaged, buy a replacement and cut it to length with a hacksaw.

Leaders are as important as downspouts in keeping basements dry, because they channel water away from the house. To secure the connection between downspout and the lower elbow (sometimes called a shoe), he attaches the pieces with a screw or rivet (the shorter the better, or else they'll snag debris).

repairing a rake On houses with gables or dormers, the rake is the trim piece that follows the pitch of the roof. It can be made of several components, including a rake board and crown molding. As with the fascia, the rake is prone to rot (p. 57), but not along its whole length. "Usually it's just the ends near the gutter that you have to worry about," says Tom, because the wood's end grain is most likely to absorb water. If that's the case, Tom cuts out the lower 2 to 5 feet of it with a reciprocating saw. When installing the new pieces, Tom staggers the cuts on any trim so that the patch is less apparent. Then he primes both faces and all edges of the new wood, as well as cut edges of the old wood. If more than half of the rake is damaged, however, Tom simply replaces the whole thing.

Just before he nails the patch into place, he smears the upper end with enough caulk to squeeze out of the joint. "The caulk squeezes out, then you smooth it with a putty knife," he adds.

Gutter system repairs. **1.** *Loose elbows that break free of the gutter let water land where it's least wanted: next to the foundation. Elbows should be connected to the gutter outlet with rivets or short screws.* **2.** *If the seams in sectional gutters leak, spread gutter seam sealant over the area, but try to minimize a lumpy repair that would impede water flowing down the gutter.* **3.** *When gutter spikes pull loose, the entire gutter sags. Renail loose spikes into fresh wood (and seal the old holes), or replace the spikes with gutter screws.* **4.** *Loose downspouts should be strapped to the house.*

improvements:
leafless gutters

Cleaning gutters is a loathsome task, but Tom has found a way around it: leafless gutters. "They've made me appreciate the beauty of a New England fall, rather than cursing at all those golden leaves that would otherwise end up in my gutters," he says.

Some systems can be retrofitted onto existing gutters, but Tom chose to have one-piece units installed on his house. These have a trough just like ordinary gutters, but they are covered by a curved roof-like plate that deflects leaves. "Water follows the curve due to natural surface tension and runs into the trough," says Tom. "I don't have to sort through soggy, half-decomposed leaves anymore." If some debris does happen to work its way into the gutter, it can be flushed it out with a garden hose. "I've had great luck with these systems, and I use them a lot now," he says. Because he doesn't have pine trees in his yard, however, Tom doesn't know how effective leafless gutters are in keeping out pine needles.

Tom doesn't care for traditional anti-leaf products such as screens. "They blow out or fall off or unravel over time," he says. "No matter how carefully you put them in, they come undone."

LEAFLESS GUTTER

types: siding

"Much as we'd like to believe it, there's no such thing as a siding that's maintenance-free," says Tom. "Everything requires at least some degree of care."
WOOD: Although this ranks as Tom's favorite, it requires perhaps more maintenance than anything else. Wood deterioriates, not just from wetness and rot, but from the sun itself, which can destroy the lignin that holds the cellulose fibers together. Paint protects the wood, but patches of peeling paint suggest problems. "That often indicates that water is getting at the wood," says Tom.
VINYL: Billed as a maintenance-free siding, it's not. Boards can break just as they do on a wood-sided house, and dingy siding should be washed. Beyond that, "the vinyl can lose its luster and dark colors can fade from the sun," says Tom. As a result, it has a shorter life span than properly maintained wood—often as little as 20 years.
CEMENT BOARD: Painted cement-based siding can look more like real wood than any other non-wood siding, says Tom, and is increasingly common. Not only did he install it on the exterior of the show's project in Salem, Mass., but he also put it on his brother's house in Billerica. The boards are heavy to work with, which is a disadvantage, "but they are available preprimed, and hold paint very well," he adds.
STUCCO: This is a type of mortar that surrounds the house with a durable shell. Stucco is prone to cracking, however, if moisture seeps behind it, so it's important to inspect the flashing and caulked joints each year, and to replace them if necessary. "Stucco should be painted with latex, rather than an oil-based paint," says Tom. Latex paint is less likely to trap moisture vapor inside the wall cavities or behind the stucco than an oil-based paint.

cleaning out gutters Gutters do more than keep the rain from splashing on your head as you walk out the door: They also protect lower walls from being splashed by cascades of water, which can stain the siding and encourage rot.

But along with channeling water away from the house, gutters collect debris; seemingly every leaf that blows in the wind will end up in the slender troughs. "If a gutter is full of junk, it can't drain water," says Tom; "It's as simple as that." The constant dampness and frequent overflows can easily rot the fascia board—the wood behind the gutters—and if that goes on for long, even the ends of the rafters can be damaged. "To prevent this, you've got to get up on a ladder, and you've got to dig in there with your hands or use a slender scrap of wood as a scoop," says Tom. "This has to be done once or twice a year, depending on how many trees are nearby." Tom rarely wears gloves for this operation but admits that most homeowners probably prefer them. He hauls a 5-gallon bucket up to contain the grunge he dredges out. "You don't want to throw this stuff down to the ground—it's a disgusting mess that will splatter all over everything," he explains. If the bucket imperils your stability, however, just toss the muck on the ground and clean it up later. The job is unavoidably messy, says Tom, "but it's a job that has to be done."

Once a gutter has been cleared, Tom flushes it with a garden hose. "This gets rid of all the little bits of debris that could later block the downspout," he explains. If the downspout is clogged, Tom snakes the hose into it. "That usually blasts away the culprit—usually a bunch of leaves dammed up by small twigs," he says. Make sure that the downspout isn't dumping water right next to the foundation, an invitation to basement leakage. Instead, install a section of downspout called a leader to divert it away from the

When cleaning a gutter, Tom keeps one arm looped around the ladder. This keeps his body centered over the ladder and prevents him from leaning too far in any direction.

sizing nails
To choose a nail for installing corner boards and other trim, Tom uses this rule of thumb: "The nail should be 2 1/2 times as long as the trim is thick." That will ensure that it gets through the sheathing.

house. If the leader is missing or damaged (lawn mowers and children have a particular talent for crushing leaders), put in a new one—they're inexpensive. "Keeping the gutters and downspouts flowing freely is probably the single most important thing you can do for the exterior of your house," Tom says.

repairing a fascia Fascia boards delineate the lower, horizontal edge of the roof and provide support for the gutters. They'll rot where gutters leak or spill over, and if the adjacent roof flashing, called drip edge, is missing or damaged. They also rot at the corners, where they join the rake board that rises up the gable end of the house. "This isn't major structural damage, but rot leads to holes, and holes offer open doors to every possible pest, from wasps and bees to squirrels," says Tom.

Before the fascia can be repaired or replaced, the gutter must be removed (or at least loosened, as on p. 62). Tom uses a prybar to remove the spikes (long nails) holding the gutter in place, though sometimes locking pliers work better. Lengths of gutter are unwieldy, so it's a good idea to enlist a helper for this part of the job. Next, using a nail puller called a cat's paw, he yanks the nails from the fascia board and pulls it off the house, working carefully to prevent damage to the drip edge. "Once it's on the ground, I'll decide whether to cut away the rotten portion and patch in new stock, or to just replace the whole board," he says. Either way, Tom searches for a piece of wood that has the same width and thickness so that it blends in with the rest of the house. Tom always primes a new fascia board on both sides, both edges, and both ends before installing it. "That's one sure way to add life to the fascia," he explains. Another is the use of galvanized or (even better) stainless-steel nails to reattach the fascia. If the damage is minor, such as that created by carpenter bees or surface rot, he simply patches the fascia in place, using a polyester-based two-part wood filling product (similar to auto-body filler), before priming and repainting the wood.

repairing stucco Stucco houses have mortar slathered over the exterior, and patching any damaged areas involves applying a

*Repairing the fascia. **1.** To remove this rotted section of fascia, Tom was able to loosen the gutter just enough to reach behind it with a reciprocating saw. **2.** After cutting a replacement piece and priming it, Tom secures it by nailing into the rafter ends.*

tom's tip: wasps, bees, bats

An attic can end up as the home for an assortment of critters ranging from bats to bees and wasps. But rather than using chemical killers, Tom prefers a good defense.

"Creatures can find their way into the littlest holes—whether it's a gap in the miter between a rake and the fascia, or a patch where crown molding doesn't actually meet the gutter," says Tom. If trim is loose, he nails it back into place. If he finds holes or gaps, he fills them with expanding foam sealant, shaves off the excess when dry, then spreads paintable caulk over the foam for a smooth patch.

Some insects actually damage the wood in a house, and small rodents—squirrels in particular—are notoriously destructive if they find a way in. "But the biggest risk from bees and wasps is getting stung by them," says Tom. "Once I opened up a fascia board and got hit by about 15 or 20 yellow jackets at once. I almost fell off the ladder."

To prevent infestations in the first place, Tom is a ruthless repairer of rot and a diligent patcher of holes and gaps. "This is one case where an ounce of prevention is worth two or three tons of cure," he says.

CARPENTER BEE

improvements:
vinyl over wood

Before installing vinyl over wood siding, there are a few things to consider. You'll have to remove deteriorating or rotted areas of wood before covering them up with vinyl. "If you don't," warns Tom, "you could be sealing a serious decay problem behind the new siding, and it will only get worse." If the wood is in good condition, however, Tom says to put the new siding right over it.

Leaving the wood in place gives future homeowners the option of removing the vinyl and restoring the wood beneath it. "I've seen more than one house where drab vinyl siding covered up beautiful cedar clapboards and detailed molding," says Tom. "Before you give up and cover the wood, make sure you've at least tried to preserve what you've got."

During installation, vinyl shouldn't be pressed tight against the wood—it should be hung a little loosely, says Tom. This is because vinyl expands and contracts at a different rate than wood. "You want the vinyl to be able to move without interference," he explains.

Repairing vinyl is a snap, literally. Tom just pries a course loose to remove it. But to install a replacement, he uses a simple device sometimes called a siding removal tool or a zip tool (below). The hooked end slips underneath the siding to disengage the interlocking edges of adjoining lengths of vinyl.

ZIP TOOL

new coat of mortar. "The hard part isn't patching the hole," says Tom. "It's making the finished area look like it's not a patch." To do this, Tom first builds up the base coat of stucco in two or three stages. If the old stucco is painted, he roughs up the area and removes any loose stucco with a wire brush in order to prepare the surface to accept the new mortar. Then he brushes a liquid bonding agent over the area to provide a good grip for the new mortar. "Without that, the new stuff will just crumble off," he says. When it comes time to butter mortar into the area, Tom chooses a trowel according to the texture he's trying to match. "It could be a metal trowel, a wooden trowel, or even a brush," he explains. To disguise the patch, Tom feathers the new mortar into undamaged sections of the wall, blending the texture so that the repair does not look quite so obvious. If the stucco is to be painted, he paints a larger area with latex to further conceal his work. "If you feather the new stucco over a big area and paint over an even bigger one, you'll end up with a patch that's not at all obvious," he says.

repairing vinyl siding Like wood, vinyl can break under stress. "You might find that it cracks from being hit with a rock, or when your extension ladder slams against it during other repairs," says Tom. "And if the weather is extremely cold, the vinyl becomes brittle, making it more susceptible to damage." Newer vinyls are more resilient than older versions of the siding. Vinyl siding won't hold up as long as wood, but it can last at least 20 to 30 years. The older the siding gets, however, the more prone it is to damage. "If old vinyl siding has to be replaced and you can't find a piece to match, then you may have to replace an entire wall of siding if you want the patch to be invisible," says Tom. That's why homeowners should stockpile siding pieces when they first have it installed.

Wood clapboard and shingles must be carefully pried out when they are replaced, but vinyl siding is easy to repair. Tom pulls off a damaged section by hand and uses a zip tool (*left*) to reinstall it. Replacement pieces can be cut to length with a utility knife guided by a straightedge, or with a circular saw fitted with a plywood blade. When renailing the piece, says Tom, the nail shouldn't be driven tight—the siding needs to move with changes in temperature.

Tom relies on a zip tool to remove and reinstall vinyl siding. The tool enables him to easily disengage the interlocking edges at the heart of the siding's weatherproof barrier.

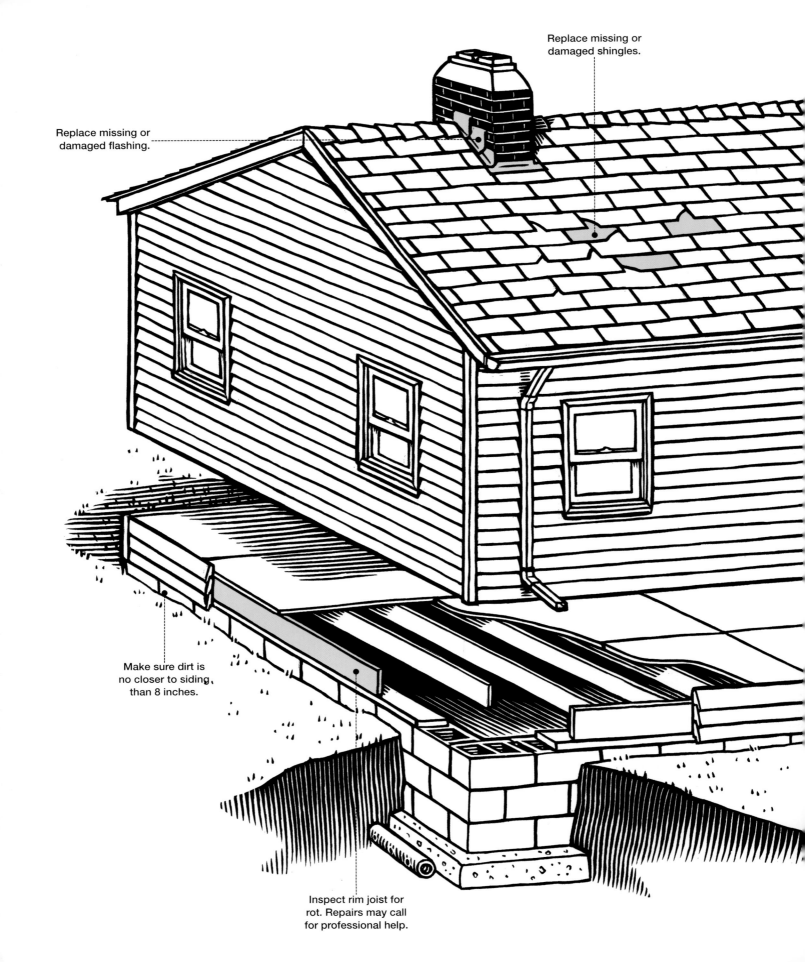

Replace missing or damaged shingles.

Replace missing or damaged flashing.

Make sure dirt is no closer to siding than 8 inches.

Inspect rim joist for rot. Repairs may call for professional help.

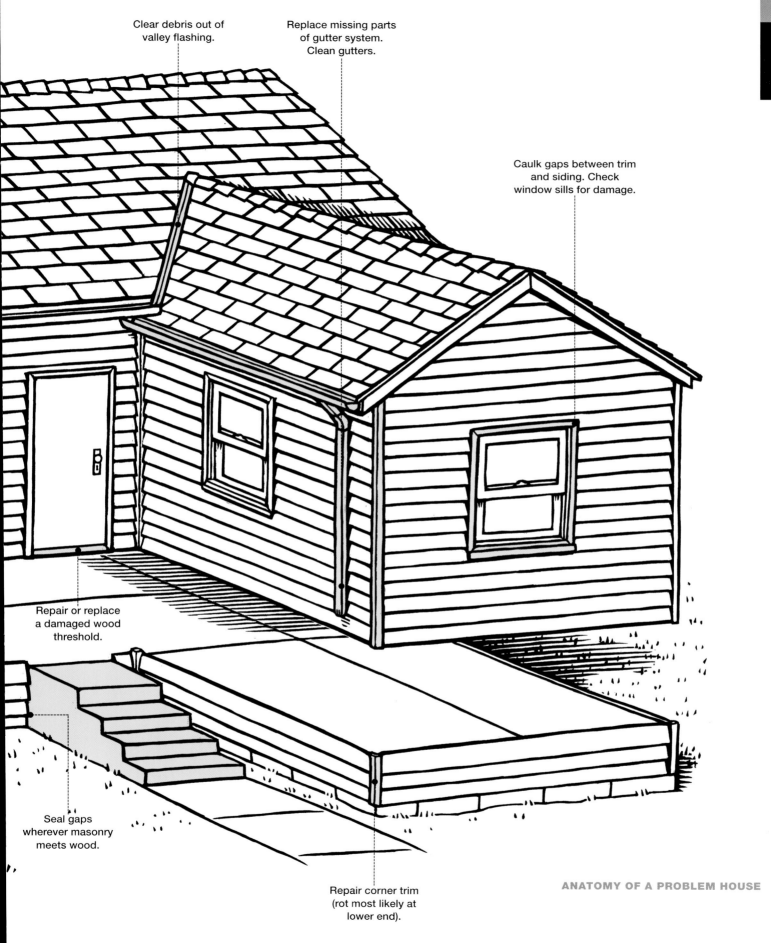

Clear debris out of
valley flashing.

Replace missing parts
of gutter system.
Clean gutters.

Caulk gaps between trim
and siding. Check
window sills for damage.

Repair or replace
a damaged wood
threshold.

Seal gaps
wherever masonry
meets wood.

Repair corner trim
(rot most likely at
lower end).

ANATOMY OF A PROBLEM HOUSE

repairing clapboard   Sometimes a damaged clapboard can be repaired in place. "If there's a small hole in the wood," says Tom, "or a gouge, it's a lot easier to fill it than to replace the board." He has found that two-part all-purpose wood filler (p. 63), available at most hardware stores, makes a permanent, solid, and invisible repair. He simply mixes the two components and butters them into the damage with a putty knife. The material dries within an hour, and can then be sanded flush with the surrounding area. Priming and painting follow. The same repair works on any outdoor wood.

replacing clapboard   Occasionally a portion of wood clapboard is beyond repair, such as when it has split lengthwise all the way to one end. That's when it should be replaced. Tom begins by cutting out the damaged piece with a utility knife, slicing horizontally right along the top and vertically on either side. "Believe it or not," he says, "that works great." The goal is to avoid damage to the boards above and below the one being removed.

The next step is to slide a flat pry bar underneath the cut piece of siding, using the house as a fulcrum and the removed piece of siding as a cushion to prevent damage to the board above. He gently works the bar back and forth to loosen all the nails a little at a time. "You may be talking about four, five, or six nails—and you just keep going back to them, loosening them a little bit more," he says. It's a process that rewards careful, patient efforts—and penalizes haste. Once the nailheads stick out enough to be extracted with the pry bar, he removes them, slips out the remaining portion of the old clapboard, and cuts a new piece to fit from stock that exactly matches the profile of the existing siding.

After he primes the new piece on all sides and edges (as well as priming cut edges of the old siding), Tom lays down a bead of acrylic latex caulk at the ends and presses the new board in position. He nails the board into place by driving new nails through the old holes in the siding above. "Angle the nails slightly downward so you're driving into fresh wood in the sheathing beneath," he says. "That will give you a better hold." When the repair is complete, the area can be repainted.

Repairing wood siding. **1.** *After scraping off loose paint and excavating loose wood with a chisel, Tom fills the hole with 2-part putty, a quick-drying and strong patching material.* **2.** *After sanding the patch smooth, he primes it and then paints it.*

improvements:
vinyl siding details

In the quest to find maintenance-free siding (there is no such thing, says Tom), many people have turned to vinyl siding and, in an earlier era, aluminum. "Because it goes on quick and easy, it can be a great choice," says Tom, "especially because the only upkeep involved is to wash it now and then. Done right, vinyl siding can look good."

Done wrong, however, it can look terrible. "I've seen more beautiful houses ruined by a bad vinyl siding job," says Tom. "The first thing people want when they call me is to have me rip it off." Still, there's a simple way to avoid a bad vinyl job. "The main thing on a classic older house is to leave the detailing intact," says Tom. "You can use vinyl for the siding, but leave the corner treatments, door treatments, and window treatments wood," he suggests. That will result in an exterior that needs some maintenance, but it will be less than having the whole house to work on.

Vinyl siding comes in an assortment of thicknesses and grades, some of which contain an embossed wood grain. Tom prefers smooth siding, however: "The embossed types tend to collect dirt."

pressure washing

On a pressure washer, a pump creates the force with which the water jets out, but it's the nozzle tip that focuses this force for particular applications. There are four basic tips (*below*), which vary according to the width of their spray; they may be color-coded. Other tips are available for special work, such as removing paint from masonry. Though Tom feels that pressure washing is generally best done by professionals, but enough people rent or own pressure-washing gear to make a quick course on tips worthwhile.

BASIC TIPS: The zero-degree tip is the most aggressive, producing a narrow, piercing stream that can pinpoint stains or penetrate hard-to-reach spots. "But an amateur can do way too much damage with this tip," says Tom. Once, when trying out a pressure washer for the first time, he drilled a hole into a 2x4. "It took a couple of minutes, but it was a pretty clean hole."

The 15- and 25-degree tips produce a fan-shaped spray that's far more controllable but still powerful enough to lift algae and grime off decks. The 40-degree nozzle produces a soft, fan-shaped spray. "Use it for rinsing a house once you've washed it," says Tom. "But a garden hose works pretty well, too."

WASHING TIPS

washing siding   Houses, like cars, get dirty, and they look worlds better when washed (as long as there's a decent paint job underneath the grime). "For some reason a lot of people never think to do this, but it makes a huge difference and it's a lot easier than repainting," says Tom. For this job, Tom picks up the same sort of brush he would use to clean a car—one with bristles stiff enough to remove dirt but not so unyielding that they'll damage the paint. Attaching it to a pole, he can scrub most of the siding from the ground, using a solution of mild household detergent mixed into a bucket of water. First he scrubs the siding—working from the bottom to the top so that the dirty water won't streak the dry boards as it drips down. Then he rinses the soap off with a hose, being careful not to squirt water up under the siding, where it could get into the wall cavities. If there's any mildew on the house, Tom mixes 3 parts water with 1 part chlorine bleach, squirts the affected areas with a spray pump, and scrubs them if the mildew doesn't wash off immediately. Then he rinses the bleach off thoroughly with the hose. "Just be careful that you don't let too much of the mixture splash on plants—they won't like the bleach much," he says. It's a good idea to wet surrounding plants before you begin work, just to dilute any bleach mixture that does hit them.

You won't damage a house by squirting it with a garden hose. A pressure washer, however, is another story. Shooting out water at anywhere from 2,000 to 4,000 pounds per square inch (compared to a measly 40 psi that jets from a garden hose), it can be a tricky tool to use. Many homeowners have rented pressure-washing gear, thinking it would make short work of cleaning their siding, only to find that they've damaged siding instead. If you're cautious and patient when using the tool, however, it can be a great help.

A professional pressure washing can cost between $300 and $500, says Tom. The process is particularly good for removing mildew, especially if chlorine bleach is added to the water (bleach kills mildew and its spores on contact). "That's great, because if you paint over mildew, it will just start growing right through the paint film again," says Tom. "But whenever you use bleach, you want to make sure you rinse, and rinse, and rinse," he warns. "Any residue will weaken the new paint's bond."

With a highly concentrated stream of water, a pressure washer is unexcelled at removing grime. Even the smaller units, however, call for some caution in their use.

doors

problems with hinges / troubleshooting hinges / fitting a strike plate / trimming a door / installing door weatherstripping / servicing garage doors / installing garage-door weatherstripping / solving threshold problems / repairing a lockset

chapter 4

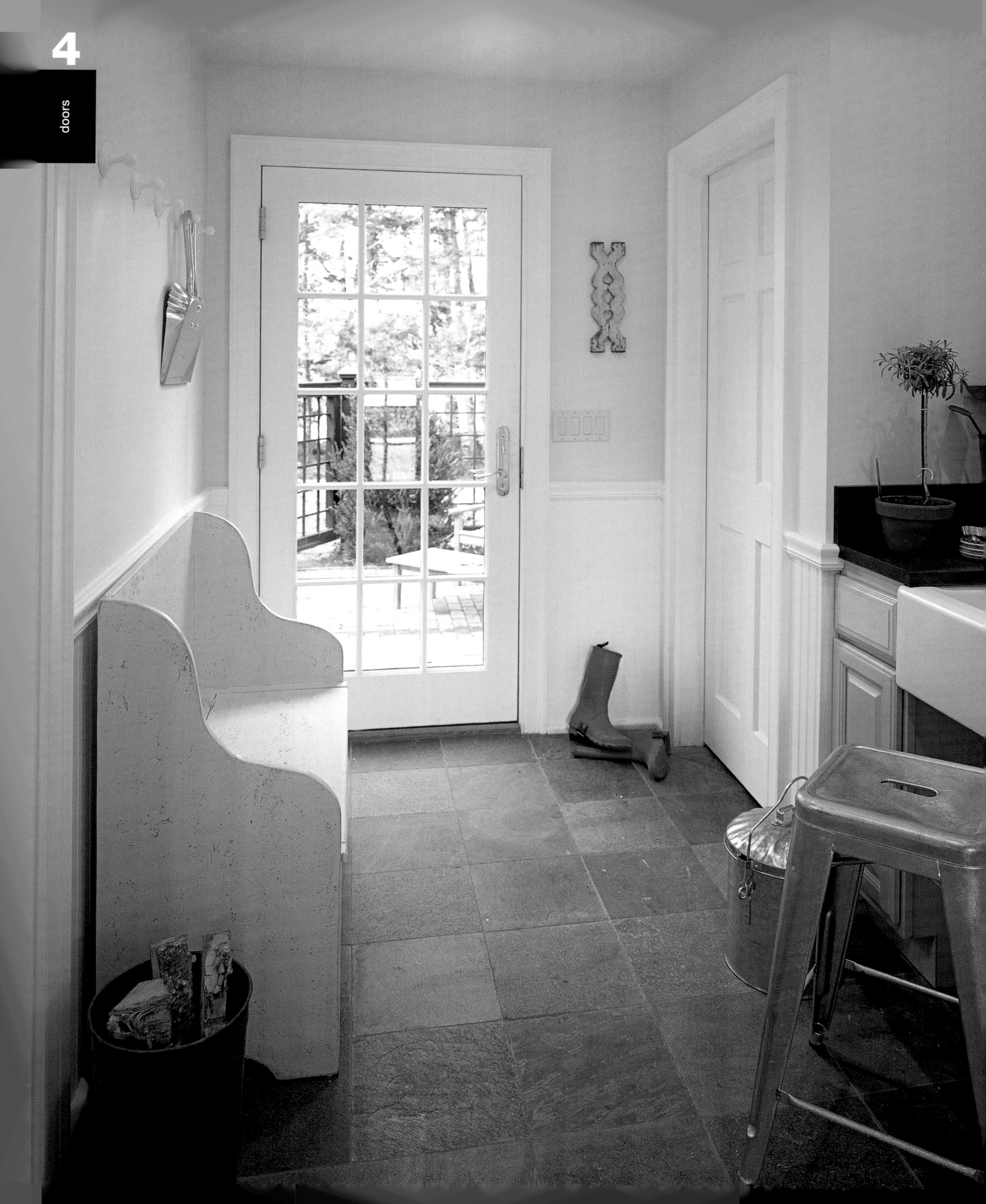

REBUILDING THE FIRE-RAVAGED HOME owned by Dick and Sandy Silva was the subject of our 1999 season, and I'll admit that throughout the project I didn't think much about the front door. But Tom did. One day he installed a beauty of solid mahogany, with a lacquer and marine-varnish finish that gleamed like a classic yacht in the afternoon sun. When we wrapped filming one day, Dickie checked out the door. He opened it, then closed and locked it a couple of times. Finally he nodded in satisfaction, opened it once more, and went inside. The door closed behind him with a deep, satisfying "thunk." The house wasn't finished, but when the front door was done, Dickie was home.

—STEVE

types: doors

There are two basic types of doors: those for interior use and those for exterior. Although wood exterior doors often look similar to wood interior doors, they're thicker—1¾ inches compared to 1⅜ inches—and contain weatherproof adhesives. "Never use an interior door outside," says Tom.

Among exterior doors, some of the choices have confusingly similar names. *Solid wood* doors are made of solid planks of wood. "Years ago, all doors were solid wood, but now you pay a premium to get them," says Tom. By contrast, *solid-core* doors consist of a wood veneer over a solid core of either a sawdust/adhesive composite or pine planks. *Insulated-core* doors are built of galvanized metal up to ⅛-inch thick, wrapped around rigid insulation. Tom prefers the look of wood on an older house, but for a maintenance-free alternative, he'll use *fiberglass* doors with a core of insulation. "They're very tough and don't rust, warp, or crack," he says.

Interior doors are similarly varied. There are *solid wood* doors, *solid-core* doors, and *hollow-core* doors (below). Hollow doors consist of wood veneer glued to a honeycomb of cardboard or stiff paper. They're inexpensive but offer little resistance to sound transmission. "Believe me," says Tom, "when they say hollow, they mean it."

HOLLOW-CORE DOOR

`MAINTENANCE` **problems with hinges** If confronted with a door that won't close properly because it either hits against the frame or fails to strike the latch, the first thing to do is to check the screws in the hinges. "Loose screws here could be the source of your problem," says Tom. Tightening them will often realign the door in its frame. Some sticking problems require more than just a screwdriver; the door may have to be trimmed (see p. 79). But be careful: A few hasty swipes with a block plane or a circular saw may create more troubles than you thought they would fix. "You might think you're getting the door to fit fine," says Tom. "But when winter comes and the door shrinks, you could end up with the opposite problem—a door that's too small for the opening." To control this, Tom always makes certain to remove as little as possible, whether he's sanding, planing, or cutting with a

Glazed doors let in natural light, a particular advantage in entries. Panes in any door must be shatter-resistant safety glass, identified by a manufacturer's logo in one corner.

types: locksets

Locksets are tailored to match different levels of security. There are two types. EXTERIOR LOCKSETS contain the doorknob and a secure locking mechanism. A version called a mortise lockset is best. "They tend to be the strongest, most durable locks—and the most expensive," says Tom. They're also the most difficult to install. Standard exterior locksets are easier to install and more common; their security can be improved considerably with the addition of a deadbolt. Tom recommends deadbolts that are keyed on the outside but have a thumb turn, not a key, inside. "If there's a fire and you have to leave in a hurry, what if the key is missing?" PASSAGE LOCKSETS are used on bedroom and bathroom doors. They have no real locking mechanism at all; at most, a button is pressed in to stop the knob from turning. "These locks are for privacy, not security," says Tom. "They can be popped open easily—good news if a child locks himself in." Simply poke a stiff, straight wire or narrow screwdriver into the hole in the outer knob.

Whatever type of lockset you choose, buy the best. "A cheap one won't last that long," says Tom. The easiest way to gauge quality? "Good ones are a lot heavier than others because they're made with thicker materials," he says. "You can literally feel the difference."

DEADBOLT LOCK

circular saw. "You can always go back and make another pass to trim a little more off, but if you pare away too much, you're stuck with it," he explains. Once he's made a wood door fit, Tom makes sure to seal the cut edges either with polyurethane or with primer and paint. Otherwise, moisture will be absorbed right into the raw cut and the door will swell again. "Sealing the door is the key to preventing problems in the future," he says. If a door fits but bare wood shows on the edges, seal them anyway.

REPAIR **troubleshooting hinges** In some cases, the problem with a door that won't stay shut lies not in the strike plate at all, but in the hinges—particularly the top hinge, which is under great tension as the weight of the door pulls against it. There usually aren't many problems with the bottom hinge, Tom reports, "but a loose, worn, or damaged hinge can throw the whole door off." Worn or damaged hinges should be replaced; loose hinges can be retightened *(right)*. If the holes behind the hinges are too sloppy to hold the original screws, Tom tries longer ones, or stuffs wood matchsticks into the holes to give the screws a better grip. Sometimes, he just replaces the problem screws with threaded inserts and machine screws *(right)*. "These hold better than anything," he says.

If a latch and strike are too far apart to engage, the entire door can be moved closer to the strike by placing shims under the hinges *(right)*. If the opposite problem occurs and the door sticks, the recesses (mortises) holding the hinges can be deepened—slightly—with a chisel. That effectively widens the gap between the latch and the strike, and it's a lot easier than trimming the entire edge of the door. "Study every part of the door to figure out where the trouble is coming from," says Tom, before rushing in to make repairs.

fitting a strike plate "Sometimes, no matter how many times you slam a door," says Tom, "it just won't latch." When that happens, he checks first to make sure all the screws are tightened in the strike plate, the small piece of metal attached to the doorjamb.

When it comes to getting doors to swing properly, Tom has a few tricks. 1. If the hinge screws can't be tightened, he replaces them with longer versions. Threaded inserts are another alternative. 2. A business card, or two, makes a handy shim to move a hinge (and the door) closer to the opposite jamb. 3. To fix a loose hinge, Tom shoves a glue-dipped wooden matchstick into the hole before driving the old screw back in. 4. If the door doesn't latch, a few strokes with a flat file might solve the problem.

If that doesn't help, he may be able to enlarge the strike plate's hole using a flat metal file (p. 77). When a latch is misaligned with the hole in the door jamb by more than ⅛-inch, however, it's time to remove the strike plate altogether, enlarge the hole in the jamb with a chisel, and reposition the plate.

trimming a door A door has to clear the finished floor—of course. "But if you buy a new carpet or replace a vinyl floor with ceramic tile, the door might not open over it," says Tom. Metal exterior doors can't be trimmed. Trimming a hollow-core door more than ¾ inch will expose the cardboard core, but solid and solid-core doors can be trimmed as needed. Trimming any wood door, however, requires care to avoid chipping the door's surface. "It's not just a matter of giving it the once-over with a circular saw," says Tom.

When Tom trims a door *(left)*, he determines exactly how much he has to cut off for the door to swing freely and adds another ⅛-inch for extra clearance. Then he removes the door, rests it on padded sawhorses, pencils a cut line along the bottom of the door, and scores the line with a utility knife. The last step prevents the wood from splintering as he cuts, particularly on the "face-up" side of veneered doors. Tom cuts just below the line, then uses a palm sander to smooth the cut to the scored line. If there's less than ¼ inch to trim off a door, Tom skips the saw altogether and uses just the belt sander. "But make sure you clamp the door down or you'll send it skidding," he says.

installing door weatherstripping Weatherstripping is as vital a part of an exterior door as the doorknob. "In addition to blocking air infiltration, a good piece of weatherstripping at the bottom of the door acts like a dam to keep out water," says Richard. Any weatherstripping is better than none, says Tom, but high-quality weatherstripping is well worth the modest extra expense. Some varieties slide into place in a wide groove cut across the bottom of the door, so that they're pushed against the threshold when the door is closed. "This gives you the best seal, and it's almost invisible," says Richard. Another type consists of interlocking pieces, one attached to the door bottom

To trim a door, Tom sometimes makes a simple layout jig that he clamps to the door. "It takes more time to find scrap to use," he says, "than to make the thing." The jig has a thin base and a raised stop that the saw's shoe rides against. After assembling the jig, he trims the base so that it ends exactly where the saw blade will cut.

improvements:
storm doors

While a perfectly aligned and weather-stripped front door keeps a house cozy in winter, it can seem visually confining. To remedy this, Tom likes to add glazed storm doors so he can open the main door and let in light on sunny days. Storm doors also block wind and driving rain on foul days. But glassed storm doors can create havoc if they're facing south. "They'll trap a lot of heat," says Tom, and the temperature can rise enough to melt vinyl or plastic grilles fitted onto the main door—or charbroil the paint. To prevent this, Tom drills two ¼-inch holes into the bottom of the storm-door frame, then two more up high. "You'll hardly notice them, but they'll vent air trapped between the doors and reduce the problem of overheating," he says. "And you'll still get insulation value from the storm door." Among storm doors, Tom's favorite material is, as always, wood; "I love the look," he says.

In the summer, Tom swaps the glass panels with screens. Screening, though, is flimsy, so he adds a push bar across the door. "That way, you're not pushing against the screen," he says.

improvements:
electric openers

It's hard to match the convenience of an electric garage-door opener—no one likes to step into foul weather in order to open the garage door by hand. But few things can be as irritating as a door opener that is uncooperative, leaving someone stranded either in the driveway or inside the garage. "People usually blame the door opener if this happens," says Tom. "But more often than not, the problem lies in the door."

The door must be correctly balanced to open properly. To test this, disengage the door from the opener by pulling the release cord hanging from the track. "If you can lift the door up yourself," says Tom, "and bring it down without a crash, then it's probably balanced right." To balance a door, adjust the tension of the extension springs (drawing, facing page). The release cord is also helpful during a power outage: It disengages the door from the opener so that it can be opened and closed manually. When power is restored, simply reengage the mechanism.

Top-of-the-line door openers last longer than cheaper versions because they have heavier-gauge metal gears and tracks and a stronger motor. But you may not need the most expensive opener for every door. "If you have a three-car garage, buy the best one for the door you use the most," says Tom. "You can use middle-of-the-line openers for the doors you use less often."

All garage doors now come equipped with a system that beams infrared light across the opening. "If that beam is broken when the door is coming down, perhaps by a child or a pet walking through, then the door automatically goes back up," says Tom. The system also prevents the door from crushing cars or bikes that obstruct the beam.

and the other to the threshold. The resulting seal is quite effective. But don't forget the rest of the door. Weatherstripping the sides and top of a door is easier than weatherstripping the bottom because compression-type products can be used (they aren't always suitable at the bottom of the door). Richard and Tom both prefer pile-type weatherstripping (see p. 122) in such locations. If there's no groove on the door, Tom uses a router to create one (see p. 123).

servicing garage doors The front door usually isn't the most popular route into the house—that title belongs to the garage door. Most door problems are caused by temperature changes and vibrations that loosen screws and bolts holding the hinges, pulleys, and tracks together. If that's the case, a quick tightening is all that's needed.

Sometimes the problem is nothing more than a dented or twisted track that is preventing the rollers from moving; just bend it back using groove-joint pliers. Driveway grit can grind the rollers to pieces over the years, but lubricating the rollers' axles with a small amount of household oil several times a year helps postpone the problem. "You don't want oil dripping all over, and you don't ever want to use grease," says Tom; "that attracts grit like a magnet." If a roller is really shot and lubrication doesn't help, replace it: Unscrew the hinge, slide the wheel off its axle, then slip a new wheel onto the old axle.

Springs, too, can wear out; look for symptoms such as the garage door suddenly seeming to gain weight. Torsion springs (they run parallel to the door) should only be serviced by a pro, but extension springs (right) are easy to adjust. Raise the door to relax the springs and then prop it securely in place. If the door has been going up too rapidly, lengthen the lifting cable and then retighten it securely. If it slams down or feels very heavy, shorten the cable.

If an electric opener refuses to operate, make sure it's still plugged in, and brush debris away from the sensors. Leave other repairs to a pro.

installing garage-door weatherstripping If a garage is attached to the house, properly weatherstripped doors actually form an air lock that defends the house against the chill of winter and the heat of summer. "The best way to seal a garage door is to attach foam strip weatherstripping to the jambs when the door is closed," Tom says.

The position and type of garage-door springs may vary, but the rest of the hardware is fairly standard. Doors are typically wood or steel; insulated doors are also available.

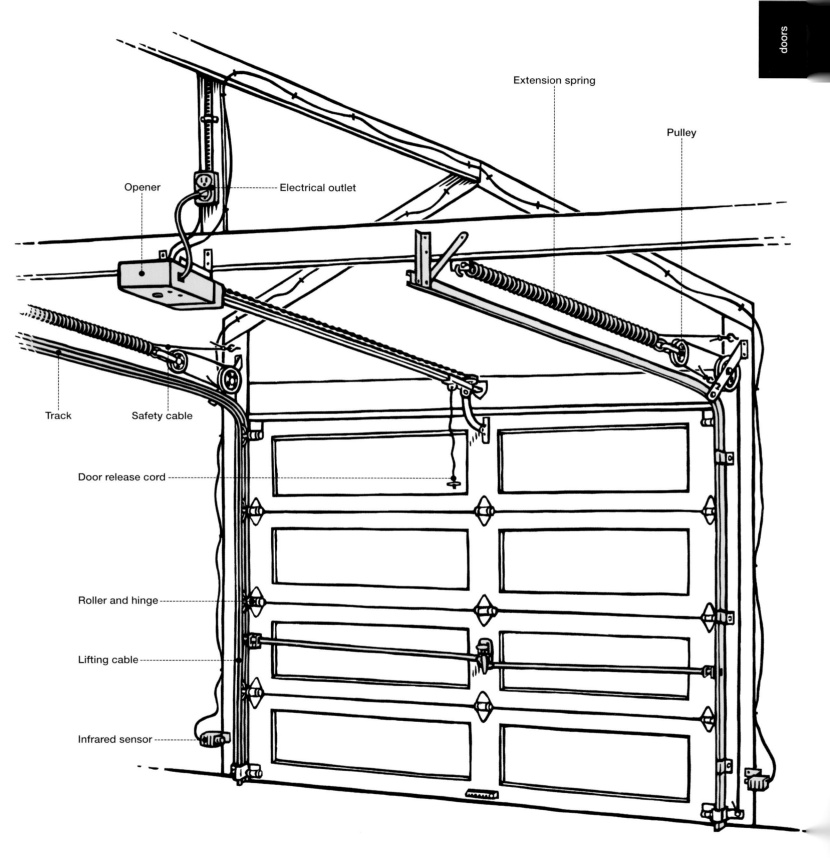

Extension spring

Pulley

Opener

Electrical outlet

Track

Safety cable

Door release cord

Roller and hinge

Lifting cable

Infrared sensor

ANATOMY OF A GARAGE-DOOR

Then open the door fully and nail a rubber garage-door weatherstripping gasket to the bottom edge. The gasket blocks cold air, wind blown rain and bugs and rodents, as well as protecting a wood door from prolonged contact with damp concrete.

solving threshold problems Because of the beating they take from sun, rain, and the steady tromping of feet, thresholds wear out sooner than doors. "When you see a gap beneath the door that weatherstripping just can't block, you know the threshold is a goner," says Tom. Deep cracks in a wood threshold are an invitation to water and rot, but they can be patched with epoxy wood filler *(left)* if they don't go entirely through the wood.

To replace a wooden threshold, Tom cuts the old one into three pieces with a handsaw or an electric reciprocating saw, then lifts the middle piece out and wiggles the end pieces loose. He uses the pieces as a template for the new threshold. "That's the biggest time-saver of all," says Tom. "Otherwise, you could spend all day trying to trim wood to fit." Before jockeying the new threshold into place, Tom coats the subfloor with polyurethane to protect it. Sometimes he'll also add a layer of self-adhesive rubberized membrane. "If water splashes against the door, it can seep beneath the threshold and cause rot," says Tom. "And then you're in for a much bigger job than you think."

repairing a lockset Every time a doorknob is turned or locked, it wears imperceptibly. "Eventually the doorknob wiggles and the lock won't work," says Tom. Other than old mortise locksets, says Tom, "I've never had to lubricate a good door lock." Most require nothing but periodic tightening of the screws to keep the mechanism working properly. When a doorknob won't turn or fails to lock, it could be that the screws have loosened behind the round escutcheon plate surrounding the doorknob's shaft. "Remove the plate first, then tighten the screws hiding beneath it," says Tom. But for anything more serious than this, it's probably time to replace the lockset. Interior locksets and many exterior units are easy to replace, but a mortise lockset isn't (see p. 76); let a locksmith work on that one.

Repairing a wood threshold—this one is at Tom's front door—is far easier than replacing it. **1.** *Tom sands the wood smooth, then fills the cracks with a two-part epoxy wood putty readily available at hardware stores.* **2.** *After sanding the filler smooth, he vacuums away the powdery dust and paints on two coats of high-gloss deck paint.*

types: thresholds

When it comes to exterior thresholds, there are two major choices: wood and aluminum. "The traditional choice is wood," says Tom, and in particular white oak: It's resistant to rot and extremely hard. The top surface should be sloped to shed water. Wood thresholds *(below, top)*, like most outdoor wood, require periodic sealing over the years. Tom prefers a good-quality deck paint or polyurethane. "Whatever it is, make sure it's something with a lot of UV protector because thresholds take a beating from the sun," he says.

Aluminum thresholds *(middle)* require no maintenance. Some are even fitted with a leveling system that makes it simple to adjust the fit with the door, which makes them easy to install. Others have a built-in channel that holds a replaceable length of weatherstripping. "Convenient as they are, the metal look can be a jarring addition to an old house," says Tom. "For me, nothing beats the appearance of wood." When a front door opens into a marble foyer, however, a marble threshold *(bottom)* offers an alternative, Tom adds. "It looks good and it's waterproof."

windows

cleaning windows / lubricating sash / patching torn screens / replacing window putty / freeing stuck windows / replacing weatherstripping / replacing screens / restringing sash weights / replacing broken glass

chapter 5

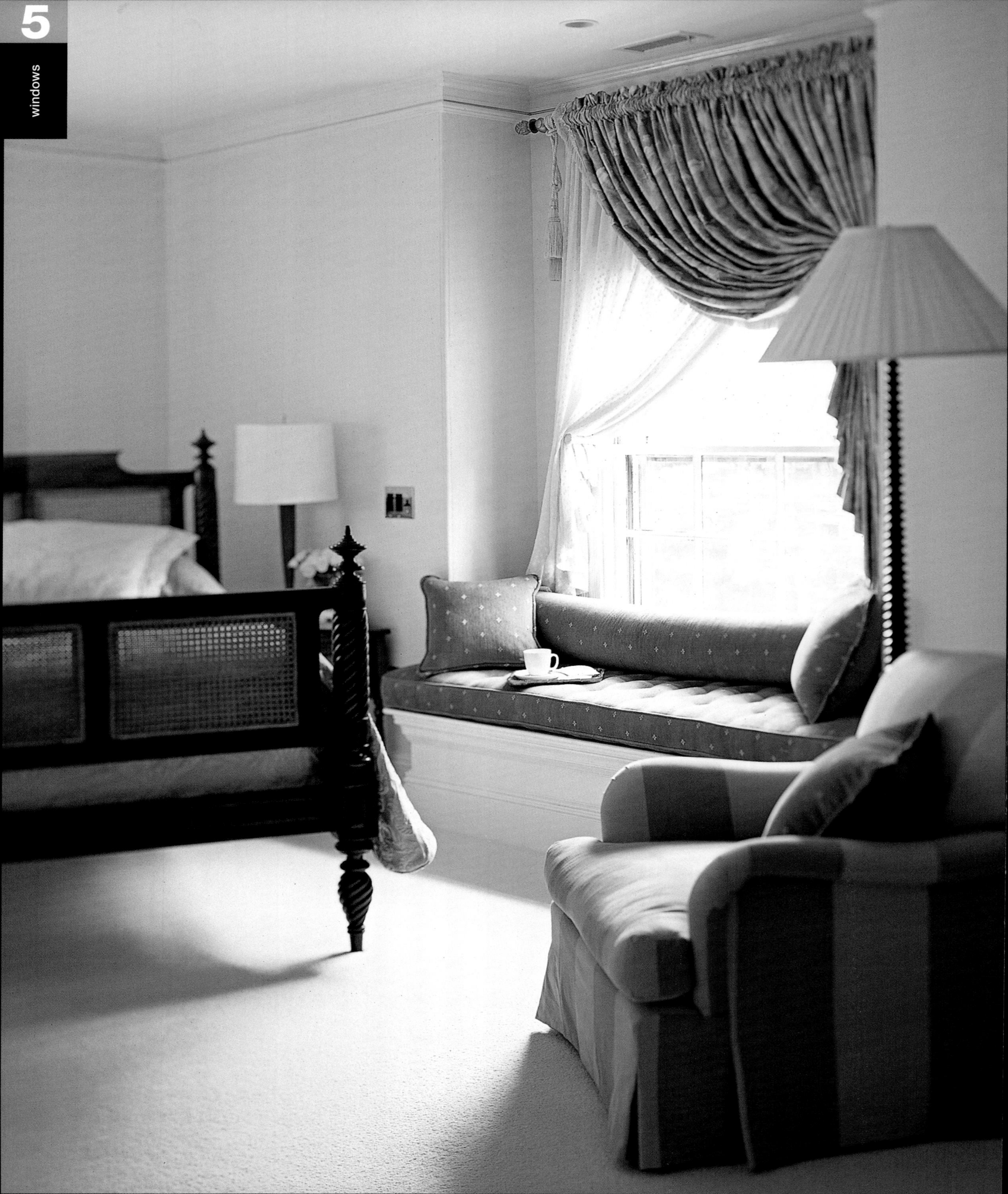

ON ONE EPISODE OF THIS OLD HOUSE we visited a state-of-the-art window factory, where a huge machine coated clear plastic film with a layer of silver exactly one atom thick. Sandwiched between two panes of glass, the film would admit light yet reflect heat. New windows may rely on technology, but old windows still call for handcraftsmanship. On a 1724 colonial we once renovated, we painstakingly rebuilt and weatherstripped the original windows. Along with the addition of storm panes, that dramatically increased the windows' efficiency without sacrificing the character of the building. Knowing your options helps you fit repairs to the house, your time, and your budget.

— STEVE

MAINTENANCE **cleaning windows** Windows give a house charm, but they can be a maintenance curse. As the seasons pass, wood windows shrink and swell, gaps form between the sash and the frame, and accumulations of paint and dirt make them difficult to open. "The single best thing you can do to make sure windows function well is to keep the various parts clean," says Tom. "You'll prevent all sorts of problems that way."

The sills and jambs of double-hung windows should be kept free of dirt by vacuuming them as needed, then sponging off grime with mild nonabrasive soap and water. If the house predates 1978, when lead paint was banned, traces of dust on the windowsills may contain lead. Vacuuming might spread the dust into the house, so clean it up instead with a sponge and soapy water.

With casement or awning windows, the operating mechanism and

A window seems such a simple device, but it can have a profound impact on the look, feel, and safety of a room. Adjacent architectural features often amplify its impact.

types: windows

Windows come in as many sizes as there are types of houses, but most can be grouped into four categories.

DOUBLE-HUNG WINDOWS contain two movable parts, called the sash, that glide up and down. When both sash are opened, says Tom, "you get a natural chimney effect as warm air flows out the top and cooler air is drawn in the bottom." But double-hung windows are the hardest to weatherstrip and the most time-consuming to maintain.

CASEMENT WINDOWS feature a single sash that pivots outward when cranked open, catching breezes as they flow by the wall and drawing them into the house. They're also very energy-efficient: "They seal as tight as a refrigerator door," as long as the weatherstripping isn't caked with paint.

AWNING WINDOWS contain a single sash that pivots outward when cranked open, like casements. But instead of opening from the side, they swing open at the bottom. Their advantage, says Tom, "is that you can leave them open on a rainy day and not end up with a wet floor." Since awning windows have the same construction as casement windows, they have similar weatherstripping and maintenance characteristics.

FIXED WINDOWS are often referred to as picture windows. This type of glazing doesn't open at all. Like framed pictures, they hang on the wall to delight the eye—by letting in sunlight and views. "You can put a much larger pane in the wall than with a window that has to open," says Tom. The disadvantage, of course, is that you don't get any ventilation. A fixed window can be paired with any other opening window, however, to solve this problem. A row of awning windows, for example, can be installed beneath a fixed window, or casements can flank it.

improvements:
effective glazing

Glass has plenty of virtues. But as an insulator against outdoor temperature extremes, it's only slightly better than a hole in the wall. In fact, heat will radiate right through the glass in either direction.

Double glazing provides a far better insulation value—as much as 50 percent greater. Windows made this way contain two layers of glass separated by a layer of trapped air or inert gas. "It's the air, not the glass, that gives the window its insulation value," explains Richard. If the seal fails, the inner surfaces of the glass fog up and the window's efficiency drops. The only solution is to replace the glass, seals and all, which usually involves replacing the entire sash.

If your existing windows are single-glazed, says Richard, don't despair. "You can improve their insulation value dramatically by adding a good-quality, tight-fitting storm window." Storm windows aren't needed over double-glazed windows, however. "That would be overkill in all but the coldest of climates," he explains.

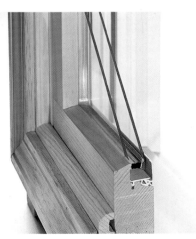

DOUBLE GLAZING

the sliding arm should be wiped free of dirt so that the window opens and closes easily. And for all types of windows, sponging the weatherstripping clean will reduce its tendency to stick to the sash.

But when it comes to window cleaning, the real satisfaction lies in liberating the glass from grime. Granted, climbing up a ladder with window-cleaning gear isn't how most people like to spend their weekend. Tom can't avoid cleaning windows, either, but he knows how to minimize the effort. His trick is to mix up an inexpensive batch of streak-free cleaning solution: a capful of paint thinner or mineral spirits mixed into 2 gallons of warm water. After wiping the glass with a rag dampened in the mixture, Tom dries the glass with a crumpled sheet of newspaper. "That eliminates streaks," he says. "And it's a good way to get rid of the Sunday *Boston Globe*."

lubricating sash Parts that rub against others often require lubrication. If window jambs and stops have thick layers of paint on them or haven't been cleaned for years, the surfaces may be too rough for the sash to glide. If the jambs are wood, Tom sands them lightly, then rubs them with a stick of paraffin wax. If they're covered with jamb liners (p. 91), Tom gently chips off any paint and sprays them with a "dry" spray lubricant. "Don't use an oil-based spray," warns Tom, "because it acts like a magnet to attract grit." But if the sash are painted shut, no lubricant will help: You'll have to cut them open (p. 91).

patching torn screens Screens may protect a house from swarming insects, but even a tiny breach foils the defense. That makes patching screens an urgent bit of maintenance. "I put it high on my own list of priorities well before warm weather hits," says Tom, "because I hate mosquitoes."

Patching kits for small holes in metal screens can be purchased at a hardware store, but Tom often makes his own patches from scraps of leftover screening. He starts by cutting a rectangular piece for the patch, making it about 2 inches larger all around than the damaged area. Then he pulls several strands of wire off each edge, leaving spiderlike "legs" at the perimeter, and bends the legs at a 90 degree angle. "All I have to do then is fit the patch over the hole

Short of replacing an entire window, various things can improve its operation and energy-efficiency, including weatherstripping it, adding storms, and replacing the sash.

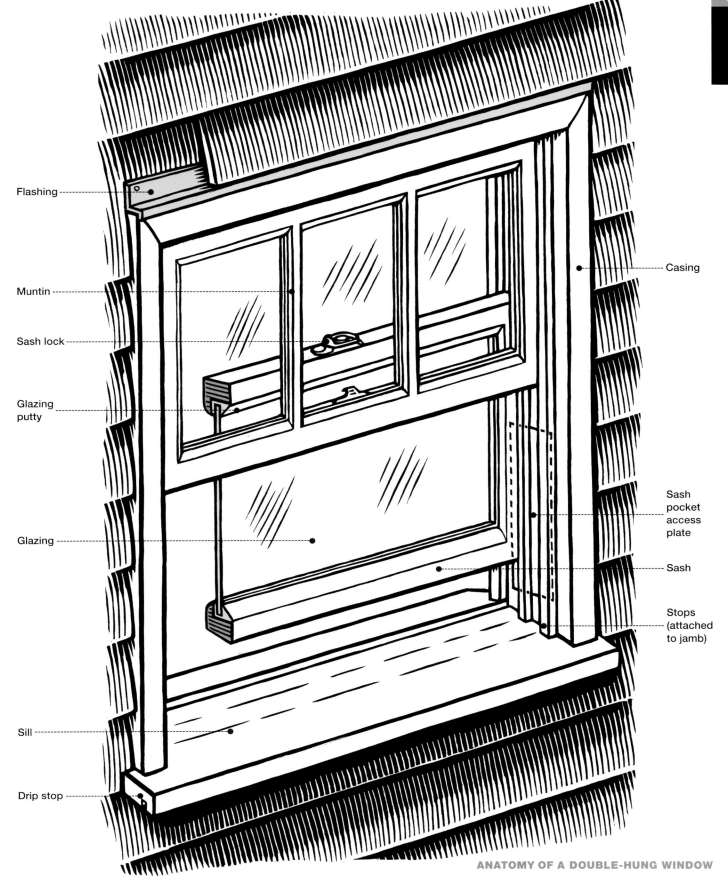

Flashing

Muntin

Sash lock

Glazing
putty

Glazing

Sill

Drip stop

Casing

Sash
pocket
access
plate

Sash

Stops
(attached
to jamb)

ANATOMY OF A DOUBLE-HUNG WINDOW

1 2

3 4

and bend the little legs over to hold it in place," says Tom. The patch isn't invisible, however: The screen looks twice as dark where the material overlaps. If a screen is torn, Tom can sometimes stitch the pieces back together with monofilament fishing line and a needle. "It's a temporary repair," he admits, "but it'll keep the mosquitoes out until you can get time to replace the whole thing."

Most new windows come fitted with corrosion-proof fiberglass screens; repairing them is a breeze. If the strands were simply pushed out of place and not broken, push them back with a straightened paper clip or a pin. If the strands are broken, Tom dabs the hole with epoxy glue and wipes away any excess before it hardens. For larger holes, it's as easy to replace the screen (see p. 95) as it is to patch it. "That way you won't have to look at a big ugly patch when you're done," says Tom.

(see p. 95)

REPAIR **replacing window putty** The weakest part of any single-glazed wood window is the putty, the substance that seals the gap between the glass and the wood. (In double-glazed windows, the glass is either built into the sash or held in place by wood stops.) Over the years, the oils in putty slowly evaporate. When this happens, the putty hardens and cracks, letting water reach the wood. "Every 20 years or so, windows have to be reputtied," says Tom. (The putty on windows facing the incoming weather may deteriorate more quickly.) "It's a fairly simple job that can save the entire sash from rotting." Some people patch a section of crumbled putty, but not Tom. "The part you didn't patch will fail soon enough," he says, "and then you'll be right back at the same window to do the job again." Instead, he removes all the old putty before adding new (*left*).

freeing stuck windows The frame of a house can shift over time as the house settles. When the framing gets too far out of plumb, windows open and close only with great difficulty, or not at

Replacing putty: 1. Tom removes the sash if he can, or works from a ladder. Working carefully, he removes loose putty with a stiff putty knife or an old chisel. 2. When the putty is gone, he smooths the muntins with 80-grit sandpaper. 3. Priming the wood is an oft-neglected but crucial step. Unprimed wood will absorb oil from the putty and shorten its life. 4. When the primer is dry, Tom scoops a wad of putty from the can, warms it in his hands, and coils it into a snake shape before pushing it into place with his thumb. With a single deft stroke, he bevels the putty; then he removes the excess.

improvements:
jamb liners

The channels that guide the sash of double-hung windows eventually wear to the point where gaps can't easily be bridged by weatherstripping. The sash may also be hard to open and close. A solution suited to many windows is to install jamb liners. A liner (*below*) is made of vinyl, aluminum, or plastic, and can make an old window more energy-efficient by sealing the area between sash and jamb.

After the liners are installed (a job for professionals), the old window sash is sometimes trimmed an inch or two in width and then pushed into place between the liners. If that's not possible, new sash will be necessary. Either way, the cost is considerably less than entirely new windows, so the payback in energy savings will be quicker. As an added benefit, liners eliminate the weights that balance old sash, so the sash pockets can be insulated.

Liners have some drawbacks, however. In old houses, the modern materials may look out of place. "And if an old sash is already weak, trimming will make it even weaker," cautions Tom.

JAMB LINER

improvements:
storm windows

Storm windows are a great way to improve the energy efficiency of single-glazed windows. "Storm windows trap air between the window and the storm window, which makes for a higher insulation value," says Tom. As an added benefit, storm windows protect the sash and jambs from weather extremes, prolonging their life.

Newer storm windows often have separate tracks for screens and storm windows. "In the summer, you slide the storm windows up and put in screens; in the winter, you do the reverse," Tom explains. Old-fashioned wood-framed storm windows must be installed each fall—an arduous task. Wooden storm windows should be weatherstripped, then attached in a way that presses the weatherstripping tight against the window stops.

One problem with storm windows, however, is condensation. In cold climates, moisture from inside the house condenses on the warmer side of a cold glass surface, and ice can even form between the layers of glass if the interior windows aren't sealed properly. That's why it's OK to seal the top and two sides of storm windows, but not the bottom. "That can trap moisture and lead to rot, not just of the sill but inside the wall beneath the window," Tom says. Condensation must be able to drain.

Metal storms often have two weep holes along the bottom edge of the frame, which allow any water that accumulates on the sill to migrate outside. "These should be ⅛ inch in diameter and be located about 3 or 4 inches in from each side," says Tom. Clean out plugged or painted-over weep holes using a straightened paper clip. Wood windows don't require weep holes if moisture can seep out beneath them.

all. "If you see an uneven gap at the top or bottom of a double-hung window when it's closed, that's probably the problem," says Tom. "To get the sash to fit better, the window frame has to be removed and straightened, and that's not a job for a homeowner."

But stuck windows seldom call for such effort. In fact, it's more likely that they've been painted shut. Even a single layer of paint can immobilize a sash, and pounding on it with your fists (or worse, a hammer) can break the glass. Tom's solution: a sash saw. The small heart-shaped blade is a flat piece of metal ringed with tiny teeth that can nibble through paint between the sash and the stops. "Once you've cut the paint free, you can open the window without having to whack it," says Tom. "It's an inexpensive tool that really works." It's also safer to use than a knife.

replacing weatherstripping Wherever windows don't fit together snugly, air will leak through the gaps. The simplest way to plug leaks for the winter is to use rolled caulking; it's available in hardware stores. Just press the puttylike material around the perimeter of the sash and into any crevices. "Then forget about it until spring, when it can easily be removed," says Tom. Just remember that you can't open the window with the caulking in place.

A better approach involves weatherstripping that fits around the sash and still allows the window to be opened. Gaps around the sash can be sealed by tacking a strip of spring bronze (p. 122) into place (*right*). Richard and Steve are big fans of this material because it's so inexpensive and easy to install. For windows with sash weights, Tom has a trick that reduces air infiltration from the sash pockets. He starts by cutting a scrap of foam carpet pad into a foot-long, 2-inch-wide strip. At the window, he pulls a sash cord

Richard nails spring-bronze weatherstripping into place on his dining room windows. A major benefit of the material: It can be installed without having to remove the sash.

removing putty

Tom uses a heat gun to soften window putty that's firmly stuck. "Just be careful," he cautions. "You can scorch the wood or shatter the glass with too much heat." He sometimes shields the glass with a piece of metal flashing to deflect excess heat.

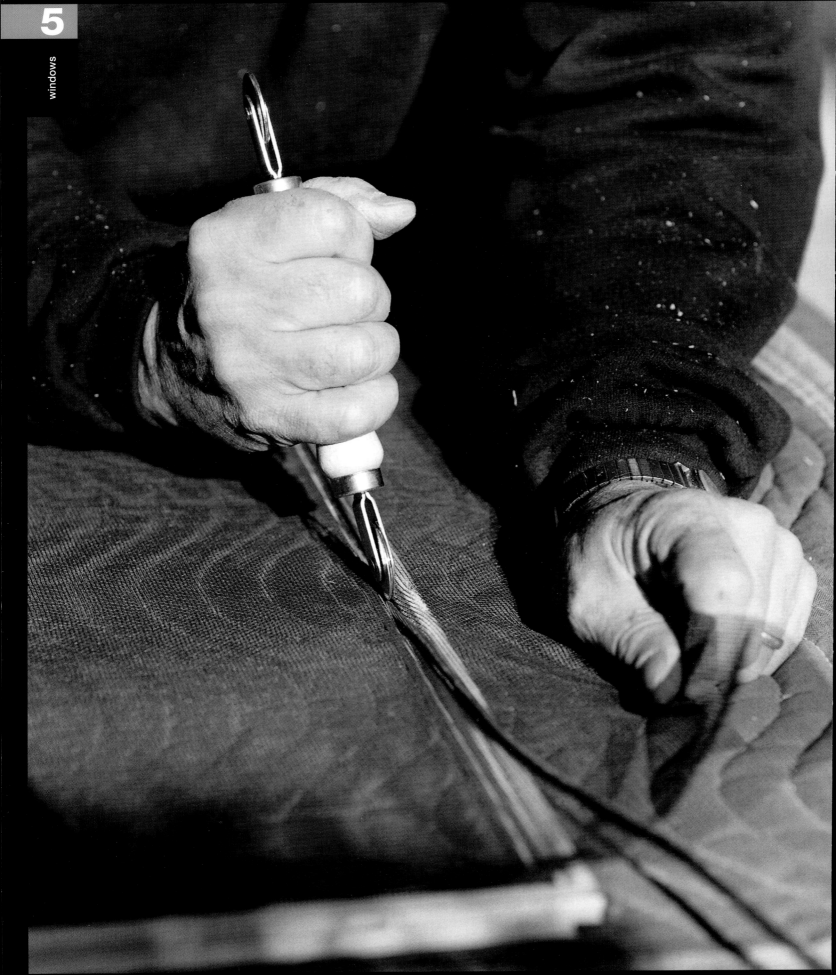

several inches out of the jamb, slips the foam strip under it, and then releases the cord slowly: The cord will pull the foam partway into the sash pocket. "It plugs the gaps around the window pulley, which can't be caulked, and cuts down on drafts," says Tom. When summer comes, he pulls the cord again, and out pops the foam. "It's not beautiful, but it sure does the job," he explains.

replacing screens   Although it's possible to patch large tears in a screen (p. 88), it's generally better to replace the material altogether—it takes about the same amount of time.

Removable screens with metal frames require an inexpensive tool called a spline roller (*right*). This double-wheeled tool is used to press a stringlike piece of rubber—the spline—into a groove that runs around the perimeter of the frame. To fit the screening material, Tom cuts it so that it is larger than the frame by about an inch all around. Pulling the material tight can be a challenge, and for this Tom has devised a clever strategy. He puts thin wood blocks under the top and bottom of the metal frame, then clamps the sides down to give the frame a gentle arc. After laying the screening over the frame, he presses the spline into the grooves at top and bottom with the spline roller, pinning the screen securely. "When I remove the side clamps, the frame springs back into its normal shape and pulls the screen tight," he says. "It's foolproof." Tom finishes by splining the sides, then trimming off the excess material with a utility knife. Be careful with the spline roller, though. "If you run it out of the groove it will slit the screen—then you'll have to start all over again," explains Tom.

restringing sash weights   Hidden behind the jambs on either side of many old windows are weights, which are connected by smooth cords to the sash. They're part of a balancing act that keeps the sash in place at any position. Over time, however, those cords—often nothing more than old bits of clothesline—fray and may even break loose, sending the weights plummeting. With no weight to counterbalance it, a sash won't stay up. Before that happens, advises Tom, replace the ropes with galvanized steel chain. The work isn't difficult, though it can be time-consuming.

The two wheels of a screen spline roller have different purposes. The concave wheel (in use here) starts the spline in its groove; the convex wheel finishes the job.

types: screening

To the untrained eye, all screens look alike: a sieve of wires that strains out insects. But various screening materials have different characteristics.

Among metals, aluminum screen is the cheapest. Over time, however, it darkens and corrodes, which makes it unsuitable near salt water. Copper, brass, and stainless steel are more durable, but not as readily available.

Among nonmetals, fiberglass screening is the most common. The matte-black fibers are inexpensive. Vinyl screening has more flexibility, making it somewhat less prone to damage.

Regardless of the type of material, screens need occasional cleaning to keep them looking fresh. "Once or twice a year, take them out of the windows, soap them gently with a car-washing brush, and hose them off," says Tom. "Then when they are dry, put them back in the window and they'll look brand-new." Tom never uses a pressure washer on screens, and he won't even use a car-washing brush on delicate fiberglass screens. "They're so soft they could tear," he says. "For fiberglass, I just hose them off."

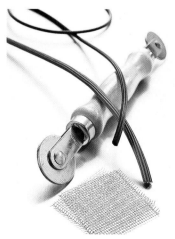

SPLINE ROLLER AND SPLINE

improvements:
sash locks

When double-hung windows are closed, the top and bottom sash are held together by a two-piece sash lock (p. 89). One piece is screwed to the top of the innermost sash; a smaller mating piece is attached to the outermost sash, near the bottom. When a curved plate on one piece slides beneath the hook of the other piece, the two sash are drawn tightly together.

The lock offers a small measure of security, but only if it is engaged fully (otherwise, it can be defeated by a putty knife). Other types of sash locks, such as those with a sliding cam-lock mechanism, offer somewhat better security.

But security isn't really a sash lock's most important role: It compresses the sash weatherstripping to reduce air leakage. If a lock no longer holds the sash together tightly, cold air can easily escape between the mating parts of the sash (the meeting rails).

To salvage a sash lock that no longer seals well, Tom unscrews both parts and fills the old holes with wood putty, then he drills new holes and repositions the lock slightly off-center on the sash. Windows more than 30 inches wide may require two locks, positioned symmetrically on the sash, to ensure a tight seal. And if the lock itself is damaged or hopelessly encrusted with paint, it can be replaced.

The standard hardware-store sash lock is an inexpensive item made of stamped metal. It suits the purpose but isn't long on style. Solid brass locks are available, but they're considerably more expensive. If you're lucky enough to have a house with old brass sash locks, they're well worth salvaging, no matter how much time it takes. You'll have to remove them in order to clean off accumulations of paint.

To begin, Tom uses a putty knife to carefully pry away the inside stops from both sides of the window. Then he lifts the sash out of the opening, pries open the access plate in the jamb (p. 88), and reaches in to fish the weight out. After attaching one end of the new chain to the weight, he cuts it to the same length as the original cord and attaches it to the sash; then he repeats the process on the other side of the window. "When one sash cord breaks or is frayed, the other one will go soon—you might as well replace both," he says.

replacing broken glass   If you have kids, learn to replace glass (Tom, Steve, and Richard know this well). Hail and falling tree limbs can break glass, too, but replacing a damaged pane is easy.

Before he starts, Tom dons safety goggles to guard against flying shards and leather work gloves to protect his hands. Carefully, he removes the broken glass, scrapes out the old putty, and plucks out any remaining glazing points with needlenosed pliers. "Putty seals gaps—it doesn't actually hold the glass in place," says Tom. "That's the job of glazing points." These tiny bits of metal pin the glass to the sash at six points, one on the top and bottom and two on each side. To determine the size of the new glass, Tom measures between the muntins, then subtracts about $1/8$ inch from the height and $1/8$ inch from the width to allow clearance between the muntins; then he buys a new pane just that size (buy two and you'll save yourself a trip the next time a pane breaks). After priming the bare wood and letting it dry, Tom beds the new glass in a narrow bead of putty (*right*), secures it with glazing points, and then adds more putty over the edges (p. 90). "The process isn't complicated once you get the hang of it," he says.

Newer double-glazed windows, however, often cannot be replaced on site—once the glass breaks, you'll have to special-order a new unit and may even need a new sash altogether. Homeowner's insurance might cover this repair. And as a precaution against further damage, says Tom, "have the kids play ball a little farther from the house."

*Replacing broken glass: **1.** After removing the broken shards and pulling out the old glazing points using needlenosed pliers, Tom sands and primes the muntins as he would when replacing putty (p. 90). Then he pushes a small rope of putty onto the muntins; this bedding layer will support the glass. **2.** Tom gently presses the new pane of glass into the bedding layer, then secures it with new glazing points pushed into the muntins with a putty knife or wide screwdriver. (Traditional triangular points, also shown here, can be used instead.) Now the glass can be puttied (step #4, p. 90).*

1
2

painting

cleaning interior paint / cleaning exterior paint / exterior paint preparation / exterior painting / painting metal / painting interior walls / painting woodwork / painting doors and windows

chapter 6

I LEARNED TO PAINT FROM MY FATHER, who painted every house we owned. Eventually he handed a brush to me (with six kids and my low labor rate, he couldn't afford not to). Later, in the summer after my first year of college, I found myself painting again. The first house I took on for pay was a little cape that consumed three long weeks of scraping, sanding, priming, caulking . . . and painting. I didn't make much money, but the experience sure drove home my father's three rules for painting success: preparation, preparation, preparation. Paint technology has changed dramatically since then, but not the rules. — STEVE

MAINTENANCE **cleaning interior paint** The sheen of a painted surface has the greatest impact on how easily it cleans. Flat paints are suitable for ceilings, but Tom avoids them on walls. "Flat paint holds dirt and dust and gets marked up really easily," he says. In his own house, Tom painted all the walls with eggshell paints, which have a subtle glossy finish that can be cleaned with a damp cloth and a mild nonabrasive cleaner. "The beauty of eggshell," notes Steve, "is that it cleans so easily." Tom's woodwork is painted in semigloss for extra durability: (The four basic paint sheens are flat, eggshell, semi-gloss, and gloss.)

cleaning exterior paint Paint protects wood by keeping out water, and its pigments block the degrading effects of ultraviolet radiation. But an exterior paint surface is constantly under siege, stretching and contracting with the weather as well as with seasonal changes in the wood. To make a good job last, Tom recommends washing the house once a year (p. 70).

Painting is a great way to accentuate architectural features. Areas exposed to moisture, such as bathrooms, should be painted with products that have a cleanable sheen.

types: paint

A can of paint contains a gumbo of ingredients that color and protect the wood. The color comes from pigments, which can be either mineral or synthetic compounds. Binders are the resins that hold the pigment to the surface. The carrier—which can be either mineral spirits or water—blends the two together. "Whatever paint you buy, buy the best you can get," Tom advises. "Price is a reasonably effective gauge of paint quality, and the extra expense is insignificant if it saves you from an early repainting job." Paints that hold up best contain a relatively high proportion of expensive binders and pigments to the carrier.

OIL PAINT: Oil-based paints contain resins made from chemically modified soy or linseed oils (known as alkyds), dissolved in mineral spirits. Oil paints level out better than their latex cousins and can be applied in weather a few degrees cooler. But they don't remain as elastic over time, and cleanup calls for the use of volatile oil-based solvents, which must be stored and disposed of with considerable care.

LATEX PAINT: Latex paints contain vinyl or acrylic resins suspended in water (acrylic resins are the more durable and flexible of the two). Because they're water-based, the paints are easier to clean up—soap and water does it—and they're less likely to trap moisture behind the paint film, which can cause the paint to peel off.

SOLID-COLOR STAIN: Exterior stains are actually thin paint, but they're more likely than paint to let the wood texture show. Thinness has its downside, however: a shorter life span. Two coats of top-quality paint might last 8 years or more; two coats of stain, only 6. As with paint, though, the performance of stain is directly related to the climate it's in.

safety: lead paint

Tom has a one approach when it comes to dealing with lead paint: "I don't touch it." If there's lead in the paint, he tells the homeowner to hire a licensed de-leader and have them deal with it.

As a paint ingredient, powdered lead carbonate once seemed ideal. It gave paint rhino-hide durability and a self-leveling smoothness that made application easy. But those benefits came at a cost. Some dried layers of paint contain up to half their weight in lead, and ingesting paint chips or dust over time can cause learning disabilities and reduced growth in children, as well as hypertension, anemia, and kidney failure in adults. That's why lead was banned as a paint ingredient in 1978.

If a house contains lead paint, the best thing is to leave it alone, say the experts: There's little hazard just from touching it and none at all if the lead is concealed beneath an intact layer of lead-free paint. But if renovation plans call for sanding, scraping, or heat-stripping old paint, beware. If you have any concerns about the paint in your house, check it with a lead test kit (*below*) or have a professional analysis done by a state-certified specialist.

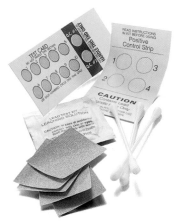

LEAD TEST KIT

exterior paint preparation The best way to keep a house properly painted is to paint before damage gets out of hand. To find out if the existing paint is solid enough to paint over, place a piece of duct tape on it, then peel it off quickly. "If the tape is clean, it's safe to repaint after washing the surface," says Tom (p. 70). If the tape pulls off paint, then the area should be scraped or sanded down to solid paint layers. Flaking paint can be removed with a carbide scraper, but Tom and Steve prefer ordinary steel scrapers because they can be sharpened quickly with a file. Steve, in fact, kept a file in his pocket when he painted houses. "I'd touch up the edge every 15 strokes or so," he recalls. If the paint contains lead, find out if local ordinances govern the stripping process. And don't use a pressure washer (p. 68) for paint removal—it'll blast paint chips all over the place.

Once loose and near-loose areas of paint have been scraped off (p. 104), feather the edges of remaining areas of paint with 80-grit sandpaper to prevent new paint from chipping there. Small areas can be sanded by hand. For large areas, painter John Dee, who has worked on several *This Old House* projects, uses a 7-inch sanding disc mounted on a 5-inch disc sander. "That allows the edge of the disc to flex a little," he says, "and lessens the chance of gouging the siding." He typically uses 60- or 80-grit discs. Any damage to the siding that's encountered during preparation should be repaired (p. 66). "Preparation always takes much longer than the actual painting," says Tom; "But if you cut corners, the paint will fail, and you'll be wasting a lot of time and money."

Next comes the real secret to a long-lasting paint job: the primer. It's really just paint formulated with a higher proportion of binder than pigment, and it adheres particularly well to wood. Dee paints it on any bare wood. "The primer holds the wood and the paint tightly together," he says. "It's the single most important element in a good exterior paint job." Oil-based primers, he adds, are the best at preventing stains from bleeding through the paint film.

*Paint problems on exterior surfaces. **1.** Mildew. Dee removes it by spraying on a mix of 3 parts water to 1 part bleach, then scrubbing with a long-handled brush. **2.** Cracking. Strip the paint down to a solid surface. **3.** Alligatoring. This is one sign of aging alkyd paint. The paint should be stripped if it is loose. **4.** Nailhead rusting. If the paint is soundly adhered, Dee spot-primes the nailheads with a rust-inhibitive exterior primer. **5.** Peeling. May be caused by moisture problems. Remove loose paint and prime bare wood. **6.** Chalking. This powder forms as paint weathers; wash it off before repainting.*

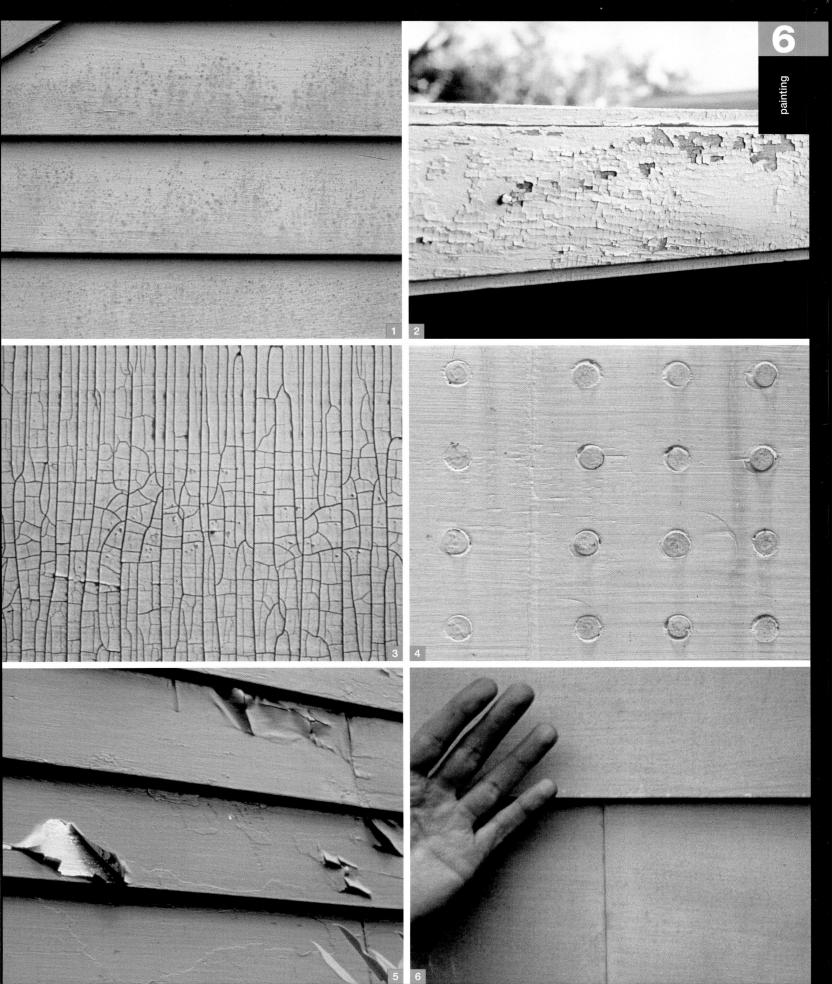

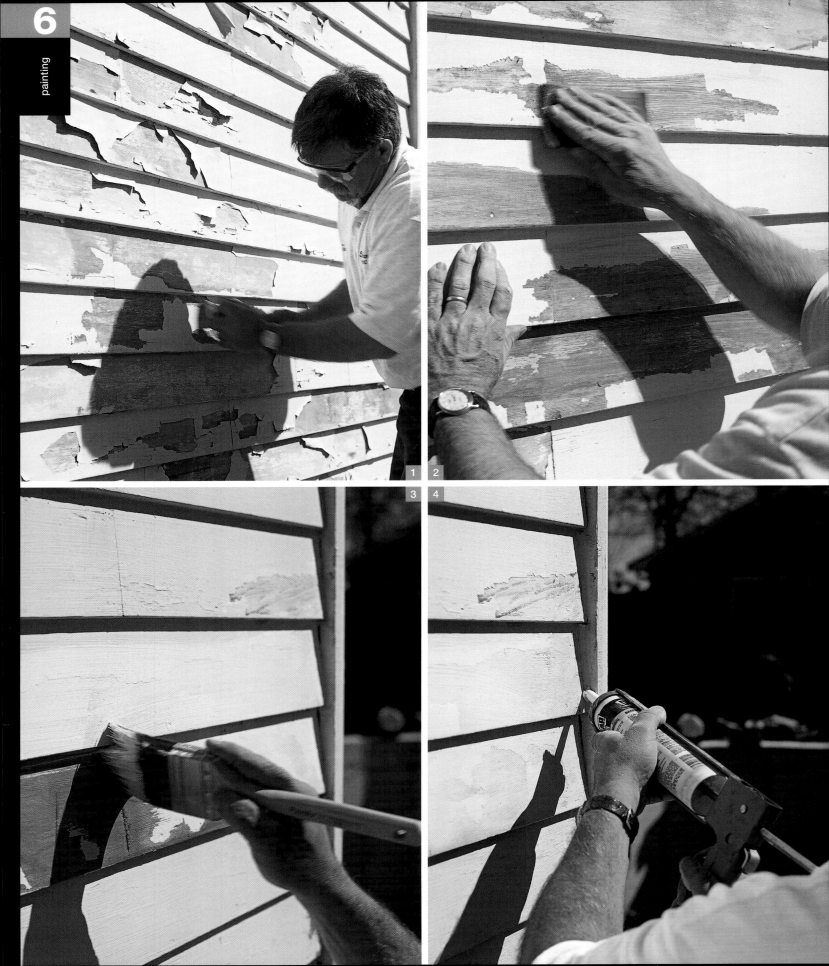

If it rains after your prep work is complete, wait a day or two for the siding to dry (wait longer for shaded portions of the house). Otherwise, moisture could cause the new paint to peel soon after application. Don't paint with latex when the temperature drops below 50 degrees, or with oil below 45 degrees: Paint won't cure properly at low temperatures unless specifically formulated to do so.

exterior painting Compared to prep work, painting goes quickly. Dee paints the uppermost areas first—fascia, rake, soffit, gutters—so drips won't mar later work. Then he moves to the walls. Working from a ladder, his strategy is to brush a horizontal stripe about 6 clapboards wide across an entire wall, then move down for another stripe. "It's the best way to maintain a wet edge," he explains, "even though I have to move the ladder around a bit more." By wet edge, he means that he never paints into an area that's already dry, a mistake that would leave ugly lap marks behind (semi-transparent stains are even less forgiving of lap marks, says Dee). After the siding is done, Dee cuts in the trim around windows and doors. "Paint should be applied liberally to encourage good leveling," says Dee, "but if you see sags and drips, lighten up."

painting metal Various metal parts of a house must be protected with paint. To do the job right, Tom first works any rust spots down to the bare metal with a wire brush, then goes over the rest of the surface with 200-grit emery cloth (a durable fabric-backed sandpaper) to smooth it. To clean off dust and any remaining dirt, he wipes the metal with a rag moistened with paint thinner (to prevent a fire hazard, rinse the rag well before disposing of it.)

The next step is crucial: brushing a coat of a rust-inhibitive metal primer over any bare metal. Once the primer dries, he brushes on two finish coats of paint: oil-based paint on wrought-iron railing (because it's a better rust inhibitor), and latex paint on aluminum gutters and storm doors.

Preparing wood siding for paint: **1.** *Tom removes loose paint with a scraper; safety glasses protect his eyes from flying paint shards. He scrapes in whatever direction removes the most paint.* **2.** *To smooth the edges of scraped areas, Tom sands with 80-grit sandpaper. Large areas would call for a power sander and a dust mask. When properly sanded, no edge should be distinct.* **3.** *After brushing off the sanding dust, Tom primes all bare wood.* **4.** *All vertical gaps, particularly those between siding and trim, should then be caulked. When this is complete, Tom is ready to paint.*

tom's tip: cleanup

Good painting tools are too expensive to throw away when the work is done. "Clean everything so that it looks like new," advises Tom. Adds Steve: "I couldn't agree more."

Brushes used in latex paint should be cleaned immediately with soapy water, or they'll be worthless. With brushes used in oil-based paints, Tom dips the brush into ½ inch of paint thinner, then brushes it out on sheets of newspaper to clean and dry the bristles. (To prevent a fire, make sure the newspaper is dry before you dispose of it.) After repeating this process several times, he wraps the brush in a newspaper sheath to hold its shape until next use.

Rollers with plastic cores may be worth cleaning (those with cardboard cores are disposable). Tom scrapes off the excess paint with a 5-in-1 tool, then washes the roller in soapy water (latex paints) or thinner (oil-based). He sticks the roller on a spinner to whirl off the residue, then lets it air-dry. "If the nap is hard after all that, it's time for a new roller," says Tom.

ROLLER SPINNER

5-IN-1 TOOL

"cutting in" paint

Flat stretches of walls and trim are easy to paint, but it's tough to paint a straight line between walls and trim of a contrasting color. Here's how:

MASKING: Some people cover, or "mask off," the area they don't want paint to get on, using various masking tapes or a paint shield (*below*). But paint often seeps beneath tape and shields, spoiling the crisp edge. And if standard masking tape stays in place more than a day, it can lift the paint when you peel it off (blue painters' tape won't).

CUTTING IN: Tom prefers (as does painter John Dee) a technique called "cutting in," which calls for painting an edge without masking it. This takes a steady hand, but it's definitely faster, says Steve. To cut in, Tom spreads the paint no closer than ¹/₁₆ inch to the edge of the surface he's outlining in long, steady passes with the brush held on edge. Then he spreads it out over an area about 12 inches wide; and finally he repeats his first strokes, this time spreading the paint right to the edge. "Once you get the hang of it, painting goes a lot faster," he says.

Steve's favorite cutting-in brush is a 2- inch sash brush with a wood handle.

TAPES AND A SHIELD

painting interior walls Done correctly, a paint job is an invisible act of craftsmanship. The eye sees smooth walls and pristine woodwork—no drips, no splatters, no ragged edges along the ceiling. "Any obvious signs that you've been there, even a brushstroke, will ruin the effect," says Tom. And though paint may work wonders for a room, it can't perform miracles. Don't expect paint to fill cracks, smooth rough surfaces, or conceal thumbtack holes.

Before starting in a room, Tom covers the floor with a canvas tarp to fend off spills and splatters (plastic tarps are less durable and dangerously slippery). He scrutinizes each wall to make sure it is smooth—playing a strong light at a low angle over the surface amplifies imperfections, which he spot-primes and later fills. When it comes to filling holes, Dee has seen them all and has several favored fillers. Joint compound is great for filling broad, shallow imperfections; vinyl spackle is ideal for small, deep holes; and lightweight spackle is best as a general filler for small holes because it dries quickly and can be painted the same day. "Really small holes, like the thumbtack holes you see all over a teenager's bedroom, can be spackled, then painted immediately." After sanding patched areas smooth, vacuum off the dust; then wipe the area with a damp rag to get rid of every last speck. If the walls are new, or if patching was extensive, Dee primes the entire wall, not just the patches, using an all-purpose latex primer. "It equalizes the porosity of the different surfaces, helping the finish paint to dry to an even sheen."

When it comes to choosing what to paint first, however, no single strategy suits all. Tom paints the ceiling, the woodwork, then the walls. "I find it easiet to cut walls into painted trim," he explains. But Steve rolls the walls before painting the trim. "That way I won't splatter the trim," he explains. Whenever you get to the walls, start with a brush, painting a 3-inch-wide swath around all doors, windows, and electrical outlets, as well as along the baseboard and in corners (*right*). That covers the areas a roller can't reach. Then load a roller and put paint on the wall, spreading it out by working the roller back and forth at various angles. Some people paint the top of the walls from a stepladder, but Dee screws an extension pole to the roller. "That gets me far enough away from the wall to see thin areas," he says, "and I don't have to bend over so much."

When Tom repainted his living room, he cut in around the windows and outlets, and along the baseboard, before rolling the walls. A "W" distributes paint evenly on the wall.

painting woodwork Painting is the reward for painstakingly scraping and sanding woodwork. When painting trim indoors or out, Tom first paints any details where paint might collect, using as dry a brush as possible so that the paint doesn't pool up and obliterate the profile. When he finishes that, he brushes the flat surfaces, completing the job with a few light finishing strokes along the length of the wood to level the paint. Another trick for ensuring a smooth finish is to keep a wet edge. With oil paint, Tom brushes it until he's got the finish that he wants, but overbrushing latex isn't good. "If you brush it too much, you'll see brushstrokes," he explains. Instead, brush latex once or twice after spreading it out; then leave it alone.

painting doors and windows A door can be removed and laid over a pair of sawhorses for painting, but Dee would rather leave it hanging. "The job goes a lot faster and the results are just as good," he says. He uses a small inspection mirror to see if the bottom edge is painted (if it isn't, the door must be removed.)

He first removes the knob and the latch so that they won't become spattered with paint. "You have to paint around the hinges, but that's not difficult," he adds. Dee's strategy calls for painting the door edges first, then the moldings around the door's center panels (he's very careful to prevent paint from puddling in the corners), then the panels themselves. Finally, he paints the rails and stiles—the horizontal and vertical parts of the door, respectively. Here, he starts painting in the center of a stile or rail and spreads the paint toward its edges. That eliminates the dripping that would occur if he touched a loaded brush to the door edge.

As for windows, Dee offers this advice: Start by painting the sash that's farthest away from you (if you're inside, in other words, paint the upper sash first). That reduces the chance of touching wet paint. "What you do next is a matter of preference," he says, "but I find that changing directions disturbs my concentration. So I paint the upper edge of all the horizontal muntins, then both edges of all the vertical muntins, then the lower edge of the horizontal muntins." When that's done, he finishes up by painting the rails and stiles.

Because of their exposure, exterior windowsills may require more frequent painting than walls and trim. **1.** *Tom scrapes off loose paint, fills surface cracks and holes (p. 66), and feathers rough edges with 80 grit sandpaper.* **2.** *After dusting off all sanding debris, he primes bare wood before painting the sill, including the area under the sash.*

stripping paint from woodwork

In old houses, accumulations of paint often obscure intricate woodwork. Before you strip paint, however, have it checked for lead (p. 102). Then, if stripping is safe, decide whether to strip the trim in place or remove it first. Stripping paint in place, says Tom, is "a ton of work," and it's often easier to remove the wood, strip it, then reinstall it. "And if the wood is nothing special," adds Steve, "you'll probably find it faster and safer just to replace it entirely." Clearly, stripping paint is no fun.

Tom sometimes uses chemical strippers, but more often he turns to electric sanders and hand scrapers. "Be careful, though—if you put a belt sander to Victorian trim, it'll end up looking Colonial." A better idea: Use an orbital pad sander (*below right*) on flat areas. "Wear a dust mask," cautions Tom, "and connect a shop vac to the tool to suck up the dust."

Fine details call for a detail sander (*below left*) or sharp paint scrapers. A heat gun can soften paint, making scraping easier. Just work carefully to avoid damage to the wood.

POWER SANDERS

building comfort

getting comfortable / cleaning filters / maintaining a forced-air heating system / maintaining hydronic heating systems / servicing air-conditioning / maintaining chimneys / maintaining fans / sealing windows and doors / caulking and sealing / insulating an attic

chapter 7

I'VE LEARNED THIS ABOUT COMFORT: You can have the most perfectly restored house in town, but if it's cold and drafty in the winter or hot and sticky in the summer, you'll come to hate the place. Over the years, I've attacked the comfort weaknesses of my own old house one by one. Now, whenever I've been away for a while, I'm welcomed home by a house that's truly comfortable. And here's the best news: Making a house feel like that is a job anyone can take on.

— STEVE

MAINTENANCE getting comfortable Of all the qualities of a house, comfort can be the most difficult to understand. "That's because if people are comfortable, they don't pay attention to the particulars," says Richard. But live inside an uncomfortable house and you'll notice them right away— from the way winter air slices through gaps around the windows to the oppressive heat of an upstairs bedroom in August.

For a human body to be comfortable, temperature and humidity must be within tolerable ranges. The average temperature of human skin is 74 degrees Fahrenheit. "So if I can make the room I'm in close to skin temperature," says Richard, "my body won't gain or lose heat." But humidity—the amount of moisture in the air— has an inverse relationship to temperature when it comes to comfort. As the humidity climbs, explains Richard, people search for cooler temperatures in order to maintain a given level of comfort; if the humidity drops, they're able to maintain that same level of comfort at higher temperatures.

Comfort can be costly to maintain if a house lets too much air in or out. But "energy efficient," as Richard notes, is one of the most misapplied terms in the English language: "Energy efficiency in one area, such as the combustion efficiency of a furnace, won't automati-

A fireplace exemplifies the trade-offs called for in the quest for comfort. Heat radiating from the fire is soothing, but warm air from the room is being lost up the chimney.

safety: air quality

Insulation, weatherstripping, and caulk create tight houses—in some cases too tight. "If you can smell the garlic scampi days after you've cooked it, and if the odors from the hamper seem to linger, then you've got a problem," says Richard. Too little fresh air coming into the house can encourage a buildup of smells as well as allergens, mold, and mildew. If your house suffers from this problem, consider adding one or both of the following devices.

HIGH-PERFORMANCE FILTERS: In forced-air heating or cooling systems, air quality can be improved by upgrading the air filter to a high-performance filter (p. 114). That doesn't bring in any more fresh air, but it does cleanse what's there, sifting out dust, allergens, even viruses and odors that can't be trapped by ordinary filters. A heating contractor can install such a filter; changing it or cleaning it periodically is a task anyone can handle.

HEAT EXCHANGER: In a tight house, bad-air problems can actually be compounded by turning on exhaust fans in the bathroom or kitchen. These fans are necessary—they exhaust moisture-laden air—but they sometimes do too good a job. "They'll pull air from wherever they can, and in extreme cases they can even draw air down the chimney or down the vent for the furnace or the boiler," says Richard. That can lead to an accumulation of deadly carbon monoxide within the house. One way to ensure a steady supply of fresh air is to install an air-to-air heat exchanger (sometimes called a heat-recovery ventilator). "The heat exchanger brings in fresh air from outside and pre-warms it by transferring the heat from the outgoing air to the incoming air, but without mixing the two," says Richard. A heating contractor can install an air-to-air heat exchanger.

types: heating systems

A heating system is classified more by how it delivers heat than by what fuel it uses. Here are four common types:

FORCED-AIR: A blower moves heated air through ducts. This system is the cheapest to install, so nearly two-thirds of U.S. homes rely on one. Maintenance includes professional tune-ups for the furnace and fan every year or two, and homeowner replacement of filters when they become clogged.

HYDRONIC: A boiler heats water and a pump circulates it throughout the house via copper or plastic pipes. At various locations, radiators extract the heat and release it into the room. The system distributes heat without creating drafts the way forced-air systems do. There are no air filters to change, but the boiler needs professional cleaning every year or two. A variant is hydronic floor heating, in which pipes embedded in the floor radiate heat.

ELECTRIC BASEBOARD: Placed at the perimeter of a room at floor level, these radiators heat up just the way a toaster does. They require no regular maintenance other than an occasional vacuuming of interior surfaces, and are used in mild climates (or for supplementary heat in cold ones). "Anywhere else, the costs to operate them are just too darn high," says Richard.

GEOTHERMAL HEAT PUMPS: A variant of forced-air, these systems capitalize on the constant 50-degree temperature of the earth below the frost line. In summer, heat drawn from the building is circulated through a piping loop and cooled; in winter, warmth is drawn from the ground and transferred to the house. "This sounds elaborate, but much of the technology is no more complicated than what's used in your refrigerator," says Richard.

cally make the whole house efficient." If heat leaks out through ducts and disappears through poorly insulated walls and ceilings, the result will be discomfort that no amount of fiddling with the thermostat can remedy. Instead, achieving true efficiency calls for a variety of improvements, including upgrading insulation, maintaining the heating and cooling system, and adding weatherstripping. It also requires proper ventilation to safeguard air quality and to protect the house from the perils of uncontrolled condensation, which can cause mold, mildew, and rot.

cleaning filters All heating and air-conditioning systems that move air rely on a filter to strain dust out of the airstream. Replacing or cleaning the filter is easy; the hard part is remembering to do it. The most common system filter is a disposable spun-fiberglass model that's about an inch thick, and Richard doesn't think much of it. "It'll sift out dust, lint, and other coarse particles, but not bacteria, mold, pollen, or pet dander. It's there to protect the equipment, not your health." An electrostatic filter is better; air moving over it creates a static charge that collects small particles. But much better, says Richard, is a high-efficiency media filter. These are replaceable 6- to 11-inch-thick cartridges made of non-woven cotton-polyester fabric, and they can cleanse the air of most contaminants, including flu viruses. At the top of the filter pyramid are electronic air cleaners. A continuous electric charge attracts particles to surfaces inside the cleaner, and not much escapes. Electronic air cleaners are not disposable, and must be cleaned periodically. Retrofitting a system to accept a high-efficiency filter or air cleaner is a job for a heating or air-conditioning contractor.

maintaining a forced-air heating system Whether they use oil, propane, or natural gas as fuel, forced-air heating systems create hot air by heating a series of enclosed tubes, called a heat exchanger, with a flame. The purpose of the heat exchanger is to ensure that heated air is kept separate from deadly flue gases. Air is drawn from the house and blown through the exchanger, then returned to the house; flue gases are sent up the chimney. A furnace works hard all winter, and regular maintenance will keep it on the

A heating system employs a blower to push heated air through ducts; gravity returns cooled air for reheating. A central air-conditioning system uses the same ducts.

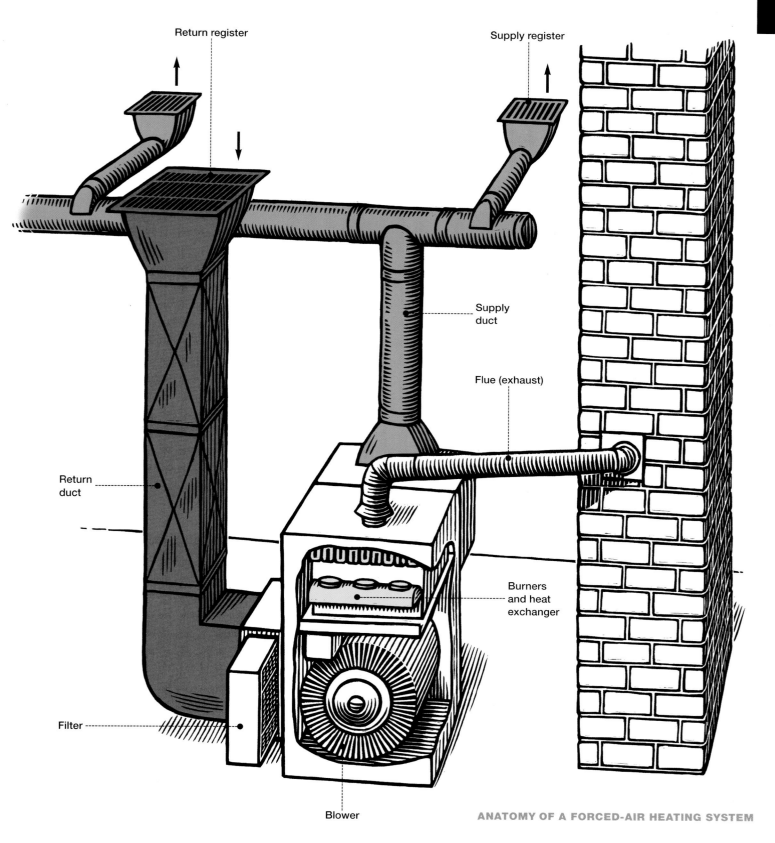

Return register

Supply register

Supply
duct

Flue (exhaust)

Return
duct

Burners
and heat
exchanger

Filter

Blower

ANATOMY OF A FORCED-AIR HEATING SYSTEM

job. Much of this should be left to your fuel supplier or a heating contractor. "Schedule a maintenance call every summer for an oil-fired system, and every other summer for a gas system," says Richard. Regardless of the type of fuel used, the heat exchanger should be checked at each service call to make sure it is free of corrosion, which could eventually allow flue gases into the house. Older systems often have a belt-driven blower; it should be checked for proper tension, also at each service call.

Homeowners, however, can take care of one crucial maintenance task: changing the air filter. Air circulates through the filter before being distributed to the house: "Filters trap everything from dust and lint to dog hair," says Richard. If a filter is clogged, the decreased airflow will reduce the overall heating efficiency of the furnace. Richard prefers heavy-duty pleated media filters that contain an accordion-like collection of cotton baffles. "They do much, much more than the standard little inch-thick filters that slide into place on the side of most furnaces," he says.

One characteristic of forced-air furnaces is that air loses moisture as it passes through the heat exchanger, where temperatures can reach 500 degrees Fahrenheit. "And dry air can be really uncomfortable, as well as unhealthy," says Richard. The problem can be solved by adding a humidifier to the furnace, which puts moisture into the airstream of the system. Many of these units, however, become maintenance headaches if supplied by mineral-laden water; if the unit cakes up regularly, it may have to be replaced periodically. "Have your water tested before you install a humidifier," suggests Richard. "Then talk to the folks who service your system to see what they recommend."

maintaining hydronic heating systems Instead of using heated air to warm a house, hydronic systems heat water in a tank like boiler and circulate it through a piping system to radiators. Unfortunately, many homeowners have an "out of sight, out of mind" attitude toward their hydronic systems. "And believe me,

*Basic hydronic-system maintenance. **1.** Modern hydronic boilers, such as this one, require regular professional maintenance but little else except periodic vacuuming to remove debris that collects beneath the burners. **2.** On older hydronic systems, the pressure tank must be drained and repressurized each year. **3.** Baseboard radiators, called convectors, should be cleaned each year. Lift the access hatches and remove the front panel. **4.** Vacuum gently; dirty or bent fins reduce the unit's efficiency.*

richard's tip: radiant floor heat

In the quest for steady, draft-free heat, one system works best of all: radiant floor heat. "There's no more comfortable form of heat on the planet," says Richard. Pioneered by the ancient Romans (they heated floors with horizontal chimney flues), the system continuously circulates warm water through coils beneath the floor. "If your feet feel warm," Richard explains, "the rest of your body will feel warm regardless of the air temperature."

Radiant floor heating systems gained in popularity in the 1940s and 50s, but the copper coils used then eventually corroded, cracked, and leaked. Now, a highly durable plastic tubing made of cross-linked polyethylene affords a safe alternative. "If you put it in correctly, the tubing is projected to last 200 years or more," says Richard, who has installed it in his own house as well as in the adjacent barn that serves as his office. One disadvantage is the fact that the system can't cool—only forced-air systems can do that practically. Also, installation costs are higher than other systems. "Those," notes Richard, "are forgotten on the first cold winter day."

RADIANT-HEAT TUBING

improvements:
system controls

One way to improve a heating or cooling system is to upgrade the thermostat. "It's like giving the system a new brain—one that's smart enough to save you money," says Richard. A thermostat turns the system on and off in response to temperature; a new one can be installed by a homeowner.

SETBACK THERMOSTAT: This unit (also called a clock or electronic thermostat) raises or lowers the indoor temperature according to a limited schedule. "In cold weather, you might want the house to settle at 60 degrees for the night, then go to 70 degrees just before everybody wakes up," says Richard. The units can result in energy savings of 10 to 20 percent on an annual fuel bill.

PROGRAMMABLE THERMOSTAT: Digital setback units are called programmable thermostats. The most expensive ones let you select a different temperature pattern for every day of the week.

RESET CONTROL: Richard thinks every boiler should have a weather-sensitive reset control that changes the water temperature to compensate for weather changes. "It's like cruise control for the boiler, and it saves energy," he says.

that's a mistake," says Richard. "I've seen horrors lurking down there." Chief among them is a poorly maintained boiler, one so crusted with soot that it barely works. "I've found some where the efficiency rating must have been down around 50 percent," says Richard. "That means that for every dollar spent on fuel, 50 cents was being wasted." The solution is regular maintenance by a professional. "That's probably the single best investment you can make for energy efficiency and comfort," he says. In addition to checking the general health of the system, the service technician will run a combustion test to check the boiler's efficiency and to make sure the air consumed by combustion is replaced with enough fresh air (called make up air) to prevent conditions that could let flue gases into the house, a particular concern in tightly sealed houses. "Simply cleaning and tuning an old boiler can raise its efficiency from 50 to about 65 percent," says Richard. And while that's still well below the 85-percent combustion efficiency attained by new boilers, it's enough of an improvement that you'd notice it on your fuel bill.

Another part of a hydronic heating system that may require maintenance is the expansion tank (p. 116). The tank provides a place for water to expand into as it's heated, like the overflow tank on a car radiator. When properly pressurized, the tank is half-filled with water, half-filled with air, but in older systems the air will gradually dissolve into the water. "Once a year you have to drain the tank and refill it," says Richard, which he concedes is something of an art that involves breaking the vacuum inside the tank. "The average person should call in a pro for this one," he says. Tanks installed after 1970, however, need little or no maintenance because an impermeable diaphragm separates the air and water. With any tank, have it checked if you notice water dripping steadily from the overflow pipe that's connected to the relief valve, particularly if the tank's pressure gauge is approaching 30 pounds (normal pressure is 12 to 15 pounds). There's no urgency to replace an old tank unless it's faulty.

Hydronic heating systems generally don't have ducts like forced-air systems, but they do include baseboards or radiators that extract heat from the circulating water. "They might not seem to need atten-

Maintaining a central air system. 1. Debris inhibits air flowing into the condenser, so each year Richard uses a shop vac to remove it from the grilles. 2. If he can see a build up of debris inside the condenser cabinet, Richard cuts power to the unit, removes a few retaining screws, and carefully pivots the top upward to vacuum it out.

tion," says Richard, "but they do." In order to warm a room efficiently, air has to circulate over or through the radiator, with cooler air being drawn in from the bottom of the unit and warmer air rising from the top. The bottom of the baseboard, however, is often blocked by carpeting, a sofa, or dust. "Either way, the result is a cold room," says Richard. Gently vacuum the inside of the baseboard regularly, and make sure nothing obstructs the airflow to it. The housing on many baseboard units can be partially removed to make the interior easier to vacuum.

servicing air-conditioning Central air-conditioning systems consist of two elements: a condenser outside the house and an air handler inside. The system takes warm air from inside the house and blows it across a series of coils containing a refrigerant. The heat from the warm air is absorbed by the cool coils, leaving cooler air to recirculate back into the house. The trick is to make sure that the air blowing over the coils remains dust-free. That's a job for a filter on the air handler, which should be changed at least once each year. Otherwise, dust will clog the refrigerant coils. "That forms an insulating layer of crud and makes it almost impossible to cool your house," says Richard. Pleated media filters do a better job of removing dust than standard fiberglass filters, but when media filters get dirty they can reduce the airflow so severely that the coils may freeze. A duct-flow meter, installed by a heating contractor, can remind you that it's time for a new filter.

Outside the house, the condenser draws in fresh air to exhaust the heat picked up by the coil. "These units aren't particularly attractive, so people like to plant shrubs really close to them," says Richard. But leaves and twigs block the vents and prevent the unit from working properly. Keep plants trimmed at least 2 feet away from the condenser, and regularly clear away leaves and other debris.

maintaining chimneys A roaring fire is romantic, but it also has a dangerous side, a fact to which many fire departments can attest. Problems with a fireplace, woodstove, or chimney typically stem from improper use or poor maintenance, and the most common problem is a buildup of creosote in the chimney. Creosote, a black

A chimney sweep has the specialized tools and skills to clean a chimney properly. This is not a job for homeowners: Improper cleaning can damage the chimney lining.

improvements:
fireplace doors

Fireplaces may have kept rooms toasty during the Colonial era, but in today's tight houses they're more like air conditioners. "They suck warm air out and send it right up the chimney," says Richard, "even when there's no fire." That's why he recommends installing a pair of tight-fitting glass doors (*below*) over the fireplace opening—they'll stop cold air from flowing down the chimney into the room and prevent heated air in the room from escaping. "You can open the doors for the most romantic moments, and then close them right up again. At least, that's what I do."

Along with the doors, however, an outside source of combustion air is needed. "If the house is reasonably tight, you've got to have a dedicated air supply from outside for the fireplace," says Richard, or it may pull air into the house through other openings, including flues. The vent should run from a screened grille in the siding to a point directly beneath the firebox.

Steve had a chimney-top flue damper installed at his house and finds that it, too, helps to keep cold air (and animals) out of the chimney.

types: weatherstripping

No home comfort product is simpler. Here's a quick guide to some common problem-solvers.

SPRING BRONZE: This flexible metal strip (*below*) must be nailed to a wood surface; it's good for double-hung windows, where surfaces slide past each other. "It's a great product," says Steve.

EPDM: A dense rubbery strip (*below*) that stays in place with a self-adhesive strip. Easy to apply, it comes in various thicknesses and profiles, and in several colors. It's ideal where surfaces compress against each other. A similar product, open-cell foam weatherstripping, is also self-adhesive, but it's not as effective as EPDM.

PILE: This polypropylene strip (*facing page*) fits into a groove cut into a wood surface; the fuzzy portion is effective where surfaces sweep across each other, such as a door against the threshold. Easy to replace when worn.

SPRING BRONZE

EPDM

residue produced by burning wood, is extremely flammable, and accumulations of the stuff can catch fire and destroy a house. Because of the risks, periodically hire a chimney sweep to remove creosote buildup. "If you heat primarily with wood," says Richard, "you may have to clean the chimney twice each year." A chimney used infrequently may have to be checked only every other year. In addition, he suggests, look up through the chimney at the start of the heating season to make sure there are no animal nests at the top and no branches stuck inside (a screened chimney cap prevents such problems). At the same time, make sure that the fireplace damper opens and closes without binding. Keep the damper closed whenever there's no fire going to prevent the loss of heated room air. A mason can replace a warped or damaged damper that doesn't seal properly.

Inspect a chimney for structural integrity each year. "Any signs of mortar falling out or loose bricks indicate trouble," says Richard. If you see that, have a mason make repairs right away.

maintaining fans Fans are an integral part of a home's comfort system. Exhaust fans whisk away moisture from steamy bathrooms and smells from kitchen stoves, and also vent the hot air from attics. Most need no maintenance, says Richard, other than perhaps a drop or two of light weight household oil each year (if the manual calls for it) and an occasional dusting of the blades. Kitchen fans, however, have a metal grease filter that should be cleaned several times each year—simply place it in the dishwasher.

Ceiling fans can help with the overall comfort of a house. In the summer they blow downward to create a comfortable breeze; in the winter the same fan can be used to gently mix the air in a room and even out temperature differentials. "Because heat rises, there can be a 7- or 8 degree difference between the top of the room and the bottom," says Richard, particularly in rooms with high ceilings. In the winter, he likes to have the fan blow downward at the lowest speed in order to pull the warmer air from above. Alternatively, some manufacturers recommend reversing the fan in winter to blend cooler air with warmer ceiling air. "Experiment to see which works best for you," says Richard. One caution: Never use a ceiling fan with radiant floor heat. "It will make the house feel very cold," he says.

The finned spine of pile weatherstripping fits into a groove cut into the edge of a door. It can be added in a continuous length as long as the door hardware doesn't interfere.

general-purpose caulks and sealants

TYPE	FLEXIBILITY	ADHESION	PAINT-ABILITY	UV RESIS-TANCE	CLEANUP	BEST USES
SILICONIZED ACRYLIC LATEX	±10% to 20%	good	excellent	good	water	interior paintable surfaces
BUTYL RUBBER	±10%	good	poor	good	solvent	sealing metal gutter joints and metal-to-masonry joints
SILICONE	±25% to 50%	excellent	poor	excellent	solvent	outdoors and in bathrooms and kitchens
POLYSULFIDE	±25%	good	good	poor	solvent	outdoors, in situations of moderate movement
POLYURETHANE	±25%	excellent	good	low; should be painted	solvent	any joint subject to abrasion, such as a driveway seam
SILICONE LATEX	±25%	excellent	good	excellent	water	for general purpose indoors and out
LATEX	±5%	fair	good	fair	water	low-movement joints indoors
ACRYLIC LATEX	±10% to 20%	good to porous surfaces; poor to nonporous surfaces	excellent	good	water	patching indoor cracks, joints, and small holes prior to painting

specialized caulks and sealants

NAME	TYPE	SPECIAL CHARACTERISTIC
MORTAR PATCH	acrylic latex	Colored to match mortar between bricks or blocks.
METAL DUCT SEALANT	vinyl acrylic terpolymer	Stops air leaks in the joints of metal ducts and flexible plastic ducts.
ROOF PATCH	asphalt	Asphalt-based caulk for temporary repairs of leaks around chimneys and holes in shingles.
TUB AND TILE SEALANT	vinyl latex	Contains additives that inhibit the growth of mildew.

The terms "caulk" and "sealants" are often used interchangeably, but "sealants" generally refers to products that stretch and compress better than caulk. Either product consists of binders, fillers, liquids, and additives. Binders, such as silicone and latex, have the greatest effect on flexibility, durability, and adhesion. Fillers control consistency, and additives give the material special characteristics or color. Liquids—water or solvents—hold the ingredients together in suspension.

sealing windows and doors

"People often ignore weatherstripping," says Richard. "But if you were to combine all the gaps around all the doors and windows in a house, you'd end up with the equivalent of a huge hole right in the side of the house." Warm air flows out through these gaps in the wintertime and flows in during the summer, leading to a drafty, uncomfortable house that no heating or air-conditioning tune-up and no amount of insulation can remedy.

As a wintertime test to see whether an opening needs new weatherstripping, moisten your hand and move it along the edges of the door or window—you'll feel cold air leaking in. In warm weather, a lit candle can do the same thing: If the flame flutters, it's time to weatherstrip. But you might not even need to test: Just listen. "If your windows rattle, you'll know you've got a big problem," says Richard. Don't assume you need new windows, however, because even old windows can be made much more efficient with weatherstripping—and for much less than the cost of replacing them.

If windows are already weatherstripped, check to see if the weatherstripping is worn. One way to tell is to lay a dollar bill across the windowsill and close the window on top of it. "If you can pull the bill out easily, it's time to put in new weatherstripping," says Richard. The same test can be used at the meeting rail, where the upper and lower sash come together. If the dollar slips through, it could be due to worn weatherstripping, or to a sash lock that should be tightened. (For more on weatherstripping doors, see Chapter 4; for more on weatherstripping windows, see Chapter 5.)

caulking and sealing Some of the biggest air infiltration problems in older houses result from gaps around wiring, ceiling-mounted light fixtures, plumbing vents, ductwork, and chimneys. "These hidden passageways pull warm air right through the house

sealing the ceiling

Doors and windows must be weatherstripped, but so should heat-leaking attic access hatches. "I took care of mine," says Steve, "by securing a piece of rigid insulation to the top and sticking strips of EPDM to the inside edges. It was a 10-minute job."

improvements:
radiant barriers

No matter how well ventilated and insulated an attic may be, summertime heat will still radiate into the rooms below. Additional insulation reduces the problem, but in climates that require more cooling than heating, there's a more cost-effective technique: attaching a radiant barrier to the underside of the roof framing (p. 127).

A radiant barrier is a thin reflective-foil sheet that comes in rolls of various widths. "It's easy to apply—just staple it to the rafters," says Richard (be sure not to block ventilation paths, however). In climates such as Florida's, radiant barriers have been found to reduce heat gain by up to 50 percent, and to cut up to 20 percent off an annual air-conditioning bill. The farther north you go, however, the less cost-effective radiant barriers become. "We never install them in New England because we just don't have enough air-conditioning days to make it worthwhile," says Richard.

Contrary to intuition, the barrier must be installed with its shiny side facing down (toward the attic floor), rather than up toward the roof. Some varieties have foil on both sides of a bubble-wrap core, eliminating the guesswork about proper installation, but research indicates that the second radiant surface doesn't add much heat-reflecting value.

Unlike insulation, which must be installed with care to eliminate any gaps that would reduce its utility, a radiant barrier doesn't have to be installed so carefully. "Gaps and seams don't really undercut its effectiveness," says Richard.

The barrier won't significantly increase the temperature of the roof itself, particularly if the attic is properly ventilated with a combination of soffit and ridge vents.

types: insulation

Insulation slows the movement of heat through walls and ceilings. Some of the more common forms of insulation:

BATTS: Inexpensive; easy to install. Can be cotton, or can be fiberglass in various densities.

BOARDS: Good for narrow or hard-to-reach areas. Easy to work with. Polystyrene is moisture-impermeable; polyisocyanurate is moisture-resistant.

SPRAY FOAM: Resists moisture and seals effectively. Available in spray cans for sealing small gaps, but can be contractor-applied to walls and ceilings. Also deadens sound transmission.

FIBERGLASS BATTS

EXTRUDED BOARDS

SPRAY FOAM

and create serious comfort problems," explains Richard, as cold outside air rushes in to replace the departing warm air. In an air-conditioned house, the same gaps leak cool air. Even a well-insulated house, says Steve, can be uncomfortable if it's leaky: "That's like wearing a heavy arctic parka but leaving all the zippers open." Professional weatherization contractors usually start their work by looking for leaks in the attic, then work their way down to the basement or crawl space, and that's a strategy that Richard recommends for anyone.

Small gaps can be sealed with acrylic latex caulk, but any gap larger than ⅜ inch, says Tom, should be filled first with a foam rope called backer rod before being caulked, or else the caulk will eventually pull away from the surfaces. Expandable foam sealant is often easier to use in such gaps. In the attic around a chimney, any flammable materials, including faced insulation, should be kept at least 2 inches away from the masonry.

Although interior walls don't require insulation, holes in the top of wall framing can vent tremendous amounts of air into the attic, right through attic insulation. "Holes for wires and pipes should be sealed with expandable foam sealant," says Richard. Attic hatches (see tip, p. 125), pull-down staircases, and whole-house fans also leak air. When not in use, stairs and fans should be covered with a box made of foil-faced insulation board (kits are available, but you can easily make your own) and then weatherstripped.

Moving down from the attic into the house itself, the most common places for air leaks are found around electrical outlets and light switches (seal them with foam gaskets), wherever pipes penetrate a wall (use expandable foam sealant), and near baseboards, where the walls often don't form a tight seal with the flooring (use caulk). Outside, all cracks and joints in the walls should be caulked, especially where two walls meet. (But never caulk the bottom edges of clapboard siding; that can trap moisture in the walls.)

If you really want to know how your house is performing, its heat loss can be analyzed professionally. Using a variety of equipment, including infrared thermographs that create an image of the house based on its temperature, it's possible to find currents of leaking air

Stapling a radiant barrier to the rafters can dramatically cut the amount of heat radiating from a roof into the house. Various products are available; this one consists of foil laminated to a core material similar to bubble-wrap packing. The product can be stapled to the inside surfaces of rafters; a ventilation channel should be maintained behind it.

that would otherwise go undetected. "We had an infrared analysis done of our San Francisco project, and it was an eye-opening experience," says Richard. "The thermographic imaging color-coded heat loss in red, and when a technician cracked open one window just a tiny bit, it looked like someone had just lit a flare at the bottom of the sash. It was like a superhighway guiding dollars out the window." If you find every last leak, the payoff in comfort and energy savings is huge. To find a professional testing contractor, check with local insulation companies.

insulating an attic After all the cracks and holes around a house have been caulked or weatherstripped, adding insulation to the attic is the next most cost-effective task to take on, and it can lead to big energy savings as well as an increase in comfort. Tom's first consideration in a cold climate is to provide a vapor barrier (p. 33), a plastic sheet about 6 mils thick. (Barriers may not be needed in warmer climates; check local building codes.) "If you don't have one between the ceiling material and the insulation, you're asking for trouble from condensation," he says.

If a house doesn't have any attic insulation, Tom sometimes adds fiberglass batts faced with kraft paper. Positioning them with the paper against the ceiling forms a reasonably effective vapor barrier, and it's more of a homeowner task than some other insulation methods, such as blown-in insulation.

More often, however, a house already has attic insulation and simply needs a bit more of it (check with your local building department to find out what's recommended). That's when Tom lays unfaced fiberglass batts perpendicular to the ceiling joists and the existing insulation. "That fills all the little gaps and voids and gives you better results," he says. Don't add faced insulation batts to existing insulation, warns Tom, or you'll create a second vapor barrier that will trap moisture within the insulation, ruining its effectiveness. Tom also cautions against jamming insulation against roof sheathing, where it can block the ventilation from soffit vents. To prevent this, he staples inexpensive foam chutes to the underside of the sheathing *(left)*. The chutes create unblockable air channels against the sheathing so he can pack in the maximum amount of insulation.

Air should flow into the attic through soffit vents. Tom uses foam chutes to prevent the cellulose insulation in this attic from blocking the airflow. He stapled them into place.

improvements:
keeping your cool

Air-conditioning can effectively cool an entire house, but installing a central air system in an existing house is expensive, particularly if the house does not already have ductwork. Here are some alternatives:

WHOLE-HOUSE FAN: A whole-house fan is a sensible and frugal alternative to central air-conditioning. The fan can be installed upstairs, preferably in the ceiling of a main hallway. "You turn it on when the weather starts to get cool outside, during the evening or first thing in the morning. It sucks out the warm air and draws cooler air from the outside," says Tom. The changeover is rapid: These powerful fans can replace all the air in a house in just a few minutes. "Then you close the windows on the sunny side of the house, draw the window shades, and pull air from the shaded side of the house."

The installation challenge is to make sure that the warm exhaust air has somewhere to go once it's sucked into the attic. "You need gable or ridge vents that are big enough to handle the flow," says Tom. Consult air volume charts that accompany the fan.

WINDOW AIR CONDITIONERS: Window units are easy to install and can make you feel more comfortable, but they won't cool a whole house. Instead, they provide what Richard calls "a cold oasis" in a hot house.

DEHUMIDIFIERS: It's the reduction in humidity, not the coolness, that actually makes a person feel more comfortable on a hot day. In a single room, a dehumidifier can reduce humidity more efficiently than a room air-conditioner, and uses less electricity. In climates where the humidity is already quite low, however, cool air is still the preferred antidote to heat.

interior walls + ceilings

cleaning walls and ceilings / patching plaster / sealing water-stained ceilings / patching holes in drywall / plugging nail pops / repairing tiled surfaces / patching wood paneling / repairing wallpaper

chapter 8

IN ONE PARTICULARLY MEMORABLE episode of *This Old House,* we stood at the edge of the largest gypsum mine in North America. A horn sounded, a series of explosions ripped the clear maritime air, and a vast ledge of chalky gray gypsum—soon to be drywall—spewed into the pit below. Over the years we've used acres of drywall on *This Old House* projects, but we've used a lot of other wall materials, too, including wood paneling and tile. No surface, however, can avoid maintenance or repair, a fact well known to my father. With three rambunctious boys in the house, he became a wall-patching expert, and I learned early about the transformational magic of paint, wallpaper, and a solid repertoire of basic repair techniques.

— STEVE

MAINTENANCE **cleaning walls and ceilings** Most houses devote more square footage to walls and ceilings than to floors, yet they get far less attention. That's because painted wall surfaces rarely need much more than a light cleaning, and then only when dirt becomes apparent. Typically, says Tom, a mild household spray cleaner works just fine to remove obvious smears. If an entire room seems dingy, lightly sponging the surfaces with water and TSP (trisodium phosphate) might brighten them up enough to stave off repainting for a while. Accumulations of dirt, however, have a way of blending in—you may not even realize how far the situation has progressed until you happen to clean a patch of wall and notice the color difference. If cleaning fails to restore life to a room, it's time to repaint (see p. 98).

Walls and ceilings are often overlooked when other architectural features take center stage. But how good would this timber frame look without the contrasting surfaces?

history: from plaster to drywall

From the earliest Colonial days until just after World War II, plaster was an almost universal wall finish. The earliest plaster came from limestone, which was burned to form quicklime, then thoroughly saturated with water for several months in a process called slaking. The resulting lime putty was mixed with sand and animal hair, spread over walls covered with wood strips called lath, and finished off with a smooth finish coat. Subsequent advances made plaster easier to work and quicker to set, and gave it a harder surface.

To further reduce the time and effort of plastering, an entrepreneur named Augustine Sackett cast plaster in a rectangular mold and reinforced it with layers of felt paper, creating a rigid board. He patented the product in 1898, and it caught on as a base for plaster. By the 1920s, drywall (plaster sandwiched between two layers of paper) surfaced as a finished wall covering in its own right. It nearly replaced plaster during the housing boom following World War II, when speed was the greatest asset in construction.

Often underappreciated, drywall has great virtues. It can be installed faster and less expensively than full plaster, requires minimal preparation, and is fire-resistant. Its main weakness is revealed on impact: Furniture, fists, and doorknobs that bounce off plaster can poke through ½-inch drywall. Fortunately, drywall has one more virtue: It is easy to repair.

To determine if your walls are made of plaster or drywall, press against the surface with your thumbnail. "If you leave a mark in the wall, it's drywall," says Tom. "But if your thumb starts to hurt and the wall is unscathed, then you've got plaster."

improvements: wall finishes

One alternative to plaster and drywall blends plaster's hardness and satin-smooth texture with the installation convenience of drywall: veneer plaster, sometimes called skimcoat plaster. A similar technique employs standard joint compound.

VENEER PLASTER: Veneer plaster can be trowel-skimmed to a depth of ⅛ inch or more over blueboard—a gypsum drywall with blue-tinted paper that is treated to accept wet plaster. "You use the same material as in standard plaster, but you apply it in a much thinner layer," says Tom. Within an hour, the plaster hardens to a smooth finish, duplicating the look of an old-style plaster wall. "Even better," adds Tom, "it's a harder surface than drywall and actually adds some rigidity to the wall."

JOINT COMPOUND SKIMCOAT: Veneer plaster isn't difficult to work with, but joint compound is a more familiar material to most people, and it can be skimmed over ordinary drywall. "You might only do this during a renovation when you'll have to tape the walls anyway, but a coat of joint compound can create a finish that looks like plaster," says Tom. Joint compound is stiffer than plaster, however—it's like peanut butter to plaster's mayonnaise—so it's harder to smooth. "You'll have to work at it," says Tom. "But after you paint it, the finished surface will look a lot nicer than painted drywall. Done correctly, you won't see any tape marks or spots where screw holes have been covered up." When dry, joint compound has a softer surface than veneer plaster, and can be smoothed with a damp sponge.

Another advantage to joint compound: "If you screw up with joint compound, you can sand out your error." says Tom. "Plaster isn't quite so forgiving."

REPAIR

patching plaster Repairing plaster involves some of the same steps as repairing drywall. For a large hole, Tom clears away loose material and fits in a piece of scrap wood (p. 136). Instead of adding a drywall inlay, however, he uses blueboard, a type of drywall suited for plaster work. Then he mixes up a small batch of plaster (adding the powder to the water, rather than vice versa, to eliminate lumps), and mists the wall with water to prevent it from sucking moisture out of the patch. After spreading on the plaster, Tom smooths it with a steel trowel. "If little bubbles form in the plaster, you're troweling it too aggressively," he says. Continually swiping a trowel over the surface as the plaster sets coaxes a fine "cream" to the surface, resulting in the best finish.

To fill a crack, first enlarge it with a utility knife to a width of about ¼ inch, creating a slight undercut to help the patching plaster stay in place. "Mist the area, butter plaster into the crack, smooth it, and you're done." To maximize the connection between new and old plaster, a bonding agent may used. It looks like white glue and is simply brushed over surfaces prior to patching them.

If a section of wall surface is loose, Tom secures it with plaster washers (*right*), staples fiberglass screening over the area, then plasters. "The screen provides reinforcement," says Tom. "I've used this trick to fix ceilings and walls that were in really bad shape."

sealing water-stained ceilings Damaged ceilings, whether drywall or plaster, can be patched just as you'd patch the walls. Sometimes, however, the damage comes from water leakage, and repairs then call for a slightly different approach. Fix the leak first. Then, if the water hasn't actually damaged the drywall, tackle the ugly brownish stain left on the surface. Before painting the area, Tom brushes on a stain-blocking primer to keep the stain from bleeding through the new paint. "The stain may look like it disappears if you just swab it with a coat or two of regular paint, but before long it will reappear if you don't use a stain blocker," he says. Stain-blocking primers are also available in spray cans, which are particularly handy for use on textured ceilings.

If a plaster surface is solid (not crumbly) but has separated from the lath beneath, it can be reattached with plaster washers and drywall screws. Once the area has been secured, Tom conceals the washers with joint compound, which he sands lightly later.

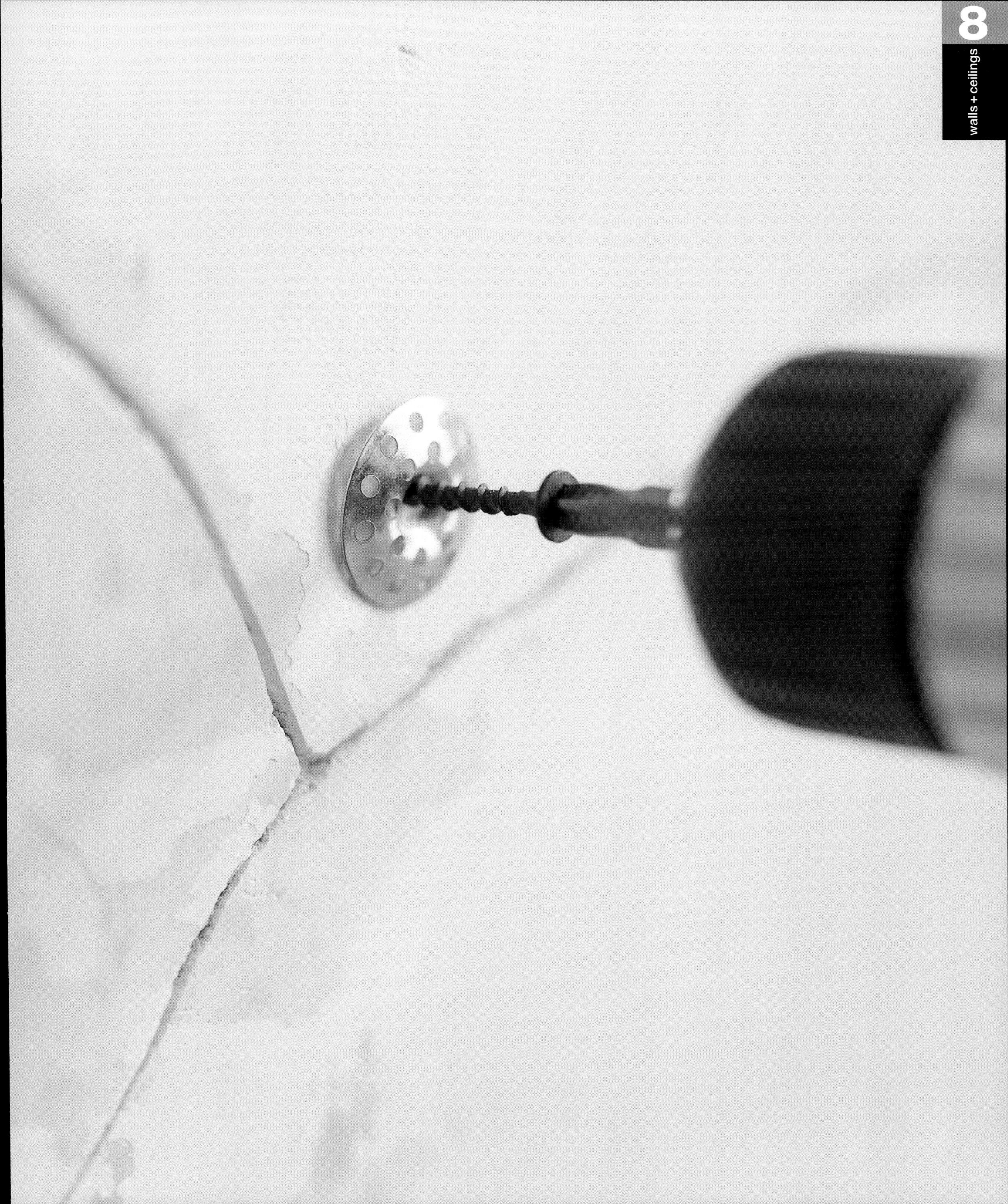

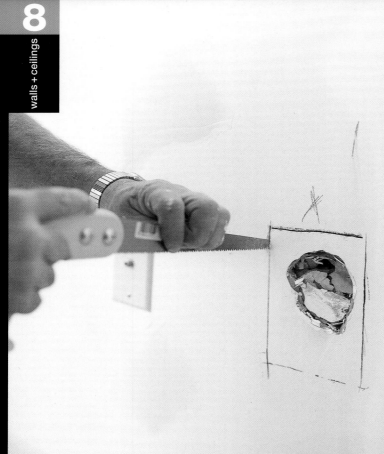

1 2

3 4

patching holes in drywall Drywall forms a smooth surface and is easy to install, but as a material it's far from strong. The smallest holes—less than the diameter of a pencil—can be repaired by swiping a putty knife loaded with premixed joint compound over them. Let the compound dry, then add another layer (compound shrinks slightly when it dries). When that layer is dry, lightly sand it smooth with fine sandpaper. To see if you've filled the hole completely, shine a light across it: Shadows will amplify any imperfection.

To repair larger holes—up to the size of a fist—stuff wadded newspaper into the hole and pack the area with joint compound, extending the compound several inches beyond the edges of the hole. Then cover the compound with lengths of paper joint tape or fiberglass mesh joint tape (Tom has no favorite), and press them into place with a wide putty knife. Wait a couple of days for this to dry; then spread on additional thin layers of compound (letting each dry before adding another) until there's no longer a depression where the hole was. When the last layer has dried, sand the area smooth. Holes beyond fist size call for the use of a drywall filler (*left*).

Joint compound, incidentally, is quite useful for repairing plaster (p. 134) as well as drywall. Its tenacious hold makes it good for use even on painted surfaces; just rough up glossy areas with sandpaper.

plugging nail pops As a house settles or the wood framing shrinks, however, drywall nails sometimes pop out a tiny bit, uncorking the joint compound and creating a small lump in a wall or ceiling. "You can cover it up again with joint compound and paint over it, but it will probably just pop out again," says Tom. To make a more lasting repair, Tom drives two drywall screws into the framing about 2 inches above and below the renegade. "That relieves the pressure and should fix the problem for good," he explains. Then he drives the popped fastener in and fills the sunken areas using a wide putty knife and joint compound.

To patch large holes, Tom installs a drywall filler. **1.** *He cuts a piece of drywall slightly larger than the damage, holds it over the hole, and traces its outline on the wall. Then he cuts out the marked area.* **2.** *If there isn't a stud behind the hole, he maneuvers a piece of scrap wood into the hole and secures it with drywall screws.* **3.** *After fitting the patch into place, Tom screws it to the scrap.* **4.** *Finally, he butters the area with joint compound, embeds a reinforcing square of fiberglass screen larger than the patch, and spreads on more compound, letting each layer dry before adding another.*

surface acoustics

Unless it's for a historic restoration, no one slathers plaster over wood lath today. But veneer plaster has become increasingly common in some areas of the country, due in part to an installation advantage. "The plus is that there's no sanding, which can be the messiest job in the world," says Tom. "An average room can be completed in one day."

"All of us at the show love the clean, hard surface of veneer plaster," says Steve, but Tom notes one major limitation. "The acoustics of drywall are more pleasing," he says, because drywall has a softer finish. Working on the show's 1997 project in Milton, Massachusetts, these differing qualities were used to advantage. Throughout most of the house, veneer plaster was applied to the walls in order to match the plaster in the 18th-century main wing. But in the media room—which contained a big-screen TV, surround-sound system, and stereo—Tom lined the walls with two layers of drywall, with the seams staggered, to prevent sound from sneaking through. "The designers didn't want that room to echo like the other rooms did," he says. "You can definitely hear the difference."

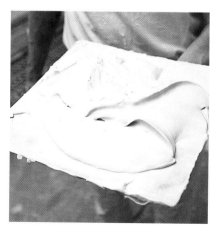

SKIMCOAT PLASTER

types: wall tiles

Ceramic tiles, made from fired clay, are grouped according to their water permeability—from nonvitreous, which readily absorbs water, to semi-vitreous, vitreous, and impervious. The more impermeable clay tiles are fired at high temperatures—2000 degrees or more—which fuses the ingredients in them and makes them suitable for use in wet locations. Most have a waterproof glaze that adds to their durability. Wall tiles also come in three distinct types.

FIELD TILES are set in the main portion of the installation.

TRIM TILES have a shaped edge, and are often used to provide a border around the field tiles. They generally cost more per tile than field tiles.

DECORATIVE TILES are used sparingly to accent an installation. They can be hand-painted, be made of unusual materials, or feature raised-relief shapes. When damaged wall tiles can't be matched, tile contractor Joe Ferrante suggests using decorative tiles. "Remove the damage and some good tiles, too, then pepper decorative tiles over the wall to disguise the patch," he says. "You won't spend a lot but the wall will look entirely new."

DECORATIVE TILE

repairing tiled surfaces Reattaching a loose tile or replacing a damaged tile (*right*) isn't difficult. Check first, however, for signs of larger problems. "If wall tiles in a wet area are loose, it's usually a sign that water is getting behind them," says Tom. To survey the damage, he gently taps every tile with the handle of a screwdriver: "Tile that's adhered poorly sounds hollow." The tiles that usually loosen first are those around the faucet and those in the first row or two around the tub. If more than a few tiles are loose outside these areas, the problems might require extensive repairs best left to a tile contractor. "Don't overlook a problem like this," warns Tom, "because it will only get worse."

If the underlying surface is sound, however, individual tiles can be replaced or reattached with ease. Where tiles are broken, Tom chisels out the pieces and looks for replacement tiles (see sidebar at left). "Look for something that's exactly right, not only in length and width but in thickness and color," he says. "Otherwise, your patch will look obvious." The original tiles may have been attached either with tile mastic, a creamy premixed adhesive, or with a mortarlike product called thinset adhesive. Mastic is usually best for reattaching tiles, says *This Old House* tile contractor Joe Ferrante. "With thinset, it's harder to get the new tile to sit flush with the ones around it—mastic spreads out better." And mastic is readily available in small containers: Why buy a big bag of thinset just to set a few tiles? To ensure that the new tile is properly positioned, glide your fingertips over the area; you might not see that a tile is too high or too low, but you'll feel it.

Grouting the tile is the last step of the repair. Sanded grout is generally used when the joints are larger than ⅛ inch; unsanded grout is best for thinner joints. Getting a color match, however, can be tough. Ferrante says that you might have to use off-white grout to match the look of white grout that has been in place for years. "Or you can even stain all the grout another color," he adds; special grout stains are available from tile distributors.

The techniques for repairing a tiled wall or floor are the same. 1. To separate a tile from its brethren, rake out the surrounding grout with a grout saw. 2. A loose tile pulls free, but a damaged tile calls for a cold chisel, a hammer, and safety glasses. Work carefully to keep the damage from spreading. 3. After scraping the old adhesive from the area, butter the tile with mastic and press it into place; keep a wall tile from slipping with a strip or two of masking tape. 4. After a day, remove the tape, butter grout into the joints, and smooth it to match surrounding grout. Seal the grout after a few days.

1 2
3 4

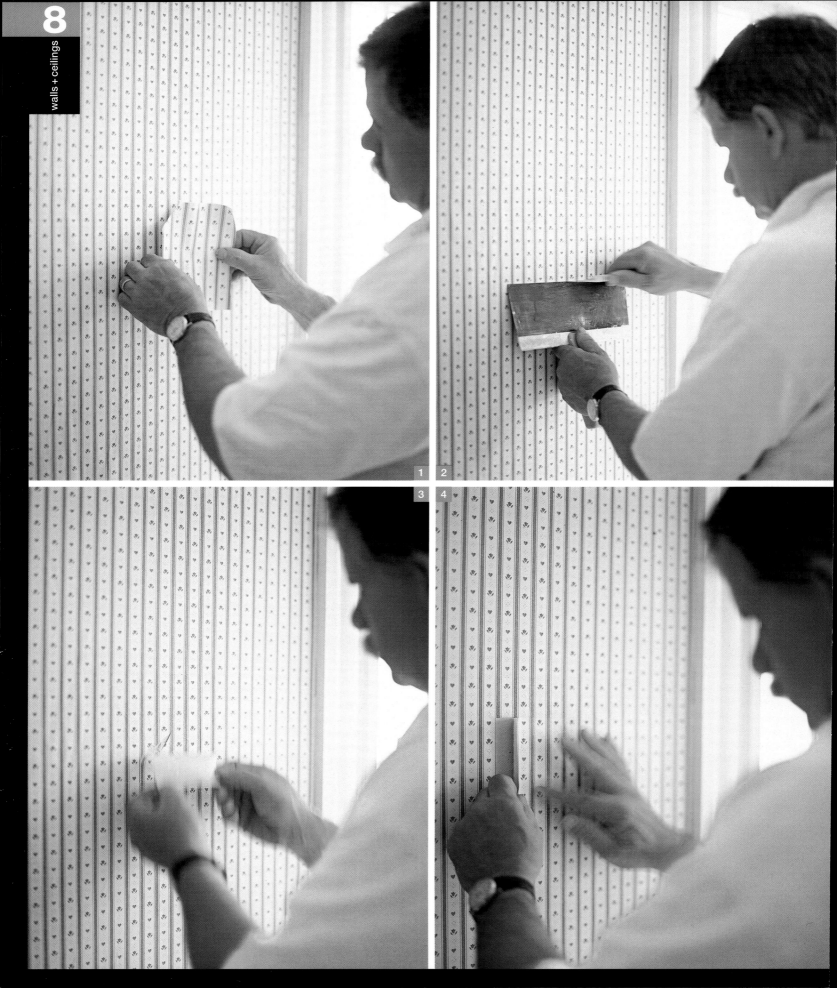

patching wood paneling Veneered sheet paneling is often no thicker than ¼ inch, which makes it prone to damage. Tom patches holes with an inlay cut from scrap paneling. Cut along the vertical grooves in the scrap, he says, to conceal the cut lines, using a utility knife with a fresh blade—it can slice through paneling in several passes. When making the cuts, Tom holds the knife at a slight angle so that the edges of the inlay will be beveled inward, like the lid of a Halloween jack-o'-lantern. After temporarily securing the patch to the damaged area with a tiny dab or two of hot-melt glue, he uses the patch as a template for cutting out the damage (the knife must be held at the same angle as before). There usually isn't a stud beneath the damaged area, so Tom slips a wood scrap into the hole to support the patch, just as he does when patching drywall (p. 136); construction adhesive holds it in place against the back side of the paneling. Finally, he fine-tunes the fit of the inlay with sandpaper, dabs the edges and center with carpenter's glue, and pushes it into place; masking tape holds it there until the glue dries.

repairing wallpaper Repairing damaged wallpaper is far easier than repapering the whole room. Patching (*left*) works best if a scrap of the original wallpaper is available (that's why you should keep scraps after a wallpapering job). If you take time to match the pattern precisely, says Tom, few people will ever notice what you've done. He uses a premixed wallpaper adhesive for repairs.

If there are no scraps of wallpaper available to make a patch, Tom tries to cannibalize a piece from a place no one will see, such as in a closet or behind a bureau. It's a last-ditch effort to avoid repapering the whole room, because getting the paper off in one piece is not easy. "You have to moisten it with hot water and coax it off slowly, and even then you might ruin it," he says.

If a wallpaper seam lifts, Tom gently works wallpaper seam adhesive under it, then rolls it flat. You may have to hold the seam down with a putty knife until the adhesive takes hold.

Patching wallpaper calls for careful, methodical work. 1. Tom obtains a scrap slightly larger than the patch he'll need, moistens it (to activate the glue), and then lines up the pattern exactly. 2. He uses a fresh utility knife, guided by a straightedge, to make four deft cuts simultaneously through the patch and the original wallpaper. Avoid repeated cuts. "That way, the patch will fit like a piece in a puzzle." 3. With the cuts complete, Tom removes the patch, peels off the old wallpaper, and scrapes the old adhesive off the wall. 4. All that's left is to fit the patch into place and smooth it out.

types: wallpaper

Modern manufacturing methods have resulted in a vast number of wallpaper products. "But whatever the wallpaper, the secret is in laying it so that the patterns match and the edges are neat," says Tom. "Otherwise, you're better off painting." Wallpapers with the following features are particularly useful.

VINYL FACING: Vinyl wallpaper stands up to scrubbing and moisture, making it a good choice for bathrooms, kitchens, and hallways. No longer is "glossy" the only finish available; matte and semi-gloss finishes are, too. "One thing I love about vinyl wallpapers is that you can use them as a vapor barrier in a house that's missing one," says Tom. "It's a great way to prevent moisture from getting into the walls."

PREPASTED BACKING: Many papers are backed with dried glue. "You soak the paper briefly in a tub of water to activate the adhesive, and that's it," says Tom. He relies on this characteristic for quick repairs (*facing page*).

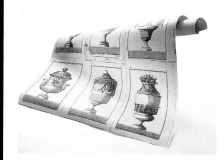

interior floors

general floor care / maintaining carpet / cleaning a carpet / maintaining ceramic tile / maintaining a wood floor / fixing a squeaky floor / repairing carpet / realigning wall-to-wall carpet / repairing a wood floor / repairing vinyl / repairing tile

chapter 9

AT THIS OLD HOUSE, WE TAKE EVERY opportunity to visit the source of products we use, and I figure we've traveled some 200,000 miles trying to learn about flooring. On one project, for example, we headed to Mexico to watch Saltillo tiles being handcrafted. During another, we visited a Georgia mill to learn about nylon carpet. And when we needed a hard-wearing but resilient floor for the Billerica project, we found linoleum. Linoleum was invented and is still produced on the banks of the Firth of Forth in Kirkcaldy, Scotland—so what could we do but go take a look? It's a tough job, sure, but someone has to do it! —STEVE

MAINTENANCE general floor care Floors bear the brunt of household living. They must withstand endless footsteps, the scraping of heavy furniture, and being the direct target of spills and other calamities that make up daily life. No surface, natural or synthetic, can match these challenges without regular maintenance. "Dirt and grit act like sandpaper when pressed against the sole of your foot," says Tom, and can eventually damage the toughest vinyl floor or the densest carpet.

Because improper cleaning of a flooring product may void the manufacturer's warranty, Tom recommends to his clients that they follow the manufacturers' recommendations for specific cleaning products and polishes: "That will really make a difference in how the floor holds up." There are some general principles to follow, however. Most important, keep the floor clean—sweeping or vacuuming frequently will remove damaging particles before they cause any harm. To reduce wear, park a slip-resistant throw rug where you stand (such as at the sink) or where you turn (near the bottom

The type of floor defines the character of any room, and is the surface most exposed to the travails of modern living, from dropped scissors to grape-juice spills.

types: floor finishes

The right finish for your wood floors depends on the look you want, the hardness you need, and the amount of effort you're willing to spend maintaining it.

Also decide upon the sheen you prefer: gloss, semigloss, or satin. Satin is the most likely to result in a natural look. A high-gloss finish will show dirt and damage more readily. It is even possible to layer finishes with differing sheens and characteristics in order to attain a particular look.

URETHANE: Urethanes (usually referred to as polyurethanes) are the hardest-wearing finishes. There are several types of the product, some of which are suitable only for application by professionals. Oil-based urethanes, however, are durable as well as suitable for homeowner application. In general, urethanes are easy to apply to bare wood but difficult to patch or repair. "It's hard to feather the edges when you apply it, so you'll see a ridge or a ring around the patch," says Tom. As a result, even small areas of damage may end up requiring that the entire floor be rescreened or refinished.

WAX: Paste wax is the traditional floor finish, but the material requires regular stripping and reapplication, boosting maintenance requirements. Also, the finish is not as durable as others.

OTHER FINISHES: Shellac, a substance based on resins secreted by lac bugs, lends a richness some prefer to urethane finishes, but it must be protected by wax. Repairs are fairly easy: Remove the wax with turpentine, apply a coat or two of shellac, then rewax.

Factory-prefinished flooring may come with a variety of finishes, making care and repair difficult to summarize. The best bet is to contact the manufacturer for specific details.

types: carpet

Wall-to-wall carpeting adds elegance, warmth, and comfort to a home. Carpets insulate against the cold and cut down on the transmission of sound in a house. But if not kept clean, they can harbor unwelcome smells as well as allergens. Of all the fibers used for carpeting, wool and nylon are the most common.

The two fibers, however, are often difficult to distinguish from each other. Knowing the difference is important because wool stains more easily than nylon, and its expense may make it more deserving of professional cleaning. One way to identify the fiber is to rub a drop or two of water into an inconspicuous spot: A wool carpet will smell musky, just the way a damp sweater does; a nylon carpet won't.

Having a professional coat any carpet with an acrylic rug protector will help prevent stains from soaking into the fibers. That won't make a carpet stainproof, but it will give you some extra time to blot up spills.

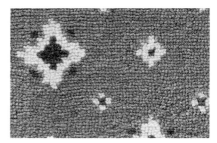

PATTERN

TEXTURE

of a set of stairs), and put carpet runners in hallways. Otherwise, the floor will show wear first in those areas. And although regular cleaning is an excellent idea, drenching a wood or resilient floor with water is not. Excess water will cause the seams in resilient floors to lift, and can damage wood floorboards as well as their finish.

maintaining carpet Keeping a carpet clean is essential to prolonging its life and maintaining its appearance. Abrasion caused by dirt particles ground into the carpet fibers by foot traffic is what does the damage. Regular vacuuming is crucial, even if the carpet doesn't look dirty. High-traffic areas, for example, might benefit from vacuuming as often as several times a week. Another way to cut down on the grit is to prevent it from getting onto the carpet in the first place, and you don't have to be a carpet expert to understand how. "Doormats inside and outside act like dirt magnets," says Tom. Some families have even adopted a "no shoes in the house" rule, which helps enormously to keep outside dirt outside. Sunlight is another enemy because it can alter a carpet's color. For heirloom carpets, keep the drapes or blinds shut during peak sunlight hours; otherwise, expect some fading. To even out wear and sun-fading, turn area rugs end for end every 2 years—they'll look better for a lot longer.

cleaning a carpet Carpets eventually need deep cleaning to remove dirt that the vacuum cleaner doesn't get, and there are three ways to go. Spray-on shampoos, available at supermarkets, contain powdered chemicals that lift dirt off the surface of a carpet. Simply spray it on, let it dry, and vacuum off the residue. This removes some dirt and may freshen the smell of a carpet, but the cleaning is superficial. A deeper cleaning comes from machines that apply wet cleaning agents to the carpet. Often rented, shampooing units contain a rotary brush that works a detergent foam into the carpet to loosen dirt particles. The dirt is suspended in the foam while the solution dries; vacuuming the carpet later removes the residue. If any detergent residue is left behind, however, it will actually attract dirt and could dull the look of the carpet.

Professional carpet cleaners rely on hot-water extraction cleaning, partly because it doesn't use the mechanical brushes that can damage yarn tufts. The machine forces hot water into the carpet, then

cleaning floors

FLOOR	MAINTENANCE	STAIN REMOVAL	REPAIR
CARPET	Vacuum frequently.	Blot up spills immediately (do not scrub) with white terrycloth towel to avoid dye transfer. Small stains yield to a carbonated-type spray cleaner. For general carpet cleaning, see p.146. Stains caused by bleach may be irreversible.	Small burns can be patched (p. 153). Rippled carpet must be restretched (p.154). A lifted seam can be repaired with heat-activated carpet seaming tape. Tears call for professional help.
CERAMIC TILE	Sweep frequently. Damp mop with water, or with water and oil-free floor cleaner. Clean mildew with a bleach-fortified all-purpose household cleanser.	Clean mildew with a bleach-fortified all-purpose cleaner.	Grout cannot be patched. Rake out loose or damaged grout (p.187) and regrout.
STONE	Sweep frequently. Damp mop with water. Seal as needed with acrylic floor sealer.	See above.	See above.
VINYL	Sweep frequently. Damp mop no-wax floors with water, or with water and vinyl-floor cleaner.	Use vinyl-floor cleaner full strength; or use rubbing alcohol or mineral spirits.	Remove damage (p.150). Replace with scrap piece cut to fit.
WOOD	Sweep frequently, or use dust mop. Mist with wood-floor spray cleaner and dry mop.	Small areas of finish are difficult to repair in most cases.	Cut out severe damage (p.158) and reweave floor; then sand and refinish entire floor.
LINOLEUM	Sweep, vacuum, or use dust mop frequently. Damp mop with linoleum-floor cleaner mixed with water. Do not use ammonia-based cleaning products.	Use concentrated linoleum-floor cleaner mixed with water. Scrub ingrained dirt with nylon brush or scrubbing sponge. Some stains may require removal of surface finish before treatment.	See vinyl.

When spills occur on any floor surface, quick action to blot up the spill can prevent stains from appearing (scrubbing may drive the spill deeper). The most important cleaning tip is to prevent dirt and grit from damaging the flooring. In carpet it will harm fibers; on a hard surface it will eventually grind off the finish. Vacuum carpet frequently. Sweep, dust mop, or vacuum hard surfaces, but do not vacuum with beater-bar attachment in place (it is for carpeting only, and can damage hard flooring). Always use cleaners recommended by the flooring manufacturer. Use a damp mop, never a wet one, on hard surfaces.

instantly pulls the water and dirt out with suction. Too much water left in the carpet, however, can cause the backing to shrink or mildew, so homeowners who rent this equipment should be careful. "The guy who cleans our carpets," notes Steve, "sets up big fans to help them dry quickly afterward."

maintaining ceramic tile Hard as they may seem, the surface of ceramic floor tiles can be worn down by the same enemy that attacks other flooring: dirt and grit. Regular sweeping and damp mopping with a little water and floor cleaner is essential.

One problem that affects some tile floors can't be helped by cleaning. "If the floor expands or contracts excessively, the grout may crack," says tile contractor Joe Ferrante, who has been involved with a number of *This Old House* projects. Cracked grout can't be patched, he says; damaged areas must be raked out with a hand tool called a grout saw (p. 139). "Removing grout is time-consuming," says Ferrante, "but the hardest part is making sure you don't chip the edge of a tile." Some saws have a blade that can be adjusted to fit grout joints of various widths; make sure the blade is skinny enough to fits between the tiles. After the debris has been vacuumed up, the floor can be regrouted as if it had just been installed.

maintaining a wood floor The wood in a wood floor is marvelously durable—it's the finish that often looks beat. To minimize wear, Tom recommends the same general precautions suitable for any floor (p. 145).

Washing a wood floor with a wet mop and a harsh cleaner will shorten its life. Not only could the cleaner damage the finish, but excessive amounts of water will sink into the floor and eventually ruin the wood as well as lift the finish. The wood floors at Steve's house—longleaf pine planks with a polyurethane finish—get their cleanup from a barely damp mop. "Then we dry them immediately with a terry-cloth towel," he says. At Tom's house, the floor-cleaning regimen is slightly different. Cleaning duty consists of misting the floor with a gentle nonabrasive cleaner specifically formulated for the purpose (they get it from their flooring contractor). The cleaner is spread around and wiped off with a terry-cloth application

Tom uses a spray cleaner specially formulated for use on wood floors to clean floors in his kitchen. A light misting with the cleaner and a few swipes with the pad does it.

how it works: the subfloor

Beneath the part of the floor you see—the finish floor—lies the real muscle of a floor: the subfloor. It provides a solid base for the finish floor, and strengthens as well as stiffens the building. The subfloor is nailed (and sometimes also glued) to horizontal floor-framing lumber, called joists, whose size and spacing determine how solid the floor feels as you walk over it. Joists are sometimes stiffened by wood (*shown below*) or metal bracing, or by solid lumber blocking. Loose stiffeners are sometimes a source of squeaks.

The subfloor is typically plywood or OSB (oriented strand board) panels, or in old houses, wood boards. Additional layers of plywood or cement-board subflooring, called underlayment, are often used to provide an extra-smooth base beneath finish floors.

Even if a finish floor is in good condition, the subfloor beneath might not be. It's vulnerable to rot caused by moisture, particularly in bathrooms. A deteriorating subfloor can usually be detected just by walking over it. "If it flexes noticeably when you step on it, you've got a problem," Tom says. Investigate.

SUBFLOOR AND UNDERLAYMENT

pad. Tough stains, such as dark heel marks, are rubbed out with a soft cloth dampened with the same cleaner.

Yet even with this care, a floor finish will eventually wear out. "You have to keep your eye on high-wear areas such as stairways and hallways," says Tom. Once he sees the telltale dulling of the finish, he calls in the floor refinisher—but not for a full sanding and refinishing. Instead, he has his floors "screened" (p. 154) and then applies two fresh coats of polyurethane. It's a process undertaken every 2 or 3 years. "The floor looks brand-new, and at a fraction of the cost of having it completely refinished," explains Tom.

REPAIR **fixing a squeaky floor** Squeaking floors can be vexing to walk on, but even more vexing to fix. Floors squeak, says Tom, whenever two materials rub against each other. "It could be a nail rubbing against the subfloor, or maybe it's the subfloor rubbing against the framing," he explains. "A lot of this happens when wood shrinks or expands as the seasons change."

If there's an unfinished basement or crawl space beneath the problemarea, that's good news. "Have someone stand near the squeak and rock back and forth so that you can find the exact spot," says Tom. Once it's been located, try to prevent the materials from rubbing by fastening them together from beneath (*right*). If the underside of a wood finish floor isn't accessible, Tom drives 8d finish nails (see page 222 for more on nail sizing) into holes drilled through the top of the finish floor. "There's always a risk that you'll hit a wire or a water pipe, so you want to consider carefully how annoying the squeak is," says Tom. "You may want to live with it instead."

repairing carpet From a repair standpoint, carpets come in two varieties: area rugs, which can be rolled up and taken to a professional for repair; and wall-to-wall carpeting, which can't be.

One method for repairing small holes in wall-to-wall carpet,

Squeak stoppers. ***1.*** *If a subfloor has separated from the floor joist (or vice versa) and the two cannot be pulled back together, small wedges secured with construction adhesive will help—but don't wedge the two farther apart.* ***2.*** *If the underside of the floor cannot be reached, drive finish nails into the subfloor through predrilled holes. Countersink the nailheads and fill the holes.* ***3.*** *A short screw driven into the flooring will secure a loose floorboard. An angled screw can reconnect subfloor and joist.* ***4.*** *A subfloor squeak under carpet can be fixed with a finish nail—if the nail hits a joist.*

1 2
3 4

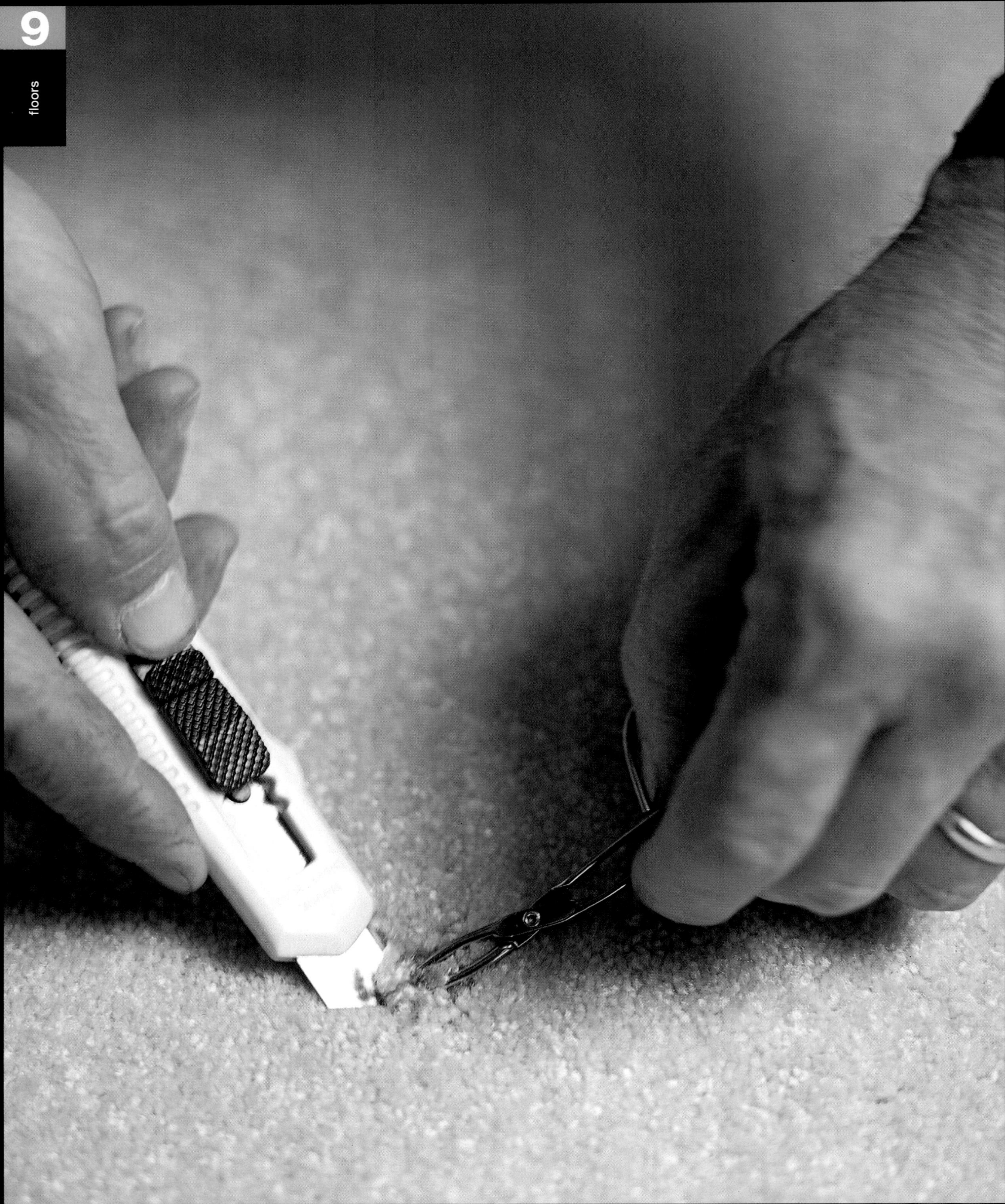

such as cigarette burn marks, involves using a kit that consists of a small metal cylinder with a razor-sharp edge. The cylinder cuts out the damage, as well as a replacement plug taken from an inconspicuous area. The new piece should be glued in place with carpet seam cement and weighted overnight. This generally works best with plush, unpatterned carpets, and not with looped-fiber carpets. "You wouldn't want to do this with a Berber or any other tightly woven carpet, because the patch would show," says Tom. "In that case, you'll be a lot better off having a professional make the repair."

In the case of a small burn mark, the affected tufts may need nothing more than a careful snipping (*left*) to remove the damage.

realigning wall-to-wall carpet Many people don't realize it, but installing a wall-to-wall carpet is a little like installing screening in a frame: The material is actually stretched across the area and secured along the perimeter. In the case of carpet, the stretching is done by specialized tools called kickers. The securing is done with slender pieces of wood called tackless (sometimes called tack stripping)—slender wooden strips with short angled, tacklike teeth that grab the back of the carpet and keep it from moving. The carpet installer first nails tackless to the subfloor, with the teeth angled toward the walls, then cuts carpet padding to fit within the toothy perimeter. The carpet comes next; after impaling one edge on the tackless, the installer "kicks" the carpet toward the opposite wall and secures it there with tackless. The process is repeated across the width of the carpet. The result: a smooth, ripple-free expanse of soft fibers.

Over time, however, the carpet can loosen, either through ordinary use or by dragging heavy furniture across it. The result can be a series of ripples in the middle of the room, and a gap along the edge

To disguise small burn marks, Tom lifts the burned tufts with tweezers (to keep his fingers out of harm's way) and slices off darkened portions with a sharp utility knife.

screw clamp
If a screw must be run through a joist and into the subfloor above, drill the hole slightly oversized, says Tom. "If the screw threads bite into the joist, they'll prevent the materials from being drawn together."

warm floors

In the course of building an addition or working on an extensive renovation, it's easy to add radiant floor heat (p. 117). But it can also be added to existing floors—including wood and vinyl—by attaching the radiant-heat tubing to the underside of the subfloor. "You can heat the house with it or just add enough tubing to warm the floors," says Richard.

Working in the basement, he attaches the tubing in a serpentine pattern to the underside of the subfloor, carefully drilling holes at the ends of the joists to link each bay. For a house where the tubing will provide the primary source of heat, he covers them with reflective metal strips to help reflect the heat upward more effectively. With the tubing in place, Richard insulates each joist bay to make sure that the heat from the coils moves up, not down. "The insulation is critical for the system to work," he says, and any type of insulation will do the job.

Under stone, tile, or vinyl floors, the water temperature in the tubing can rise to 120 degrees without hurting the floors. Under wood floors, however, Richard is careful to set the temperature so that the wood surface never exceeds 85 degrees Fahrenheit. "If it goes higher, there's a danger that the wood might cup or crack," he explains. The floors in Steve's house are longleaf pine planks, and he loves the radiant heat beneath them. "I'd definitely do it again," he reports.

About the only common floor not suited to radiant heating is thick carpeting: It will actually insulate the floor and prevent the heat from rising efficiently. "If you want plush wall-to-wall carpeting, then radiant floor heating isn't for you," says Richard. "But area rugs, or even thin carpeting with padding, should present no trouble at all."

refinishing a wood floor

Completely refinishing a wood floor is a job for professionals: The old finish must be sanded off first, and the equipment used to do this can seriously damage a floor in an instant if used by an inexperienced operator.

Two main pieces of equipment are needed to sand a floor. The first is a drum sander, which is a cross between a giant belt sander and a lawnmower. As it is guided over the floor, the sanding drum scours off the finish along with a slight amount of the wood. "The drum sander has to be kept moving at an even rate," says Tom, "or it will grind a big trough right into the floor."

To sand around the perimeter of the floor, an edger is required. Unlike the drum sander, the edger is fitted with a swirling abrasive disk. If the disk is held in one place too long, it will create dips and valleys—instead of a smooth surface—all around the edges of the room. "When you put a finish on that floor," says Tom, "it will just look awful."

Marrying the effects of these machines to create a smooth, seamless surface is not easy. "Unless you've got some experience doing this, leave it to a professional," says Tom. "And a good one—this is definitely a time you'd want to check somebody's references and actually visit some work they've done."

Even a careful professional sanding will inevitably remove some of the wood itself, which reduces the life of the floor. Instead of a complete stripping, a floor that looks worn may benefit from an intermediate step, called screening.

Using a buffer and a mildly abrasive pad, a professional can scour off just enough of the existing finish to provide a suitable base for new finish, saving the expense and effort of a complete stripping.

where the tackless has been exposed. The remedy is to restretch the carpet and reattach it to the tackless. "If the carpet is in good condition and you don't plan to replace it soon, kicking it back into place is a good way to get a lot more life out of it," says Tom. "But this is something you should hire a carpet installer to do."

repairing a wood floor Even though a wood floor is quite durable, it is not indestructible. If damaged boards must be replaced, there are two ways to approach the problem. The least desirable is to cut out only the damage, then insert short pieces of flooring to fill the area. "You'll end up with a square patch that looks more like a trapdoor," says Tom. The better way is to stagger the replacement boards and reweave them into the existing flooring (*right*), which produces a patch that's more likely to blend with adjacent wood.

To patch a floor, you'll need flooring of the same dimensions, the same species, and the same cut as the existing flooring. "It may be oak, for example, but there's a big difference in look between flat-sawn or quartersawn, and white oak or red," says Tom. After removing a piece, suggests Steve, take it to the lumberyard or a wood-flooring supplier to ensure a good match.

With the boards on hand, it's time to remove the damaged wood from the floor. To do this, Tom uses a framing square and a pencil to mark lines on each board he intends to cut. "The idea is to stagger the cuts so that you're not creating an obvious pattern," he says. After he's made his pencil marks, he carefully scores the wood with a utility knife to reduce splintering as he cuts.

Tom has several ways of cutting out the boards. The easiest is to fit an electric drill with a $1/8$ inch bit and bore 3 to 5 holes across the width of each board to be cut. The holes are lined up along the inside of the score mark, and don't penetrate the subfloor. He then rests a sharp chisel on the scored line and taps it to knock out a neatly cut piece of wood. With a circular saw, Tom cuts lengthwise down the middle of the board (being careful not to cut into the subfloor); then he carefully pries each half out, repeating the process with each remaining board.

*Repairing a wood floor: **1.** A sharp chisel can be used to cross-cut each floor board; starter holes help. **2.** To disguise the repairs, new boards are "woven" between existing boards. **3.** Most of the new boards can be toenailed into place, but the last one must be facenailed. **4.** To further disguise repairs, the entire floor should be refinished.*

1
2
3
4

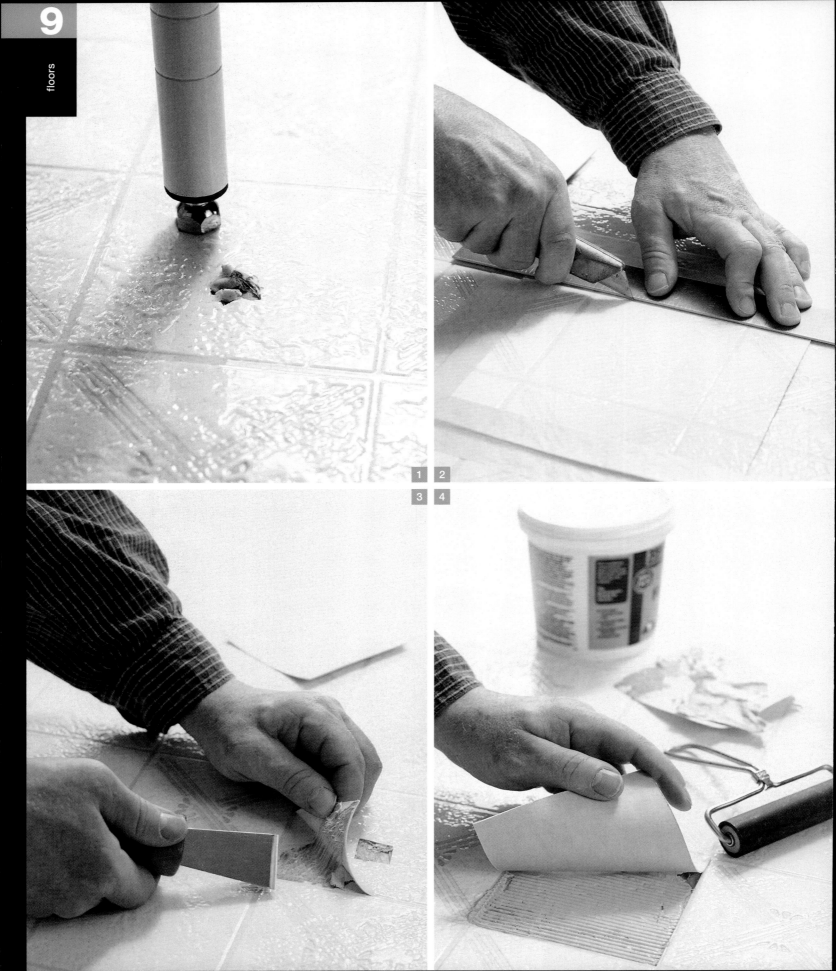

1 2
3 4

To install the new wood, Tom drops each board into place and either nails it or glues it—or both. "If you have tongue-and-groove boards, you may have to break off the bottom side of the groove in order to slide the piece in," he says. When the boards fit, he sands their surface and finishes it to match the floor. "Done right, the patch will almost disappear," he says.

repairing vinyl A gouged or burned piece of vinyl flooring can be replaced with ease, particularly if it's an individual tile. "You pop the damaged piece out by first warming it with a heat gun or a hair dryer, then gradually pry it out with a putty knife," says Tom. "Check the manufacturer's recommendation for the right adhesive— usually floor mastic—then put the new tile in place." Sheet vinyl, however, requires a more complicated approach. The first challenge is to find a patch. "If you're lucky, you'll find a leftover remnant in the attic or the basement," he says. If not, roll the refrigerator out from the wall. "Nine times out of ten you'll find a piece you can use as a patch," Tom says. A closet floor might also surrender a suitable piece of vinyl scrap.

Once the patch has been located, decide on a cutting strategy (*left*). "Vinyl usually has a pattern to it," says Tom, "and any cuts look less conspicuous if you cut along that pattern, even if you have to cut out an area bigger than the area to be patched," says Tom. If the vinyl pattern incorporates "grout" lines, he cuts along that line because it hides the cuts nicely. "Cut the patch with a utility knife that has a sharp, fresh blade, holding it on a slight angle toward the center of the patch," he says. That produces a bevel that will help the patch to blend in. Don't expect an absolutely invisible repair, however. "You might see the patch if you know where to look for it, but at least it will save you from having to buy a whole new floor," he says. To avoid leaving a dirt-catching depression under the refrigerator (or wherever the patch came from), Tom fills it in with non-matching scrap—check with a local flooring supplier to get scraps.

Patching a vinyl floor. 1. Vinyl floors are sturdy but can be gouged by heavy furniture. 2. The first repair step is to align a scrap of vinyl exactly with the pattern of the floor. Tape it down, then cut through the patch and into the existing floor. (This is called double-cutting.) 3. Remove the patch and pry out the damaged flooring, being careful not to damage adjacent material. 4. Spread floor mastic over the subfloor and press the patch firmly into place. Wipe off any mastic that squeezes out; then use a roller to press out excess adhesive. Weight the patch until the mastic cures.

types: resilient surfaces

Wood, tile, and stone floors have many virtues, but softness isn't among them. By contrast, resilient floors offer some of the durability of hard surfaces but without the glass-shattering hardness. The term "resilient" refers broadly to any tile or sheet that is flexible. "Resilient floors have traditionally been used in kitchens and baths," says Tom, who installed linoleum in those areas when building his brother's house. Resilient products come in wide sheets (best installed by professionals) or as individual tiles (perfectly suited for homeowner installation).

VINYL: This PVC-based product dominates the resilient-flooring market. There's great variety in styles, from solid vinyl to vinyl backed with a soft, high-density vinyl foam. The most expensive and longest-lasting vinyl floor products contain inlaid chips that hold up well to foot traffic.

LINOLEUM: Invented in England in 1860, this flooring was among the most popular kitchen surfaces through the first half of the 20th century, until it was superceded by vinyl. But linoleum is making a comeback, and for good reason. An all-natural product, it's composed of linseed oil, cork, limestone, and tree resin. Because of the cork content, it's highly dent-resistant. And because the color goes all the way through, it can wear without showing and can last from 20 to 30 years, depending on the traffic.

CORK: Another natural product, cork is harvested from cork oak trees, then ground up, mixed with wood glue, and applied to a backing. Cork provides natural insulation that can help make floors feel warm, and it absorbs sound well. Like wood, it must be finished periodically with wax or sealers.

types: hard floors

Carpet and resilient flooring are per-vasive, but many people prefer the durability and stain resistance of hard surfaces such as stone or ceramic tile. Choices of color and shape are vast, but installation calls for particular skill. There's a downside, at least in cold climates: "Stone and ceramic tiles conduct heat easily," says tile contractor Joe Ferrante. "That's why they feel cool to the touch."

STONE: Shapes vary from irregular to rectilinear, and surfaces may be smooth or naturally cleaved. Slate scratches easily; coat it with a slate sealer and add protective pads to the underside of furniture, especially chairs. Granite can be slippery; floors should have a honed rather than polished finish. The best stone sealers are called impregnators.

GLAZED CERAMIC: Floor tiles tend to be thicker and harder than wall tiles. Glazes that are slippery when wet make a poor choice for bathrooms. Glazed tiles require no sealers, but the grout should be sealed every 5 years or so. Tile durability is rated numerically, with 1 being the least durable for flooring and 5 the most durable.

repairing tile Cracked or broken floor tiles are more than just ugly; they can expose a floor to water seepage that can rot the subfloor or drip through to the floor below. "Repair the damage right away," says Tom, even if the new tiles don't match the old ones (sidebar, p. 138)." The hardest part of this project comes in removing the broken tile. "If you just start banging on it with a hammer, you'll probably damage the surrounding tiles—and then you'll have an even bigger problem," warns Tom.

To remove a broken tile, tile contractor Joe Ferrante starts by removing the grout around it first. "That helps to isolate the tile from the ones around it," he explains, and reduces the chance that other tiles will be damaged as he removes it. Then he uses a center punch and a ball-peen hammer to chip away at the middle of the tile, gradually breaking the tile from the center out to the grout line. Once the tile's out, Ferrante chisels away remaining adhesive and vacuums up all the debris.

Replacing a floor tile is much the same as repairing any tiled surface (p. 138). Tile mastic—a creamy premixed adhesive with the consistency of mayonnaise—is spread on the back of the tile, and the tile is pushed into place until its surface is flush with its neighbors. Any adhesive smudges should be wiped off with a damp sponge before they harden. "It's a lot easier," says Ferrante, "to remove the adhesive when it's still wet than to have to scrape it off when it's dry. You can scratch the face of the tile if you wait too long to remove the adhesive, and then you'll have to replace the tile all over again." While the adhesive is curing, be sure that nobody steps on the repair.

After the mastic has set up for at least 24 hours, Ferrante regrouts the tile. The wide joints (greater than $1/8$ inch) typical of floor tiles should be filled with sanded grout (in contrast to unsanded grout, which is suited to narrower joints). Ferrante uses a grout float—a steel trowel with a rubber face—to spread the grout and work it into the joints between tiles (*right*). If only a few tiles are being regrouted, however, other tools will suffice, even a rubber spatula (p. 139). Within a half hour or so after spreading the grout, the excess material can be removed with a damp sponge.

After a damaged tile (or a section of tiles) has been removed and replaced, the tiles must be grouted. Sanded grout is the material most suited to the wide joints typical of floors; unsanded grout is best for the narrower joints typical of other tiled surfaces.

cabinets + woodwork

cleaning cabinets / matching stains / repairing cabinet drawers / servicing cabinet doors / patching holes in woodwork / fixing a squeaky step / replacing door and window trim / replacing stair balusters / securing a stair rail and newel

chapter 10

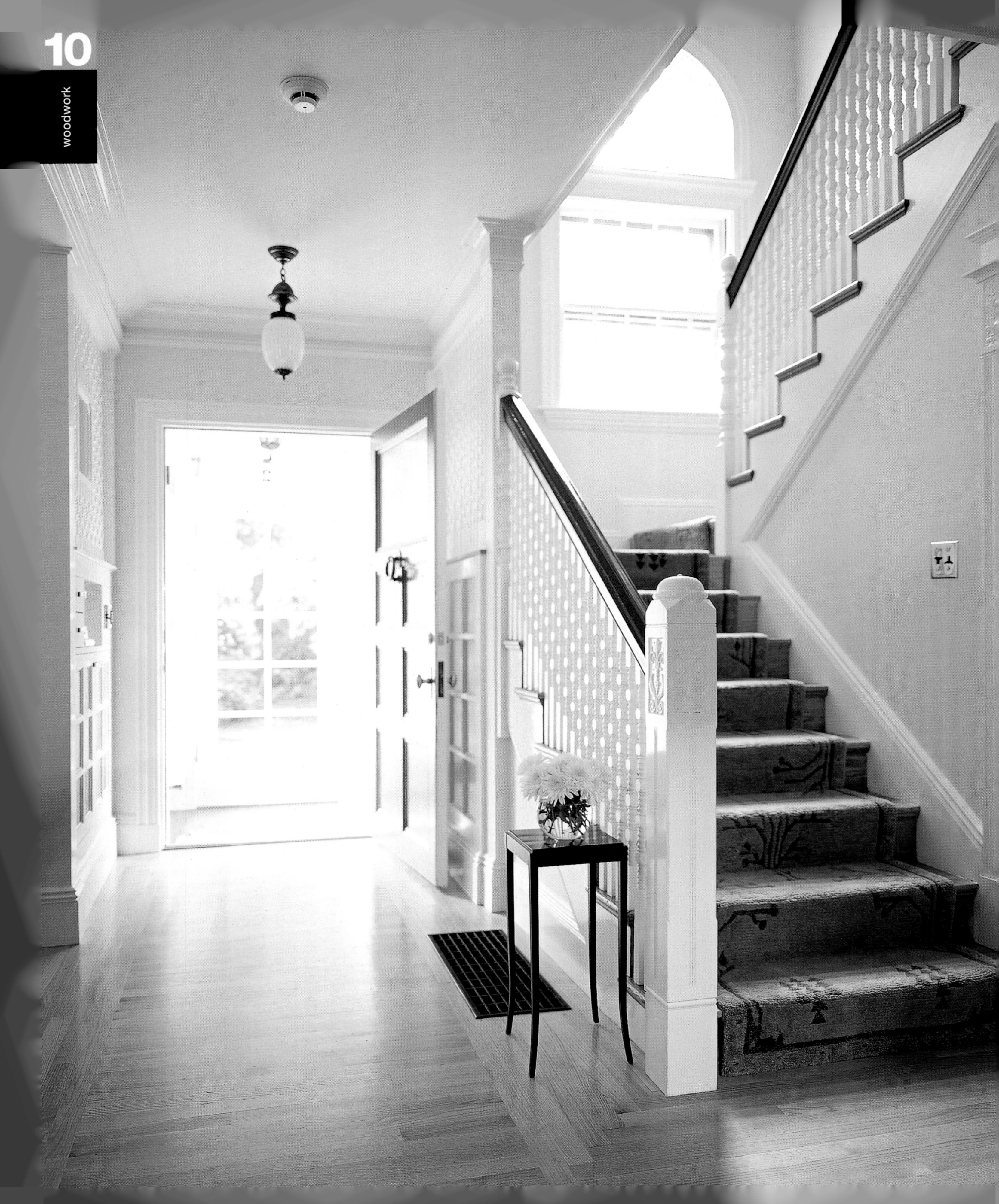

DEMOLITION IS DIRTY, SWEATY, AND often dangerous. Framing is great sport for young knees and strong backs. Insulation and drywall? Sub it out if you can. Finish carpentry? Now *that's* worth savoring. People often ask which skills offer the greatest payback, and I usually suggest honing one's painting and papering technique. But as far as getting the most satisfaction, I'd vote for finish carpentry any day. —STEVE

MAINTENANCE **cleaning cabinets** As with any piece of fine furniture, cabinetry requires special care. "People take care of their furniture, but they often neglect their cabinets," says Tom. "But they need attention, too." In fact, they may require more of it because of all the abuse they get.

The best way to take care of cabinets, according to Tom, is to keep them clean. "If you spill something, wipe the cabinet immediately with a damp cloth and then dry it off." For bigger cleaning jobs, he recommends a mild solution of soap and water or—for extra clout—powdered trisodium phosphate (TSP) and water. Be careful, however, because too heavy a concentration can eat through some finishes. "I follow the manufacturer's instructions, then dilute it by half just to be on the safe side," says Tom.

A heavy buildup of dirt and grime dulls a cabinet's finish, and usually shows up as a dull or dirty patch around drawer pulls and doorknobs. Tom cleans the wood with furniture wax remover or with a rag lightly moistened in paint thinner or turpentine. These latter two are particularly effective at removing the stickiness that sometimes clings to cabinet surfaces. Then he follows up with a furniture polish for protection (not paste wax, which is more difficult to use and may cause yellowing over some urethane finishes). Scratches and other dings can be filled in with colored paste wax. "Pick the right color, and you'll never see where the scratch was."

A grand staircase is the hallmark of master finish carpenters, but even simple stairs and modest spaces can benefit from the thoughtful application of wood molding.

improvements:
countertop options

Countertops are the most used and abused surface in any kitchen or bath. "That's where you really need something durable," says Tom. Here are some alternatives to plastic laminate:

NATURAL STONE: From the gleam of granite to the matte finish of soapstone, stone provides a beautiful counterpoint to wood cabinets. Tom's kitchen countertops are granite: "It'll last forever," he says. But even mighty granite stains if not sealed at installation. "You have to apply two or three coats of a non-yellowing, solvent-based sealer called impregnator," says Tom.

WOOD: Chopping-block countertops made of laminated wood strips add charm to a kitchen but they stain easily. Tom seals the wood lightly with mineral oil when the surface looks dull. Frequent wetness harms even sealed wood, so don't use it near sinks.

SOLID SURFACE: This man-made material can be assembled with nearly invisible seams, making it a good choice for long countertops or broad islands. "It's durable and stain-resistant," says Tom. Steve likes the material, too: "It's warm to the touch—not cold like tile and granite—and it's easy to clean."

MARBLE: Because it stains easily even when sealed, Tom avoids using marble for kitchens, except where pastry dough will be worked. "It's great for bathrooms, however," he says.

CERAMIC TILE: Ceramic countertops aren't on Tom's list of favorites. "I just don't like the look of all those grout lines on a countertop," he says. "And trying to keep them clean is a maintenance task I'd rather avoid." Steve tends to agree with Tom. Epoxy grout reduces cleaning headaches, he says, and big tiles installed with thin grout lines help, too.

types: cabinets

The appearance of a cabinet is shaped almost as much by its hardware as by the materials it is made from. Cabinets fall into two categories: face-frame and frameless.

FACE-FRAME: On face-frame cabinets, door hinges are mounted on slender wood surfaces called face frames. Various types of hinges can be used, including butt hinges or partially concealed pivot hinges, but they are usually visible to some degree. Overlay and lip doors rest against the outside surface of the face frame when they close; inset doors fit into the opening.

FRAMELESS: On frameless, or European-style cabinets, the doors are attached to the side of the cabinet in a way that makes the hinge invisible when the door is closed. Though various door types can be accommodated, a flat panel, covered with veneer or plastic laminate, is the most common.

FACE-FRAME

FRAMELESS

REPAIR

matching stains Great kitchens are designed to last the ages, but they can rarely avoid some reworking. "In my kitchen, the built-in microwave died and the new one was smaller, so I had to reframe the opening," says Tom. The carpentry part was straightforward, but matching the new wood wasn't. He couldn't remember what stain he had used when he first built the cabinets back in 1985, so he laid out some wood scraps and began experimenting.

First he blended together three different stains to lay down a light brown base. Then he brushed over them with darker cherry, followed by an even darker mahogany until he produced the right color. "You want to make sure you have plenty of wood for the job and stain it all at once," Tom says. "You don't want to just do a little bit, hit the color right, then wonder, 'Gee, how did I do this?'"

Matching a color is one challenge; matching the finish is another. "I like to work with stains that have urethane in them, so you're basically adding a sheen to the wood as you're staining it." Using this approach, Tom is able to make a suitable match even with wood that's been lacquered or shellacked. "Ideally, you'd want to use the exact finish, but the the critical thing is to get the color right."

repairing cabinet drawers Cabinet drawers can occasionally stick shut. "Most of these problems are seasonal and are related to the humidity in the air," says Tom, but understanding the cause makes them no less frustrating. Drawers fitted with up-to-date drawer guides (see p. 167) seldom stick, but older units—especially those on wooden runners—frequently do. To repair them, Tom empties the drawer and then pulls it out to investigate. Shiny spots on the sliding portions of a wood runner are indications of rubbing, often caused when a drawer carries too much weight. He lubricates wood runners with wax, but if that doesn't remedy things, he lightly sands or planes the runner to make a better fit. "Worn or uneven runners may have to be replaced entirely," he says.

Common painted finish flaws: **1.** *Cracked paint over caulk indicates a poor match with the paint. Scrape out the old caulk, then recaulk with a product suited to the paint type.* **2.** *Sagging paint is often caused by a brush too heavily laden with paint. Brush out the drips if the paint is wet; otherwise sand off the drips and repaint.* **3.** *Mildew appears as dark splotches on surfaces that are frequently damp. Scrub it off with a solution of 3 parts water to 1 part household bleach.* **4.** *Surfactant leaching occurs when water-soluble ingredients in latex paint rise to the surface. Wash it off with soap and water.*

1 2
3 4

When the sliding mechanism is metal or plastic, Tom lubricates it with spray silicone; if that doesn't help, he checks the alignment of the parts by removing the drawer and looking at the runner for any signs of damage. "The runner is attached to the side of the cabinet with screws, and some may be loose or missing," he says, causing the drawer to sag and stick. And if the joints of the drawer itself loosen, it won't close completely or open easily. This can sometimes be remedied by reinforcing the drawer with small rectangular blocks of wood glued to the inside corners. "If the inside of the drawer has a finish, you'll have to sand down to bare wood or else the glue won't grab," says Tom. "Sometimes I use screws to hold the blocks in place, but only if the drawer sides are at least ⅜ inch thick."

If a drawer slides too far into the cabinet, add wood stops behind the drawer to position it correctly when it's closed. "The easiest way to figure out how big the stop should be is to push the drawer in and then measure the difference between the face and the front of the cabinet," says Tom. "If it's ⅛ inch, for example, you'll know you need a ⅛-inch filler in the back."

servicing cabinet doors Cabinet doors fall victim to the same ills that plague regular doors (see p. 72): They swell in humid weather, and their hinges loosen. "People don't realize it, but as they bend down to pull pots and pans out of their cabinets, they're actually leaning on the doors," explains Tom. "And by doing that, they're causing them to pull loose." If retightening the existing screws doesn't secure the hinge, Tom replaces them with longer screws in hopes that they'll hold. In some cases, doors can be realigned by shimming their hinges (see p. 77). If a hinge is damaged, however, it should be replaced; take the old one to a hardware store or home center to find an exact match.

Cabinet doors sometimes stick in their openings because the house has settled. "When that happens, you have to plane the door or belt-sand it lightly so that it fits," says Tom. He refinishes sanded areas to match the surrounding wood. "You don't want to leave raw wood exposed, or it will swell from moisture."

Diagnosing drawers: 1. Tom checks for misaligned drawers in his kitchen by looking for uneven gaps between them and the surrounding face frame. 2. If a drawer doesn't work properly, screws in the supporting drawer guides may be loose or even missing. If loose screws don't tighten, Tom simply repositions them into nearby holes in the guide.

improvements:
drawer guides

Installing new drawer guides on old drawers is a good way to improve the utility of an old kitchen, says Tom, because older drawers with wood guides often stick. Wood guides (or flimsy metal guides) can be replaced with durable metal extension guides that operate far more smoothly.

The mechanisms slide on nylon rollers or ball bearings (Tom's favorite). Those attached to the underside of a drawer, says Tom, "are OK for most purposes and easy to install." But if there's space to mount them, he far prefers side-mounted drawer guides. "They're more work to install, but much stronger." Full-extension models allow the drawer to be pulled completely clear of the cabinet, making the contents very accessible. Partial-extension models leave the back of the drawer obstructed within the cabinet.

NYLON ROLLER, PARTIAL EXTENSION

BALL BEARINGS, FULL EXTENSION

types: wood stains

As a finish material, wood's beauty is unmatched. Its colors warm up a room, its grain adds textural beauty, and the material is satisfying to the touch. "Depending on the species of wood, the cut, and the stain that's used to highlight it, you can create a variety of looks for any room," says Tom.

Stain enhances the wood grain and unifies the color among different pieces of wood. "But you don't always have to use oak stain on oak, or mahogany stain on mahogany," he adds. Also, it's possible to experiment and custom-mix batches of your own choice. Test these concoctions first, however, and be sure to mix up more than enough. "You don't want to run out in the middle of a job and then have to replicate the recipe," says Tom.

Stains come in two basic varieties. Penetrating stains are absorbed into the fibers of the wood, resulting in a pure clear color that accents the grain. Pigmented stains, which are essentially a diluted paint, deposit a thin, protective film of color on top of the wood, creating a semi-opaque finish that somewhat obscures the grain. Regardless of the variety, Tom prefers oil-based stains to water-based types. "There's something about them that accents the grain of a wood in a way that nothing else does," he says.

If the cabinets seem so tired that no amount of maintenance revives them, some level of replacement is called for. But replacing the cabinets entirely is expensive. A more frugal and far less disruptive alternative is to have a cabinetmaker replace just the doors and drawer fronts, and resurface the face frames with paint or veneer. "You can end up with cabinets that look brand-new for less than half the cost," says Tom. "This is work best left to a professional, but it's a great way to go."

patching holes in woodwork Woodwork takes a beating from children, errant vacuum cleaners, and the moving of furniture and appliances. Minor damage to painted woodwork requires nothing more than a little wood putty, followed by sanding and repainting. "If it's stained woodwork, buy a colored putty stick that matches the stain," Tom advises.

With bigger holes, Tom's approach depends on how the wood is finished. "With a painted surface, the easiest way to patch big holes is to use auto-body filler," he says. He mixes up the two-part polyester filler and overfills the hole slightly. "You want to build it up a little bit above the surface of the hole," he explains. When it's dry, Tom takes a flat rasp or sanding block and levels it off. Then he sands it smooth, using progressively finer grits from 80 to 220 grit. Finally, Tom primes the area with an oil or latex primer and finishes it with a coat of paint.

If the damage is on a stained or natural wood finish, Tom actually cuts away the damage and fits in a new piece—called a "dutchman"—that matches the grain and color of the original. He uses a two-piece jig attached to a router in order to cut a precise hole in the woodwork, then cuts a corresponding wood patch that's slightly thicker but exactly the same shape. "Spread carpenter's glue on the patch, drop it in place, let it set for 30 minutes, plane the surface flush, and refinish it," says Tom. If a piece of trim is pockmarked with damage, Tom might replace it altogether. "But that's a judgment

Filling old hinge mortises on a door, like patching damaged woodwork in any other location, calls for a dutchman patch. 1. After finding a wood scrap slightly thicker than the depth of the mortise, Tom marks it to fit. 2. Using a square to ensure a straight cut, he trims off one edge of the scrap with a sharp utility knife. 3. After test-fitting the piece, he butters it with carpenter's glue and presses it into place. If the fit is tight, Tom shaves it flush with the surrounding area right away, using a well-tuned hand plane. 4. A favored antique rabbet plane trims off the remaining edge. Paint or stain finishes the job.

1 2
3 4

call based on the extent of the damage and the historic value of the house." The more historic the house, the more likely he is to go to the extra effort of installing a dutchman.

fixing a squeaky step Squeaks in a staircase, like squeaks in a car, can be a maddening irritation. "You think you hear where it's coming from, but stopping it is another matter," says Tom. Squeaks are caused by wood rubbing against wood or against a nail. So one way to stop the noise after locating the source is to apply some lubrication in the form of dry graphite powder (it comes in a small tube and can be found in most hardware stores).

A more permanent approach is to pound a pair of finishing nails at opposing angles down through the tread and into the stringer—the hidden structural part of the staircase beneath it. That will tighten the connection and stop the squeak. "The way to locate the stringer is to look for a nail hole in the riser or the tread," says Tom. Before nailing, he drills two pilot holes to prevent the tread from splitting. "Make sure someone stands on the tread while you work—that will make the connection as tight as possible," Tom says.

If you can get to the underside of the staircase, you can insert a glue-coated wooden shim between the tread and the riser to eliminate the noise. Another under-stair approach is to glue in a block of wood 6 to 8 inches long where the squeaky tread intersects the riser. "You may have to screw the block into the underside of the tread and into the support framing," says Tom. "Just be sure the screw points don't poke through." When all else fails, Tom concedes, "you might just live with the squeak—it adds to that old house charm."

replacing door and window trim The molding, called casing, that runs around doors and windows does more than just look good: It covers a gap between the wall and the window or door frame. Small holes in the casing can be filled, but when the damage is extensive, replacement is usually more efficient (see steps at left).

Replacing damaged casing is a straightforward operation. 1. Hold a length of casing in place ⅛ inch away from the inside edge of the jamb, and mark a point ⅛ inch above the intersecting jamb. 2. Cut a 45-degree angle at that mark and tack the casing in place. 3. Fit a corresponding piece of casing to the first. Tom cuts slots in the end of each casing and inserts a small wood wafer called a biscuit—it strengthens and aligns the joint—before joining the pieces. 4. When all three pieces of casing are in place, drive the nails slightly below the wood surface with a nail set, then putty the holes.

improvements:
wood molding

Moldings solve problems: They can enhance a nondescript room, protect walls from damage, and conceal the gap between adjacent surfaces. "You can make them out of two or more pieces of wood if you want," says Tom, though that means making lots of extra cuts. "Dollar for dollar," says Tom, "moldings are a great home improvement."

Moldings that will be stained call for the best wood: a grade called "clear," which has no knots. If the molding will be painted, Tom uses less expensive grades of wood, such as pine or poplar, or finger-jointed wood in which the knots have been removed. Installation techniques, however, don't change even if a lesser wood is used. "Painting molding doesn't mean you can get away with sloppy joints," explains Tom.

Corner moldings generally bridge surfaces that meet at 90 degrees; crown molding is one example. Flat moldings cover gaps between surfaces that are in the same plane, such as window and door casings.

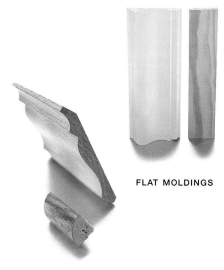

FLAT MOLDINGS

CORNER MOLDINGS

safety: stairs

Whether or not it makes a grand architectural statement, a staircase can be the most treacherous part of a home. Old staircases weren't always built with safety in mind. "They're narrow and steep in a lot of cases," Tom says. "That's because people wanted as much space as possible to live in, so they crammed the staircases in as tight as they could."

Building codes now regulate every aspect of stair construction, but there's not much that can be done, short of major reconstruction, to correct not-to-current-code treads and risers. Home owners can, however, improve the safety of other stair features, such as balusters, handrails, and stair surfaces.

"Years ago, the building codes were lax—a railing could be 28 or 30 inches high, and could even be built without balusters," says Tom. "That doesn't offer enough protection for kids." Now some codes require balcony railings to be 36 inches high or more. Balusters should be spaced so that a 4-inch-diameter sphere cannot pass between them. Every stair should have a handrail that's between 32 inches and 38 inches high, measured vertically from the front edge of each step.

The surface of a staircase can also affect how safe it is. "Never, ever wax a staircase," says Tom. "That sounds so obvious, but it's amazing how often people do it anyway." Carpeting, too, should be installed carefully because thick pads can soften the edge of a step, giving the illusion of a steppable surface where in fact there's nothing but fuzz. In the basement, many home owners paint steps with high-gloss paint. "It can be slippery to walk on, especially if it gets wet," warns Tom. For these surfaces, he recommends using paint textured with sand to provide extra traction.

replacing stair balusters Despite appearances, the slender balusters between the staircase treads and the handrail are not there for support; that's the job of the newel post. Instead, they protect people—particularly children—from falling off the stairs. As a house settles or when bulky furniture is lugged upstairs, balusters can loosen or break, a condition that compromises the safety of the stair.

A loose baluster can be tightened with a dab of carpenter's glue and a shim at the top, where repairs are hidden beneath the railing. Another method is to drill at an angle through the baluster and up into the handrail, then drive a finish nail through the hole. "Unless you predrill the hole, you'll more than likely split it," says Tom.

If a baluster is missing, remove an adjacent one and try to match it at a lumberyard or architectural salvage yard; if you can't find a match, take it to a wood turner for duplication. Some balusters fit top and bottom into holes; others fit into a hole in the handrail and a dovetail in the step (see p. 173). If you can't fit the former back into place, cut off the baluster's bottom pin and run two angled finish nails through pre-drilled holes into the step to secure the new piece.

securing a stair rail and newel If a stair rail wobbles, it may be due to a loose newel post. Fixing a solid wood newel may involve nothing more than inserting a glued wooden wedge beneath it or securing the connection with finishing nails. But take a different approach if the newel is hollow.

The wooden cap on top of a hollow newel post conceals a bolted connection to the floor framing. "Beneath the cap is a nut at the end of a threaded metal rod, and all you have to do is tighten it," says Tom. In older houses, however, the newel posts are usually attached from underneath. "If there's an open ceiling beneath it, see how the thing is put together," Tom says, and tighten what you can.

A loose baluster may rotate in place and sometimes even rattle. If it is otherwise undamaged, Tom secures it with a dab of carpenter's glue or a few finish nails.

split-free connections
When nailing through moldings and hardwood, says Tom, "drill a pilot hole slightly smaller than the nail's shank, or blunt the nail's tip slightly." Both tricks reduce the chances of splitting the wood.

electricity

understanding electricity / troubleshooting an electrical system / testing
circuits / looking for problems / replacing a wall switch / installing a
dimmer / replacing a smoke detector / replacing a GFCI receptacle /
replacing a standard receptacle / replacing light fixtures

chapter 11

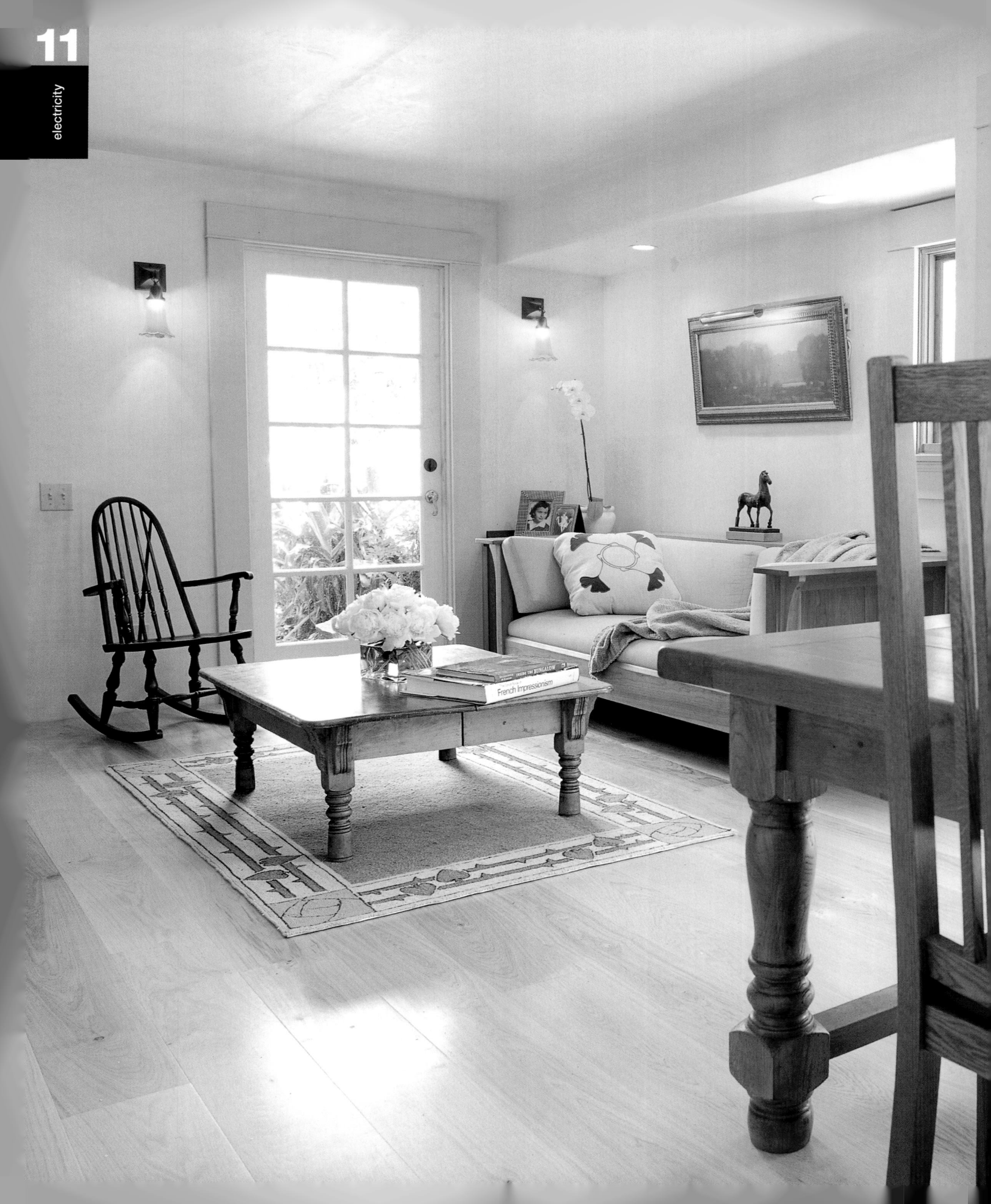
INSIDE THE BUNGALOW
French Impressionism

CUT OFF THE ELECTRICITY IN MOST ANY modern house and nearly everything stops. Even my natural-gas cooktop won't fire up unless electricity flows to the solenoid controlling the gas valve. Since we rely on electricity to run our households, it behooves us to learn something about it. Though we at *This Old House* don't advocate that you tackle complex electrical projects, you'll find that the easy ones can be satisfying and quite safe . . . if you're careful. —STEVE

MAINTENANCE **understanding electricity** Though Tom, Steve, and Richard each have a good working knowledge of electrical systems, they rely on electricians for everything except simple repairs and maintenance on their own homes. Most homeowners should do likewise. *This Old House* master electrician Allen Gallant has seen—and solved—plenty of electrical problems over the years and knows how most people feel about electricity. "Electricity is pretty much responsible for life as we know it inside our homes, but it's feared," says Gallant. "I know lots of people who'd scamper up a ladder to clean their gutters, but they'd never check the wiring on a light switch." Yet the actual work of making electrical repairs isn't difficult. To be safe, however, electrical work must meet or exceed the strict guidelines of the National Electrical Code, published by the National Fire Protection Association. The code has been adopted in every state.

Electricity is made up of electrons that move along one wire—called the hot wire, then flow back to their source along a neutral wire. This route is called a circuit (p. 179). A third wire, called a ground wire, ordinarily carries no electricity; but in the event of an overload or short circuit, it conducts excess electrical current harmlessly to earth. Switches, receptacles, lights, and other devices may be located on a circuit to make use of the electricity.

Electricity is more than a household convenience—it makes a house livable in any season and at any time of day. Lighting can have a profound effect on the feel of a room.

improvements:
electrical upgrades

Nowadays, power utilities run two hot wires to houses, providing 200 amperes —or amps—of electricity. "Older houses might have only one hot wire bringing in 100 amps or less. And some houses might have only 60 amps," says Gallant. "So the first thing everybody wants to do when they move into an old place is to bring in a new wire to upgrade service to 200 amps."

UPGRADED SERVICE This may not always make the best sense, Gallant says, because simply bringing extra power to the service panel won't solve any wiring problems within the house itself. "What matters is how the individual circuits are wired," he explains. "If you have too much plugged into one circuit, the breaker is going to trip— whether your service is 100 amps or 200 amps."

But if a household has paltry 60-amp service, Gallant always recommends an upgrade; it's a job that involves an electrician working in coordination with the local utility company. "But if you already have 100 amps, you'll probably be fine— especially if you have some gas appliances that reduce the need for electricity," he says.

NEW OUTLETS If the existing wiring is in good condition, what Gallant likes to do instead of increasing amperage to the house is to run an extra circuit for new outlets to serve specific energy-hungry appliances, such as the refrigerator and window air conditioners. "By doing this, you take the heavy loads off the existing wiring and greatly reduce the problem of overloaded circuits," says Gallant. "To me, this is the least expensive way to cure a lot of electrical problems in an old house, and it can be done without smashing through walls to rewire everything," he says.

safety: working smart

When it comes to working on a household electrical system, the penalties for making mistakes are delivered swiftly.

Even professionals can get a nasty jolt. "I was working and accidentally touched the hot wire and the neutral wire with the fingers of one hand," recounts Gallant. "The electricity passed through my fingers to complete the circuit," he says. It was a painful reminder, not a lethal one.

But if two hands instead of two fingers had completed the circuit, Gallant might have been in real trouble. "Then the current wouldn't just flow through my hand, it would flow up my arm and across my heart and out the other arm," he explains. "That can cause heart failure. It's not so much the amount of electricity that kills you, it's whether it passes over your heart," he explains.

The best way to avoid a shock is to turn the circuit breaker off before working on any part of a circuit. To verify that there's no current in the circuit, Gallant probes with a voltage tester (p.180) to make sure an outlet is truly dead. "If you're not sure you've flipped off the right breaker, turn off the main breaker at the top of the box—that cuts power to the whole house," Gallant says. Sure, you'll have to reset every digital clock when power comes back on, but that's a small inconvenience if it means you can work safely.

If a receptacle is switched (one or both outlets are controlled by a switch), the circuit tester might show that the circuit is dead when it really isn't. That's why Gallant also checks for current between the hot wire (black) and the neutral wire (white), then checks for current between the hot wire and the ground wire (or the metal box, if there's no ground wire).

In the service entrance panel (a metal box sometimes called the distribution panel), electrical current is divided into smaller circuits, and from there it flows throughout the house (*right*). One or two circuit breakers (or a fuse) govern each circuit, and cut power to the circuit if they sense conditions that could lead to a fire.

Tripped circuit breakers can be reset, but tripped (blown) fuses must be replaced. To reset a tripped circuit breaker, turn it all the way off before turning it back on.

troubleshooting an electrical system Electrical problems can cause fires—especially in houses built before 1965 that were fitted with rubber-insulated wire. Over time, that insulation can deteriorate, especially when wires heat up because of overloaded circuits. "If it's crumbling, you've got problems that can't just be stuffed back into the wall." That's why Gallant recommends hiring an electrician to check old wiring. Renovations, too, can create hazards if wiring is accidentally pinched between materials or punctured by a nail. "If the hot and neutral wires touch one another, they'll cause a spark," says Gallant. "And that spark can start a fire."

While tending to the general condition of the wiring is an electrician's domain, managing individual outlets and switches falls to the homeowner. "The most common call I get is from someone telling me that a receptacle doesn't work or a light doesn't turn on," Gallant says. There can be a number of reasons for this, but the most obvious ones are often overlooked by flustered homeowners. "You wouldn't believe how many times I've made house calls only to discover that a bulb was burned out or a switch wasn't turned on." Another non-problem occurs when something is plugged into a "switched" receptacle but doesn't seem to work. These receptacles often have one outlet that's always live, and one that's controlled by a wall switch. They're commonly installed in living rooms so that table lamps can be turned on as someone enters the room. "People feel really, really stupid when I 'fix' things just by flicking on the switch or moving a plug to the unswitched outlet."

Other problems can be serious, however. It may be that the circuit breaker has tripped. The breaker can be reset, says Gallant. "But you have to figure out what caused the overload in the first place—

An electrical system is a collection of circuits through which electricity flows. Electricity is routed first to a meter, then to the service panel, and then throughout the house.

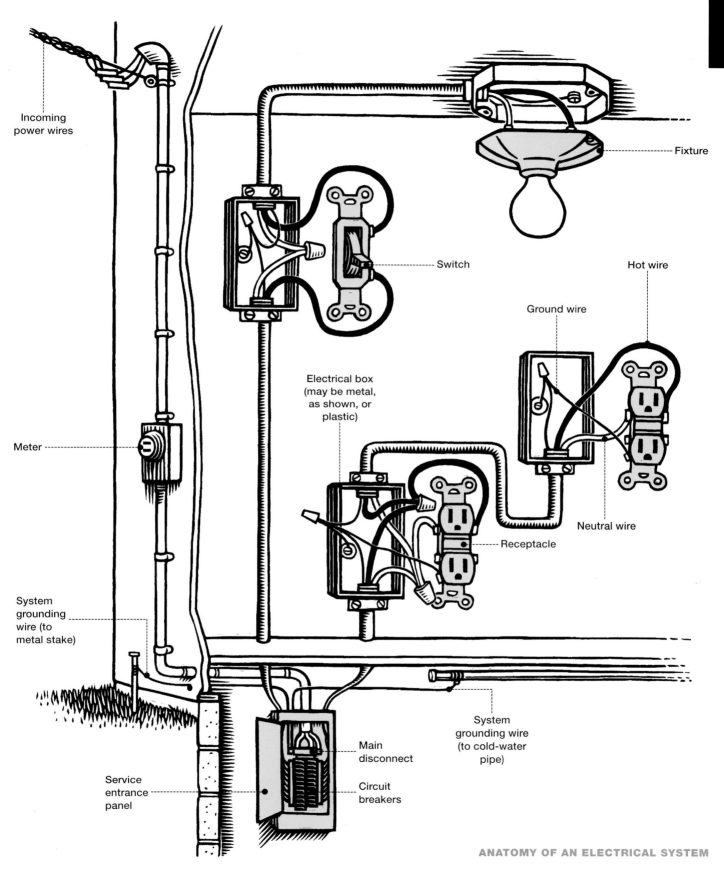

Incoming
power wires

Fixture

Switch

Hot wire

Ground wire

Electrical box
(may be metal,
as shown, or
plastic)

Neutral wire

Receptacle

Meter

System
grounding
wire (to
metal stake)

System
grounding wire
(to cold-water
pipe)

Main
disconnect

Circuit
breakers

Service
entrance
panel

ANATOMY OF AN ELECTRICAL SYSTEM

and fix it." Too many items plugged into one receptacle can overload the circuit if they're all on at once, for example. In addition, take a look at the receptacle itself. "Any sign of blackness on a receptacle means it shorted out," warns Gallant. "That can be extremely dangerous, because a short is like a brief fire, and if it happened once, it can happen again."

If a switch or an outlet doesn't work and the circuit breaker hasn't tripped, the problem probably is with a broken switch or worn-out receptacle. Replacing them is easy, as long as a homeowner first turns the power off, then double-checks to make sure it's off with a voltage tester of some sort (*left*). "If you're at all squeamish about it, stop." says Gallant. "There's no shame in calling an electrician."

testing circuits "Each wire connected to a switch or receptacle," Gallant explains, "is a different color, but with old wiring—especially where dirt and dust have obscured the colors—it's easy to connect the wrong wire to a terminal." That can leave a device functioning but dangerously ungrounded. Testing whether a circuit is wired correctly is easy, and starts with a voltage tester.

The light-up voltage tester (*left*) shows if a circuit is receiving power. To use it, insert one probe of the tester into each slot of the receptacle (be sure that your fingers aren't touching the metal probes). "If the tester lights up, the power is on," says Gallant. That could mean you've turned off the wrong circuit breaker. But a no-power reading could also mean that the wires have loosened inside the outlet—even though the wires themselves continue to have power. To check further, Gallant removes the receptacle cover plate and unscrews and pulls the receptacle from its box, taking care not to touch the screw terminals on the side. Then he touches the probes to the two terminals where the wires attach. As a rule, says Gallant, "Test twice, touch once."

After reinstalling an outlet, Gallant plugs in a simple circuit analyzer. The device alerts him to various wiring problems, such as the absence of a ground wire; labeling on the tool explains what the test results mean.

Allen Gallant uses a voltage tester to determine whether or not an outlet is "hot." He inserts one probe into each slot of an outlet, taking care to keep his hands away from the tips of each probe, and checks for a reading on the face of the tool. The model here is similar to simple testers that light up when they detect voltage. A plug-in circuit analyzer (on the floor) shows whether wires in a receptacle are properly connected.

how it works:
electrical basics

Electricity is nothing more than a flow of electrons that can be used to power appliances, make bulbs light up, and create heat. This flow is called the current. "For electric current to flow, it needs a continuous path from start to finish, like a circle," Gallant explains. This path is called a circuit.

Current is measured in a unit called amperes (amps). Every device, whether it's a lamp or a dryer, has an ampere rating, and each circuit is rated according to the total number of amperes it can handle safely.

The pressure driving the current is measured in volts. For household circuits, the most common rating is 15 amps and 120 volts. Refrigerators and kitchen appliances run on 20-amp circuits and 120 volts, while electric dryers may require 30-amp / 240-volt circuits. The greater the amperage, the thicker the wire must be to handle it.

Finally, the term watts is a measure of the rate at which electrical devices consume energy. Wattage is cumulative in a circuit: The more things you plug in, the greater the wattage.

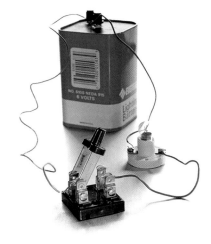

A SIMPLE CIRCUIT

joining wire

Different methods have been used to connect wires over the years. Here's what you might encounter in a house:

SOLDER: No longer allowed by code, solder was once a common way of making household electrical connections. "The problem is that vibrations cause soldered connections to disconnect easily," says Gallant.

COMPRESSION CONNECTOR: Better than solder, this outdated connection held wires together with a metal sleeve and a screw. "The wires were always coming loose," says Gallant, "and they still do, if you're unlucky enough to have these connections in your house."

WIRE NUTS: These are the connectors currently approved by electrical codes. "To use them, strip off some insulation at the ends of the wires and twist the wires together," says Gallant, using linesman's pliers. Then screw a suitably-sized wire nut over the connection. The nut covers the bare copper and holds the wires together. Manufacturers of wire nuts say twisting the wires isn't necessary, but Gallant believes it makes a stronger connection. "I doubt anything will ever improve on it," says Gallant.

WIRE NUTS

looking for problems Unlike water leaks that signal plumbing problems or a peeling surface that hints of paint woes, electrical problems remain invisible—until the day they cause a fire. "That's why preventive maintenance is so important," says Gallant.

For his customers in all but the newest homes, Gallant makes an inspection of the electrical system every 5 years. The process begins at the circuit-breaker box. "We take the panel cover off and look inside for signs of rust," he says, which he often finds if a basement or crawl space is chronically damp. "There shouldn't be any rust." If he sees rust on the screws that hold the wires to a circuit breaker, he assumes that rust has corroded the inside of the breaker as well. "And that's the worst," warns Gallant. Inside each circuit breaker lies a bimetallic steel-copper strip that deforms when heated by excess current, causing the breaker to trip. "If that's corroded, the breaker might not trip when it's supposed to and the overloaded circuit could cause a fire," he explains. Leave these repairs to a pro.

In addition, Gallant recommends that homeowners switch all the circuit breakers in the box off and back on once a year. "That way you can check to make sure they're functioning," he says. "If you find that one is stuck into a particular position, call an electrician and have it replaced."

Plugs and cords on appliances, lamps, and tools can be a fire hazard if they're worn out or damaged. Inspect plugs to make sure they haven't pulled loose from the cords, and look for even slight chips or cracks—all conditions that are hazardous. Cord insulation that is cracked or scuffed could allow wires inside to touch. Don't try to repair cords and plugs: Replace them. Extension cords are particularly susceptible to damage and should *never* be placed beneath carpets. "Check them once a year, and replace them if you even suspect damage," Gallant says.

| REPAIR | **replacing a wall switch** Most |

replacing a wall switch Most light switches are extremely durable, but if a switch breaks or wears out, it can be replaced easily. "More often, people just want a different color to match the decor of their room,"

A combination tool is a versatile device that can remove a wire's insulation without damaging the wire itself. Here it is being use to make sample connections on 12-gauge wire. Real connections, however, must be housed in a metal or plastic electrical box, says Gallant. A few turns of electrical tape make wire nut connections more secure.

1

2

says Gallant. Inside the electrical box, the switch links two wires—a hot one from the circuit-breaker panel and another that connects to the light. "There are two screw terminals on the switch, and all you have to do is turn the power off, loop one wire clockwise around each terminal, and screw it tight," says Gallant. "That's it."

One variation of the light switch is the three-pole (or three-way) switch, which allows one light to be operated from two separate locations. These switches have three screw terminals. One is set apart from the other two, and is called the common terminal. A single wire (called a traveler) is connected to the common terminal on each of two switches. The other two wires in each box can be attached in any order to the other terminals. "Label the traveler before you remove it from the old switch," says Gallant, "or you'll screw up the connection. If a three-way switch has to be on for the other switch to operate, somebody got the wires mixed up."

installing a dimmer Dimmers contain circuitry that reduces the voltage flowing to a light by a specific amount. "If it's on full, you get 120 volts. But if you turn it down halfway, you only get 60 volts—and half the light," says Gallant. Installing or replacing a dimmer (*left*) is just as easy as replacing a regular switch. Gallant turns the circuit breaker off, tests the circuit for power (p. 181), then connects the two black wires inside the electrical box to the two wires on the dimmer, using small wire nuts often supplied with the dimmer. "People hire me to do this, then they want to kick themselves when they find out how simple it is," Gallant says.

replacing a smoke detector After about 15 years, according to one safety study, the chances are better than 50/50 that a smoke detector will no longer operate correctly. That's why the National Fire Protection Association recommends that every smoke detector be replaced within 10 years of installation. Battery-operated detectors can be replaced easily. But even units wired into the electrical system can be replaced without calling an electrician. "First turn the power off at the circuit-breaker box, then test to make sure it's off. That's our mantra," Gallant says. He then removes the detector's

Installing a dimmer: **1.** *After cutting the power, Richard carefully pulls the old switch out and tests for power.* **2.** *He disconnects the old switch, then connects the wires to a dimmer. If the dimmer has a green grounding screw or strap, be sure to use it.*

how it works:
switches

Flick a switch and it turns on a light— but how? "All switches are mechanical devices that simply make a connection between two wires, or break it," explains Gallant. Specifically, they connect the hot wire coming from the electrical panel to a black wire coming from a light or another device. When the switch is on, the connection is made and current flows. When the switch is off, the connection is broken and current stops. Switches come in an assortment of types, but the following two are found most often in a house.

SINGLE-POLE: The most common switches are called single-pole switches; they sometimes have on-off markings printed on them. "These are what instantly come to mind when you think of a switch," says Gallant. They contain two wire terminals, both of which are connected to the black hot wires.

THREE-POLE: A similar type of switch is called a three-pole switch. When installed in pairs, three-pole switches allow you to turn a light on or off from two different locations. "They're good to use at the top and bottom of a staircase, for instance," Gallant says, "or at the two ends of a hallway." They resemble single-pole switches, but instead of two screw terminals, each one has a third, called the common terminal. You'll find it on one side of each switch; it holds the wire that connects the separate switches together.

SINGLE-POLE SWITCH

how it works:
receptacles

A typical electrical receptacle has two outlets, and thus is called a duplex receptacle. There are three openings in each outlet. The short slot is the hot slot, from which electricity flows; the long one is the neutral slot. The third opening, is U-shaped and accepts the grounding prong of a three-prong plug. "By inserting a plug into the receptacle, you complete the electrical circuit—and electricity flows," says Gallant.

Receptacles are rated for the voltage and amperage they'll handle—15-amp receptacles are standard; 20-amp receptacles are for devices such as air conditioners and refrigerators. Modern receptacles accept three- prong plugs, but old ones don't. In these, a ground wire is connected to the screw that holds the cover plate in place. In some, there's no ground wire at all.

It's not possible, Gallant warns, to upgrade a receptacle without upgrading the wiring behind it. "You can't just stick in a new receptacle to replace a two-prong one, or a 20-amp receptacle to replace a 15-amp one," he says. "You need the wiring to go with it—and for that, you need an electrician."

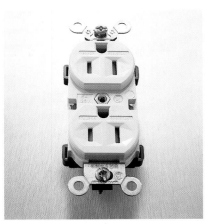

STANDARD RECEPTACLE

outer housing to expose four wires: one ground wire and three conductors. "All you do with the new detector is connect the ground, then connect the white wire to the white wire, and the black wire to the black wire," says Gallant. "There's also a yellow wire—join it to the red one coming out of the electrical box." These interconnect various smoke detectors, so that if one sounds they all sound.

replacing a GFCI receptacle Required by code in all new houses and all major renovations, ground-fault circuit interrupter (GFCI) receptacles should be installed in bathrooms, kitchens, and outdoor locations—wherever there's a risk that electric equipment will be used near water. They're harder to install than ordinary receptacles, however. "To install these you absolutely need a circuit analyzer, so that you can make sure you have the correct polarity," cautions Gallant. "If the polarity is wrong, the GFCI will supply power, but it won't offer any protection." Once the correct polarity is established, the installation is similar to other receptacles: The black (hot) wires connect, the white (neutral) wires connect, the green or bare copper grounding wires connect, and then they can all be folded neatly into the box as the GFCI is pushed into place and secured. "This is something that a homeowner can do easily enough," says Gallant. "But pay attention and follow the instructions that come with a GFCI—you don't want to discover that you've done it wrong when you're outdoors with an electric weed whacker in the wet grass."

replacing a standard receptacle If you find that a plug won't stay in an outlet, says Gallant, replace the outlet—don't bend the plug's prongs to make it hold better. "That's just covering up a problem, and it's dangerous because it results in a poor connection that might overheat."

To change a receptacle, Gallant shuts off the power at the circuit breaker and tests the outlet to make sure power is off (p. 181). Then

Richard replaced a standard receptacle near the sink in his kitchen with a GFCI. 1. Before removing the old receptacle, he cut power to the circuit and then checked to make sure it was off, using a voltage tester. 2. This receptacle was wired through the back, so Richard inserted a small screwdriver into slots to release the wire. Screw terminals on the side offer a better connection. 3. After checking for correct polarity, Richard connected the supply wires to the GFCI's terminals. 4. He then carefully folded the wires behind the device, pushed it back into place, and secured it to the box.

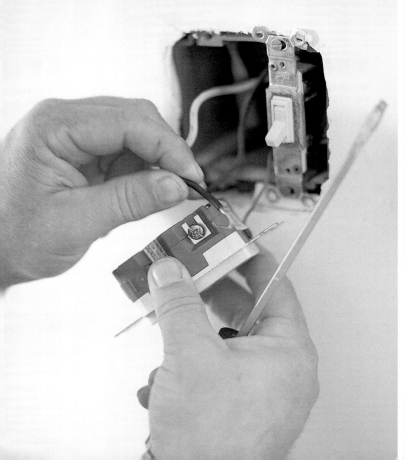

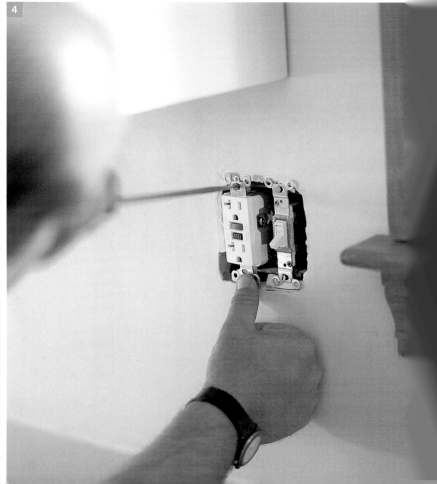

he removes the cover plate and carefully pulls the receptacle from the box. When the receptacle is out, he confirms that the power is off. Then he disconnects the three wires—the black hot wire, the white neutral wire, and a bare copper (or green insulated) ground wire. Using wire nuts (p. 182), he reattaches the wires to the new receptacle, making sure he has chosen one rated for the same amperage and voltage as the one he's replacing. "In most places in a house, it will probably be 15 amps and 120 volts," says Gallant. "If it's in a kitchen, it will most likely be 20 amps and 120 volts." To determine the amperage and voltage of a receptacle, remove the cover plate and look for the ratings (amperage is sometimes abbreviated by the letter "a") on the center of the receptacle, near the hole for the cover plate mounting-screw.

replacing light fixtures Replacing a light fixture is not usually difficult. After the circuit breaker has been switched off, the fixture can be released by unscrewing one or more mounting nuts on its housing (some may look like decorative finials). "It's a good idea to have a helper support a heavy light while you do this," Gallant advises. He disconnects the black and white wires coming from the box from those on the fixture, then disconnects the ground wires and pulls the fixture free. After lifting the new fixture into place, he reconnects the wires using wire nuts, and fastens the fixture to the electrical box with whatever hardware came with it.

Even simple jobs can be complicated by unexpected conditions, however. If wire insulation crumbles as you work with it, that's a sure sign of trouble—call in an electrician. "When people put in a lightbulb that's larger than the fixture was built to handle," says Gallant, "the excess heat can make old cloth-insulated wire very brittle." Another complication is weight. "The electrical box has to be able to hold the weight of the new light," says Gallant. "If you're replacing a light that weighs 2 pounds with a fan that weighs 30, someone had better replace the box with one suited for ceiling fans. Spend a few dollars and be safe rather than risk having a ceiling fan crash down at dinnertime."

Replacing one light with another of about the same weight is simple (a heavier fixture might require special hardware). After ensuring that the power was off, Richard loosened the coverplate of his dining room light, disconnected the wires and unfastened the light from the fixture mounting strap. Then he reversed the steps to install a new light.

types: plugs and cords

Electrical fires often involve faulty plugs and cords, rather than a sudden catastrophic failure of the house's wiring system. "You can have a brand-new house, but if you plug a bunch of lamps and some stereo equipment into a shoddy little extension cord, you're asking for trouble," says Gallant. "The problem is that everybody thinks all cords and plugs are the same, but they're not."

CORDS: The thin extension cords that are common in so many households are usually rated at 6 amps. But the outlet and the circuit breaker that they connect to may be rated for 15 or even 20 amps. "That means the cord itself can become overloaded and get dangerously hot without the circuit breaker tripping," Gallant says. "If you connect a light-duty extension cord to a heavy-duty appliance such as an air conditioner or a refrigerator, the cord's insulation will start breaking down, and you could end up with a real problem." One solution is never to use an extension cord rated at less than 15 amps. "That's the only way to guarantee that you won't overload the circuit," says Gallant.

PLUGS: Plugs also can vary. A plug must suit the type and size of cord it goes on, so bring the cord with you when shopping for a replacement plug. Small appliances and lamps operate safely with two-prong plugs, but larger appliances require three-prong plugs for proper grounding. "The stupidest thing that any homeowner can do is to clip off the third prong to try to get the appliance to fit into a two-prong outlet or extension cord," says Gallant. "If you do that, the appliance will work but you'll be operating it with absolutely no grounding protection." If anything goes wrong inside the appliance, an electrical shock could kill you.

plumbing

understanding plumbing / basic troubleshooting / taking care of the system / cleaning filter screens / faucets and washers / maintaining water heaters / maintaining drains and traps / working with copper pipe / repairing and installing shutoff valves / servicing a showerhead / replacing faucets / unclogging drains and traps / adjusting the flush of a toilet / troubleshooting sump pumps / replacing a toilet seat / anti-scald valves / installing a freeze-proof faucet

chapter 12

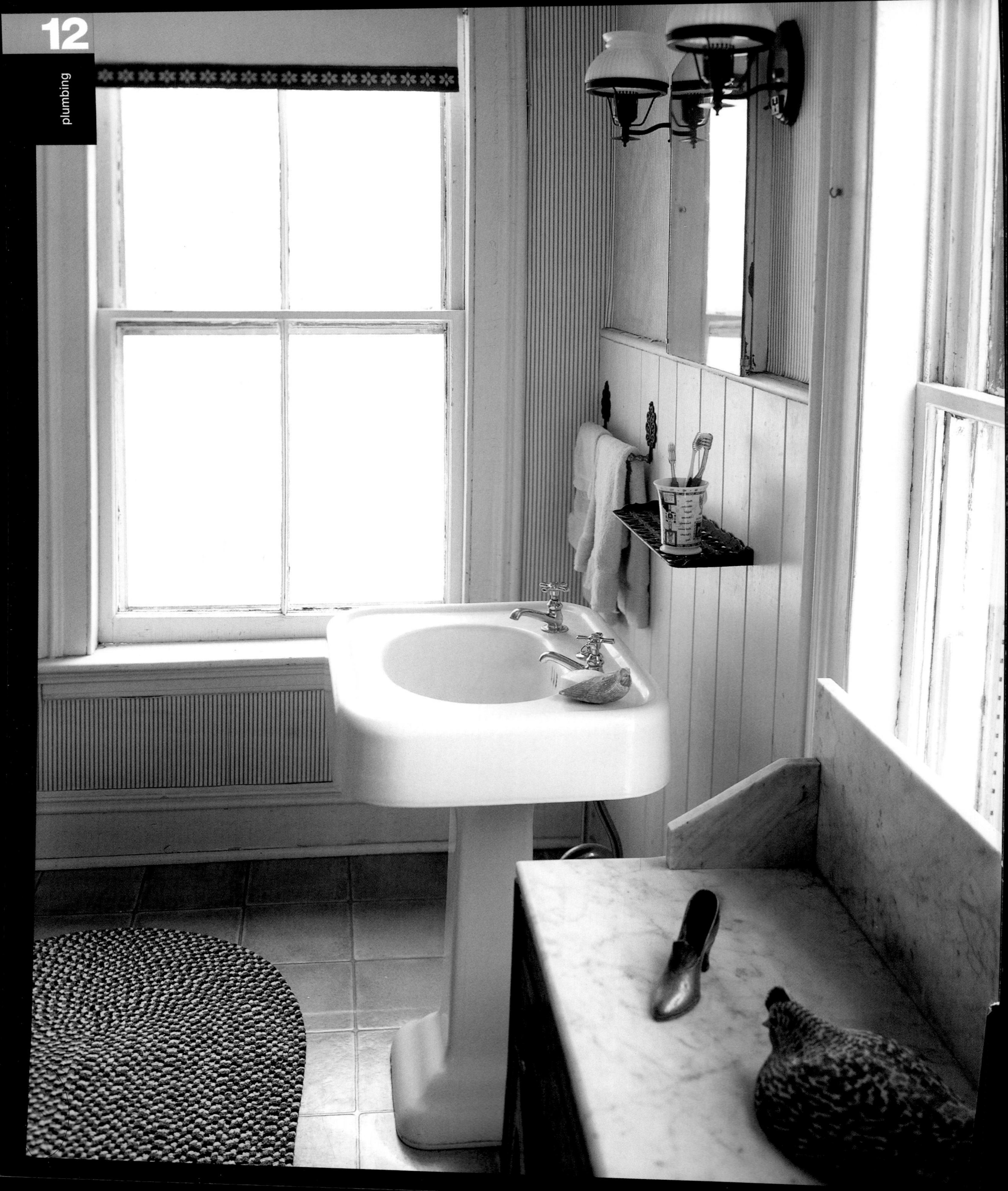

FORTUNATELY I KNOW EMIL, WHO DOES nothing but clean out drains and sewers, and at 10 p.m. on a Sunday night I'm real glad he chose this profession. After Emil arrived to fix an overflowing toilet, I helped as he probed the main sewer line with a metal snake. "Whatever you do," he said, "don't flush!," a warning I dutifully relayed to my family. Later, as we peered into the cleanout, we heard a distant echo like an ocean wave in a dream. But we were too intent on our work to realize what it meant . . . until too late. A young boy's timid voice soon reached us from upstairs: "Sorry, Dad." Working with pipes, I've learned, can be pretty exciting sometimes. —STEVE

MAINTENANCE **understanding plumbing** Most homeowners can see how windows and doors and other home mechanisms work. "But they completely fall apart when it comes to the plumbing, which remains one of the great mysteries of the household," says Richard. "The less you know about your plumbing system, the more damage you're likely to inflict on it if you try to fix it."

Water enters a house either from a municipal water supply or from a well drilled somewhere on the property. With municipal water, large pumps and a water tower provide water under pressure for an entire community. A well, on the other hand, requires a small pump to lift water from the depths to serve a single household.

Bringing water in is only half the job of a plumbing system, however; getting rid of it is the other. A network of drainpipes connects to sinks, toilets, bathtubs, and showers and removes water and waste by gravity (p.195). "If that was it, then sewer gases would

A typical household plumbing system is often ignored, at least until something goes wrong. But it provides a variety of amenities that few could imagine living without.

safety: emergencies

"By the time you call a plumber to fix a pipe that has suddenly turned into a fountain, you could be swimming in the basement," says Richard. To prevent this disaster, know where to find the main water shutoff valve.

Whether water comes from a municipal supply or a well, it passes through a valve just inside the foundation wall. When the valve is off, it prevents water from flowing into the house. "The day you buy your house, make sure you find that valve," says Richard. Simply turning it off won't stop a leak instantly, however: Water in the pipes above the leak will continue to drain out. That's when an empty 5-gallon bucket comes in handy.

The main valve shouldn't be used to shut off water to individual fixtures when making repairs, however. "You don't want wear it out; instead, turn off the fixture supply valve," Richard advises. "That way, you'll still have water elsewhere in the house." To prevent trouble in the first place, examine pipes and valves periodically for signs of corrosion. Tiny leaks often leave mineral deposits (*below*) on hot-water pipes, a sign that trouble is brewing.

how it works: the septic system

When a house is not served by a municipal sewer system, a septic system takes care of waste and wastewater. Of all the seemingly mysterious parts of a plumbing system, the septic system is, to many, the most mysterious of all.

The system consists of two basic components. The main waste pipe from the house empties into a buried *septic tank* about the size of a couch. Inside, anaerobic bacteria—those that don't require oxygen—decompose waste products; undecomposed material slowly settles to the bottom. The liquid eventually runs off into a sewage *leaching field*, an underground network of porous pipes in the yard. Water—now called effluent—seeps into the earth, where it is further cleansed by bacteria. Purified, the water eventually makes its way into the water table.

A septic tank must be pumped every 3 to 5 years, depending on use, to remove accumulated solids. "One sign that the tank should be pumped is if the drains back up. If you ignore that, you can destroy the leaching field," says Richard. "That will be a major repair."

Coffee grounds and celery strings are decay-resistant and can hasten the need for the tank to be pumped, so don't dump them down the drain. And chemicals such as bleach or paint thinner can kill anaerobic bacteria. Enzymes specially formulated for septic tanks can encourage the breakdown of organic material. "They can make the inside of a tank look new," says Richard.

The location of a septic tank is sometimes marked by a flat stone. It might also be visible on a frosty day: Decomposition generates frost-melting heat. Or call local tank-pumping companies—one of them probably has a record of where the tank is.

belch back into the house . . . not a pleasant thing," says Richard. To prevent this, near every fixture there is a bend, called a trap, in the drainpipe; the trap is always filled with water and thus prevents odors from getting into the house. The odors are exhausted by pipes called vents, which connect to the drainage pipes and rise up through the roof of the house. Vents not only exhaust foul odors but also help sinks, toilets, and tubs drain faster by drawing air into the waste pipes. "It's like pouring juice," Richard explains. "If you make only one hole in the can, the juice will come out very slowly. But if you make two holes, the air flowing in helps the liquid to flow out."

basic troubleshooting Knowing how a plumbing system works makes it possible to figure out the cause of various problems. A sluggish sink, for instance, could be a sign of a soap or hair buildup in the trap, a blocked vent, or an improperly sloped pipe. Normally, drainpipes should slope downward at a rate of at least $\frac{1}{8}$ to $\frac{1}{4}$ inch per foot so that the water drains naturally. "Anything that reduces the slant could interfere with drainage," says Richard. "I visited one house and found that the teenage son had been doing chin-ups in the basement by hanging on a drainpipe. Instead of draining away, wastewater just sat in the bent section."

On the supply side, rust-colored stains in sinks and toilets could indicate high mineral content in the water or corrosion in the water supply pipes. Water that flows weakly from a specific faucet or showerhead could indicate a mineral buildup in the aerator—the series of small screens at the end of every spout. But if every faucet in the house yields only a trickle when turned on, then the problem most likely lies in something that affects the entire system, such as a clog in the water meter or main shutoff. "You have to be a detective to figure out where a plumbing problem is. Absolute common sense is your best guide," says Richard.

taking care of the system One of the best ways to avoid costly repairs is to prevent problems in the first place. Many things that go down the drain, accidentally or not, have the capacity to cause a clog. For example, don't park small items such as makeup and jewelry on top of the toilet tank. "Anything placed there is just

Once inside the house, the water supply splits into hot and cold branches to serve various fixtures. A system of drains and vents ensures that waste is removed efficiently.

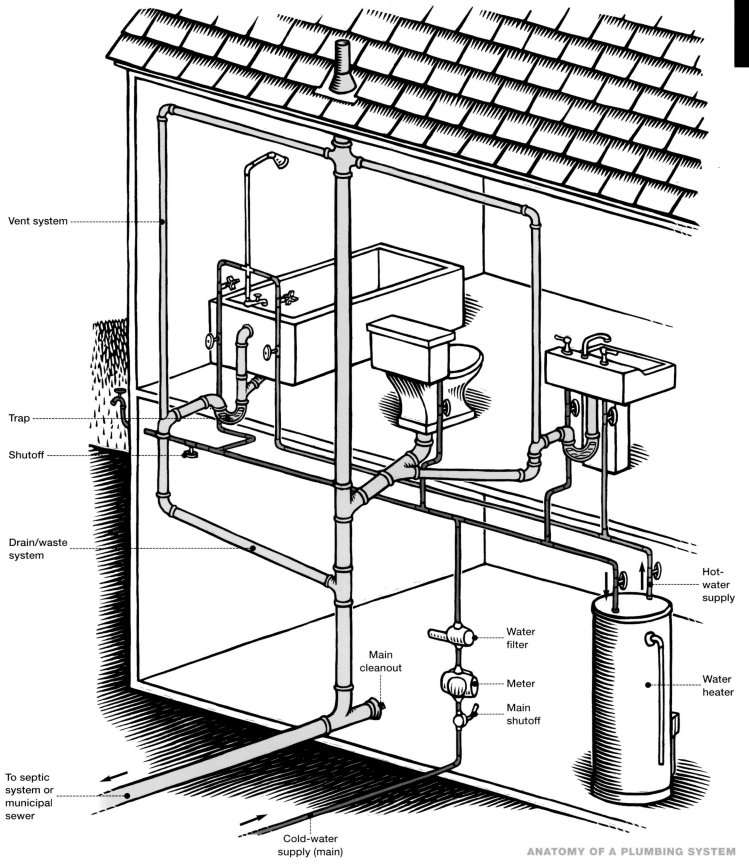

Vent system

Trap

Shutoff

Drain/waste
system

Main
cleanout

Water
filter

Meter

Main
shutoff

Hot-
water
supply

Water
heater

To septic
system or
municipal
sewer

Cold-water
supply (main)

ANATOMY OF A PLUMBING SYSTEM

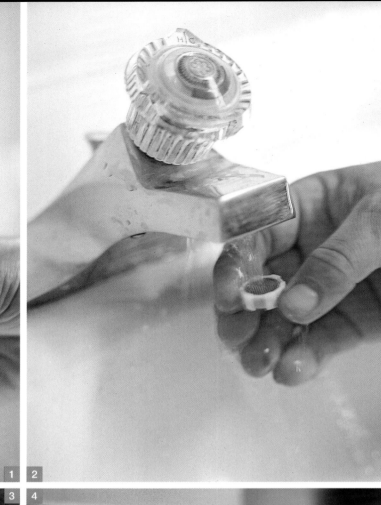

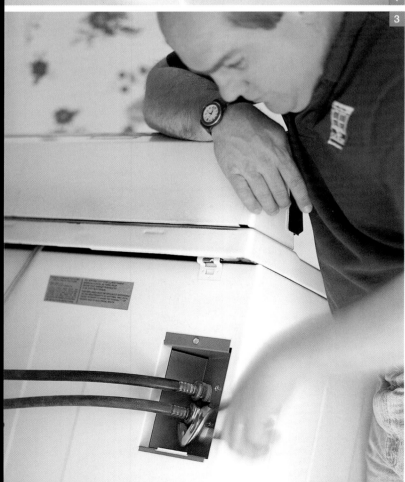

waiting to jump into the bowl," says Richard, who once spent 4 hours trying to clear a mysterious toilet blockage that turned out to be a plastic bracelet. Severe blockages that resist toilet plunging and augering (p. 209) can be cleared only by removing the toilet.

Pouring grease down the kitchen sink is asking for trouble: It can cause a drain-slowing buildup. Hair is the most common clog (which is why Richard insists upon strainers for shower and tub drains). "People are grossed out by clogs, so they're willing to pay a plumber to fix big problems instead of reaching in there for the small ones," he says. "Plumbers don't mind, but your wallet might."

REPAIR **cleaning filter screens** When a faucet delivers a dribble instead of its usual torrent of water, or when the clothes washer takes forever to fill, the problem is probably a clogged filter screen. It's one of the easiest of all plumbing problems to solve *(left)*. "Screens are so simple," says Richard, "but lots of people have no idea that such a tiny device can do such a good job of choking off their water." Some screens can't be removed, and in such cases Richard recommends vacuuming the debris or dislodging it with a toothpick.

faucets and washers Since the early days of plumbing, the standard faucet design has contained a rubber washer—a configuration known as a compression-type faucet. The faucet handle is set on top of a screwlike stem, and when it is turned off, it drives the stem against the washer, which closes off the water supply. Eventually the washer wears out. "When that happens, you'll notice a slow drip out of the spout that eventually can't be stopped just by turning the faucet tighter." That's when the washer must be replaced.

First, turn off the faucet's water supply by turning the shutoff valve located under the sink (clockwise closes it), or the main supply valve if you can't find a separate shutoff. "This is an amazingly obvious step, but you wouldn't believe the number of people who forget

A filter screen prevents rust flakes, sand, and other common water system contaminants from reaching an appliance—or your next glass of water. 1. Each faucet has an aerator that simply unscrews from the faucet; it contains a filter screen. 2. Richard turns the aerator upside down to flush out debris, being careful to prevent the screen from coming out. 3. Filter screens can also be found in the hot and cold inlet ports of a clothes washer. 4. After unscrewing the supply hoses, Richard vacuums out the debris (the screens are notoriously difficult to clean any other way because of their location).

water quality and filtration

The municipal water supply in the United States may be among the finest in the world, says Richard, but people are rightfully concerned about the water they drink. "In most cases, it's not the quality of the water coming to us that we're worried about," he says. "It's what happens inside the house that causes us concern." Lead leaching from old solder joints, rust, even dirt and sand, can make the water quality less than appetizing, if not toxic.

Water drawn from wells can be contaminated from chemicals that leach into the water table, as well as from bacteria leaching from faulty septic systems or—in agricultural areas—livestock pastures. By law, municipalities guarantee the quality of public drinking water with round-the-clock testing. "But you don't have that luxury with your own well: You have to be your own water-quality agent," says Richard. "Have your water tested every year by an independent lab—not a potentially biased water filter salesman—to figure out what, if any, steps you need to take."

Water filtration can take many forms, from simple to elaborate. Some carbon systems, such as countertop and under-the-sink filters, can eliminate the taste of chlorine; reverse-osmosis systems can remove everything. Bacteria in well water can be killed with filters that employ ozone or ultraviolet radiation. Even if your water tests pure, Richard recommends installing what he calls a pre-filter, which is attached right next to the main shutoff valve. "This traps any particles or sediment that comes through the water main or from the well," says Richard. "A pre-filter is inexpensive and easy to install, and the filter cartridges are easy to replace. To me, they make total sense."

water conservation

Motivated by federal regulations, manufacturers have modified almost every plumbing fixture to limit the amount of water used. "By reducing the flow, you can save a tremendous amount of water," says Richard. For instance, toilets now use 1.6 gallons per flush, compared to 3.5 gallons a few years ago. And kitchen faucets, on average, have dropped from a flow of as much as 7 gallons per minute to about 2.5 gpm. When it comes to showerheads, "You can have a showerhead that gives you 2½ gallons a minute that feels terrific," says Richard. "Yet some people want body sprays with multiple nozzles that put out 30 gallons per minute. I don't get it—what a waste."

Occasionally, some water-saving fixtures (notably toilets) won't work as well as the older models. "Some of the earlier low-flow toilets, specially those made in the late 1980s, tended to clog more easily," says Richard. Since that time, manufacturers have figured out how get good results with less water. Some even incorporate an air-charged tank that pushes waste more effectively through the toilet. "So you don't have to suffer anymore in the name of water conservation." One of the best water-saving strategies is also the easiest: installing new washers or cartridges *(below)* to fix leaking faucets.

it—and end up facing a geyser," says Richard. With the faucet handles open to let water drain out, remove the screws holding the handles onto the stems (they are often located under the caps labeled *H* or *C,* for *hot* or *cold*) and lift off the handles. (To remove handles on an old faucet, which may be fused to the stem by corrosion, Richard uses a special tool called a handle puller.) "Now you have to take off the bonnet packing nut. And when you do that, out comes the stem with the bonnet assembly." The washer is held in place by a screw, which can be tricky to remove. "The screw might have been sitting in water for 10 to 25 years. As soon as you take a screwdriver to it, it disintegrates," says Richard. Instead of trying to repair these really old faucets, Richard saves time, effort, and aggravation by buying a replacement stem from a plumbing supply house.

One way to reduce the tendency of a faucet to leak is to use it more carefully. "When you turn off a faucet, don't crank down hard on the handle. That just wears out the washer sooner," says Richard. Instead, lighten up and turn the faucet just until the water stops. "That causes a lot less wear and tear on the washer—it's something I've been trying to explain to my kids."

maintaining water heaters Water heaters seem simple enough. Sitting in a basement or crawl space, all they have to do is heat water. But they aren't problem-free. "Water heaters end up being the great collection point in the water supply system," says Richard. "We think of water as absolutely pure, but in fact it's filled with particles—from grit to calcium or magnesium—that can form deposits known as lime scale. And all of that can end up as sediment at the bottom of the water heater." Because minerals reduce the heating efficiency of the appliance, it's important to remove the sediment once a year or so. To do this, Richard drains off several gallons of water through a valve at the bottom of the water heater *(right)*. "This will extend the life of the heater," he says.

The inside of a water heater is usually glass-coated steel, which is subject to a chemical reaction known as electrolysis that literally eats the metal away. To guard the tank lining, a sacrificial anode rod, usually made of magnesium or aluminum, is suspended in the tank. Electrolysis eats away at the rod instead of the tank lining.

Richard connects a garden hose to the water heater in order to drain off sediment. The hose can lead either to a bucket or to a sump pump pit, where it will be drained.

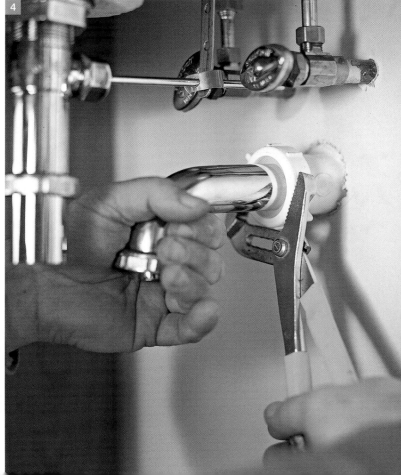

"Eventually the rod will be eaten away—a process that takes anywhere from 2 to 8 years—and when it's gone, the tank goes in a couple of months," Richard says. Replacing the anode rod periodically would extend the life of the water heater, but this is seldom done. "Everyone's accustomed to water heaters being disposable: If I called 100 plumbers, 80 would say they don't change anodes," says Richard, who suggests that homeowners might do it themselves. Short of that, he says, if you drain the water out at the bottom each year and find someone to replace the anode with enough regularity to head off electrolysis, you could double the water heater's life expectancy. One sure sign that an anode needs replacement: a rotten-egg smell emanating from the faucets.

Gas- or oil-fueled water heaters need one extra bit of maintenance: The intake port at the bottom, where air is drawn in to fuel the fire, must be kept free of dust. "Vacuum it carefully if you see dirt and dust, and it won't cause you any problems," Richard advises.

maintaining drains and traps The curved pipe beneath every sink, called the trap, is both essential and annoying. It contains water that prevents sewer smells from entering the house, but it's also the site of frequent blockages. Luckily, clogged traps are easy to clean with a plumbing snake (p. 206) or to remove *(left)*.

Sink, tub, and shower drains also require care. Regularly clean hair out of the strainer in the tub drain: it can easily ball up and form an impasse in the trap. Unless there's a garbage disposal in the kitchen, avoid letting bits of food run down the sink drain. And if there is a disposal, don't put in stringy vegetables, such as celery, because they too can clog the pipes.

Richard also cautions against pouring grease down the drain. When it hits the cool water in the trap, it congeals and sticks to the sides of the drainpipe, obstructing the flow of water. He also warns against pouring a caustic acid drain opener down the pipes—including the kinds that can be bought in supermarkets and hardware

Clogged traps are a common source of plumbing system aggravation, whether they're made of plastic or, as here, metal. 1. If the nuts securing a metal trap are difficult to remove, Richard gives them a quick blast with a propane torch. 2. Before he loosens the nuts completely, he places a bucket beneath the trap to catch the water that will spill from it. It's helpful to keep a towel handy, too. 3. When both nuts are loose, the trap can be removed. 4. In cases where the trap is too corroded to warrant reuse, Richard replaces it. This calls for removing the trap arm that extends from the wall.

improvements: quiet drainpipes

Large-diameter cast-iron pipe is often found in older homes. The pipe is heavy, tough to install, and has one other potential shortcoming: It can rust over time and leak, usually along the bottom of horizontal pipes. "If I tap a cast-iron pipe lightly with a hammer, I expect it to ring," says Richard. "But if I hear a dull tone, that tells me that the pipe has corroded and is about to fail."

The most common drainpipe replacements are PVC (polyvinyl chloride) and ABS (acrylonitrile butadiene styrene). Though not approved for use in water supply pipes, they work well for drain and vent pipes. They're also easy to work with and inexpensive.

Plastic does, however, transmit noise more freely than cast-iron pipes. "That can be troubling, especially if a pipe runs behind the ceilings or wall of a bedroom or living area," says Richard. One solution is to insulate plastic pipe with foam, rigid board, or fiberglass batting to try to deaden the sound. "But in places where silence is really critical—such as a TV room with a bathroom right above it—I'd go for cast iron, even though it costs more," he says.

CAST IRON *(LEFT)* AND PLASTIC

types: valves

A shutoff valve does exactly what its name suggests, but not all shutoffs are the same. "For pretty much the same price you can have stop valves, ball valves, or gate valves," says Richard. "But I'd take a ball valve any day." Here's why:

STOP VALVE: **This is the most widely used shutoff valve** (below right, shown partially disassembled). **With its compact handle, the stop valve seals off water by compressing a washer (which eventually must be replaced) against a metal seat. Some have a small threaded drain port on the side that can be used for draining water from nearby pipes or fixtures during repairs. Stop valves are generally the least expensive type of valve.**

GATE VALVE: **With a round, knurled handle like that of an outdoor spigot, a gate valve** (below left) **is the original shutoff and creates a metal-to-metal seal. Corrosion can cause valves to fail, however, either because the shaft inside breaks or because the inner parts bind.**

BALL VALVE: **Identifiable by its lever handle, the ball valve** (center) **contains a stainless-steel sphere that presses against a Teflon or rubber washer to create a long-lasting, dripproof seal. It's easy to tell how far open the valve is by looking at the position of the lever.**

stores. "I've never heard of a case where they've opened up a completely plugged drain," he says. Instead, the material will coagulate and harden, making life difficult for the person who ultimately has to go in and clear the blockage. Worse, these caustic drain openers may actually eat away at metallic pipes over time, and could also upset the delicate bacterial balance in septic tanks. "Nothing," he explains, "beats a snake that goes down and physically scrapes a clogged or sluggish drain back to health."

working with copper pipe Among the materials used for water supply pipes, copper is the king. "Copper is a time-proven commodity," says Richard. Unlike galvanized or cast iron, it resists corrosion; and unlike some plastics, it can safely be used to carry drinking water—and unlike plastic, it's approved for this use by all local building codes. Because of this, Richard usually relies on copper to repair deteriorating pipes in old systems.

To cut copper pipe, Richard uses a tubing cutter, which makes a straight, smooth edge—that's the surest way to guarantee a watertight connection. Then he reams the cut edges with a wedge-shaped fitting on the cutter to remove any metal burrs caused by the cutter. Once the new piping has been cut and the fit tested, Richard prepares it for soldering (right).

If a small section of galvanized pipe leaks, Richard usually opts for replacing the entire stretch of pipe. "It takes a lot of effort to get in there and replace a small section, and if the whole pipe's going, it's a waste of time and money to do it again and again," he says. "The cost of the piping is nothing compared to the cost of the labor, so you might as well replace as big a piece as you can."

repairing and installing shutoff valves Beneath a sink lies a pair of valves that make it possible to turn off the supply of hot and cold water to the faucet. "Old sinks never had individual shutoff valves, but they come in handy because you can shut off

Soldering basics: ***1.*** *The most important step is to clean the outside of the pipe and the inside of all fittings to a shiny copper color, using emery cloth. Any imperfection in the mating surfaces will prevent solder from adhering.* ***2.*** *Richard then brushes on a thin layer of paste, called flux: It's a catalyst that allows solder to bond to the copper.* ***3.*** *Using a propane torch, Richard heats one side of the fitting until the flux bubbles, then touches the solder to the opposite side. As the solder melts, it will be drawn into the hotter side of the joint.* ***4.*** *For a finishing touch, Richard wipes off excess solder.*

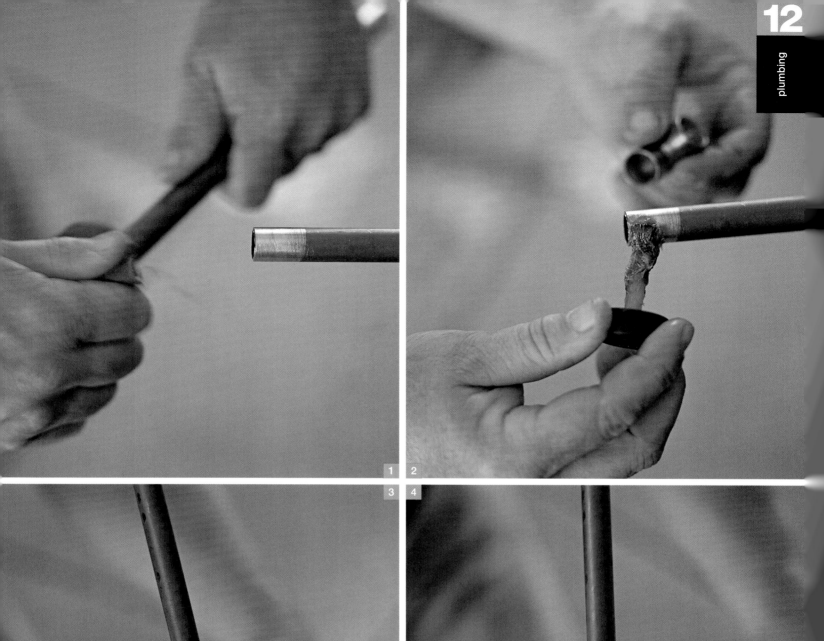

1

2

3

4

1

2

water to an individual fixture so it can be repaired," says Richard. Toilets have a single shutoff valve for the same reason. "If a worn shutoff valve is dripping at the handle, you can tighten the dome-shaped bonnet nut directly beneath the handle," says Richard. If the valve still leaks, it should be replaced.

To replace the valve, Richard turns the main water supply off, cuts the supply pipe just below the valve, then solders on a new valve. "Or you can use a compression-type valve, which slides over the end of the pipe. When tightened with two wrenches, it makes a water-tight seal without soldering," says Richard. When he's finished, he attaches a flexible water supply tube to the tailpiece of the faucet and connects it to the new valve. "Under the best conditions, this should be a 1-hour job," says Richard. "Famous last words . . ."

servicing a showerhead When water is "hard," as it is in most parts of the country, mineral deposits accumulate inside show-erheads and reduce the flow. "If water just sort of drips out of the showerhead, this may very well be the cause," says Richard.

To fix the problem, Richard starts by brushing the nozzle, using an old toothbrush soaked in vinegar to loosen the clogging. Then he delicately inserts a thin wire, such as an unwound paper clip, into each of the shower nozzle holes. "You just poke gently at the block-age, then flush it out by turning on the shower for a second," says Richard "If you really jam the wire up there, you might push the blockage in even tighter."

The showerhead can be removed *(left)* if the clogs persist, but this seemingly simple task can give a homeowner headaches. "People think they can just unscrew the showerhead like the lid of a jar," he says. "But what often happens is that the shower arm breaks out of a threaded fitting inside the wall. If the fitting is damaged, you could be talking about a huge job: You'll have to tear off the wall covering and open the wall to fix it." To avoid this, Richard removes a showerhead very cautiously. The trick is to prevent the shower arm from turning as you unscrew the head. Often, Richard will put a second wrench on the arm to resist the turning force of the first wrench.

Removing a showerhead: **1.** *Holding the shower arm steady, Richard unscrews the showerhead using an adjustable wrench (duct tape protects the chrome).* **2.** *Before reinstalling the showerhead, he wraps the arm's threads with Teflon sealant tape.*

improvements:
curtains vs. doors

Without some sort of barrier, water will splash from a shower and cause not just wet floors but serious mold and mildew problems as well. Even worse, water that regularly splashes against the edge of a tub will eventually rot out the sub-floor, and that's a repair nobody likes to make. "You need to block the water with something, but whether it should be a shower curtain or a door is a matter of personal preference," says Richard, who admits to being a curtain man. "I just don't like showering behind a door—it makes me feel like I'm locked up inside a shower capsule," he says. Curtains, however, must be washed or replaced with some regularity to keep them fresh-looking and free of mold.

Another downside to doors is that they require more maintenance than a shower curtain does, mostly to keep the guide track they slide in free of dirt and soap scum. "That can be a surprisingly labor-intensive proposi-tion," says Richard. And positioning a door requires a lot more precision than simply hanging a curtain. "There's an art to installing these things, because as much as contractors try, bathroom walls, ceilings, and tubs usually are not level and plumb."

One way to reduce the maintenance headaches of shower doors, says Richard, is to install European-inspired sliding doors. Richard likes the way they look, a purely personal reaction, but he's even more pleased with how they work. "What they have is a simple flip-down track that exposes every place where scum used to collect in the old rollers," he says. "That makes all the difference in the world for maintaining things." When something is easy to clean, it is far more likely to be kept in good working order.

types: kitchen and bath faucets

You have to understand the inner workings of a faucet to make the right repairs. The major types include:

COMPRESSION VALVE: In this faucet, a soft washer is pressed against a harder valve seat to keep water from seeping out. Faucets containing these valves are easy to identify: The handles turn 180 degrees or more.

BALL-TYPE CONTROL: This faucet controls the flow of hot and cold water with a perforated brass or plastic sphere that moves like a hip joint.

CARTRIDGE VALVE: Here, water flow is controlled by a plastic or brass cylinder within an outer housing. Turning the handle or lever lines up the holes so the water flows. Faucets with these valves have a single handle that is pulled straight up to turn on the water.

DISC VALVE: The handles of these faucets turn only 90 degrees. The valve contains a pair of perforated ceramic discs so smooth that no water can pass between them when they're pressed together. When holes in the discs line up, water flows. "I'm a big fan of these faucets," says Richard. "They seem to last forever."

replacing faucets Worn-out or outdated faucets can be replaced *(right)*, as long as the tailpieces of the new faucet fit through the mounting holes in the sink or countertop. (The tailpieces are those cylindrical parts that extend below the sink and connect to the hot- and cold-water supplies.) The standard arrangement is for the tailpieces to be either 4 or 8 inches apart on center (from centerline to centerline), though some faucets have tailpieces that fit through a single hole. The diameter of the holes can vary, too, which can further complicate replacement. "Some of the really old lavatories have tiny mounting holes, and there's no way a homeowner can add a modern faucet to them," says Richard. To check the size and spacing of the mounting holes, take a look from beneath the sink.

Getting the old faucet out can be tough. The first step is to disconnect the water supply tubes from the faucet. If the nuts holding the old faucet in place from below are corroded, Richard sprays on a penetrating oil to loosen them or heats them with a 3-second blast from a propane torch. Then he takes them off with a basin wrench, a long-handled tool that can be used easily in tight areas. "A standard wrench can work," says Richard, "but your knuckles will end up as raw as your patience." The job should take about an hour, he adds. "Leave yourself more time if you don't know what you're doing, or hire someone who does and watch over his shoulder so you'll know what to do next time."

When replacing a faucet, Richard always installs new supply tubes that connect the supply pipe to the tailpiece of the faucet. "Old ones wear out, and there's no point in going through this effort only to have them spring a leak when you're all done," he says. He prefers to use supply tubing made of chrome-plated brass because it's visually less obtrusive than flexible supply tubes, and because it's a traditional product with many leak-free years behind it.

unclogging drains and traps When a drain clogs, the first weapon should be a plunger, which breaks up clogs by creating

Replacing a faucet: 1. Once the original faucet is gone, Richard removes all traces of old putty on the sink and then inserts the new faucet (this one includes a sealing gasket; otherwise Richard would seal the area with plumber's putty). 2. Down below, he slips friction washers and mounting nuts onto the mounting bolts, then tightens the nuts with a basin wrench. 3. Richard cuts new supply tubing to fit (or uses flexible supply tubes). Before tightening the nuts, he dabs pipe joint compound on the threads to ensure a watertight seal. 4. Finally, he connects the faucet's pop-up mechanism.

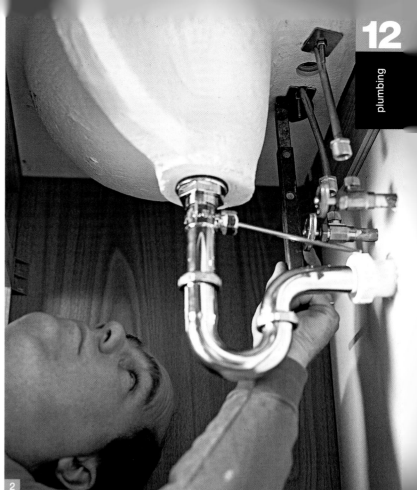

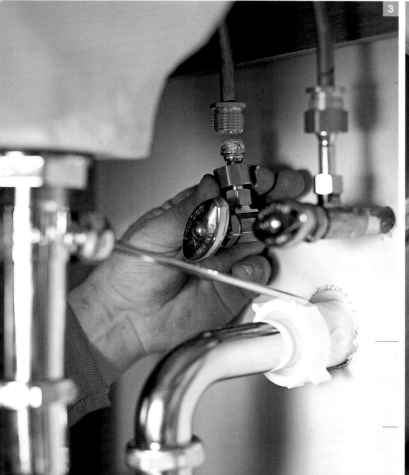

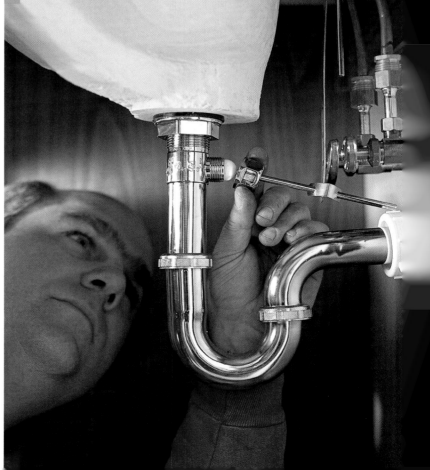

a partial vacuum in the drain line. "It's simple to use, and it's usually effective," says Richard, but most people use it improperly, particularly when unclogging a toilet. Because a toilet trap narrows as it leaves the bowl, the idea is to suck the clog upward so it can be removed. "The last thing you want is to push it farther into the pipe, where it might make the situation worse." If a clogged sink or tub has an overflow opening, plug the overflow with a wet rag before plunging to prevent air from breaking the suction of the plunger. Otherwise, you could plunge away all day with nothing to show for your efforts.

If plunging fails, Richard resorts to mechanical methods. A closet auger *(left)* is specifically for use on toilets; its design prevents damage to the porcelain. A hand snake, on the other hand, is just for sink and tub drains. The tool has a flexible steel cable that can be pushed into the drain to break up or remove obstructions. "It takes some skill to manipulate the auger through bends in pipes," says Richard. The right way is to keep the cable retracted until the snake has been pushed into the trap. Otherwise, the flexible cable will flop around and could scratch sink and tub surfaces.

adjusting the flush of a toilet As with many portions of a plumbing system, toilets depend on gravity. When the handle is pushed down, it lifts a chain inside the toilet tank that raises a rubber seal, and that in turn allows water to rush down into the toilet bowl. This forces wastewater out of the bowl, through the trap, and into the main drain. When the tank is empty, the rubber seal flaps shut and a water valve releases water into the tank. As the water rises, it lifts a hollow float ball that's connected to the valve by a metal rod. When the tank is full, the rod causes the valve to shut off. If you take the lid off a toilet and flush, you'll see how this all works.

Several problems can occur in this simple succession of events, and many of them are related to the length of the chain that connects the handle to the rubber seal at the base of the tank. If the chain has

*Clogged drains are among the most common of plumbing problems. **1.** To unclog a toilet, Richard seats the plunger over the toilet's trap, then gives it a steady push downward followed by a sharp pull back up. "Pulling up rather than pushing down," he says, "does most to break up the clog." **2.** If plunging doesn't clear up the problem, Richard employs a special type of snake called a closet auger. **3.** To unclog a tub drain, Richard pulls the stopper assembly free and removes accumulations of hair. **4.** If the drain still runs slowly, he'll insert the cable of a hand snake to bust up the clog.*

improvements:
flush mechanisms

The flush mechanism inside a toilet tank will wear out after 15 or 20 years, depending on the amount of use and the mineral content of the water. Most can be replaced part by part, and often with a trip to any hardware store. If the part is old, a more diligent search might be called for. "If you can, take the mechanism to a plumbing supply store so you can test the fit there," says Richard. "Plumbing suppliers won't be able to help you if you walk in and ask for 'a doohickey that connects to the watchammacallit.'" Old mechanisms can be replaced entirely, but in a period home, says Richard, "it's a shame not to look for the parts that can offer continued life to a beautiful antique toilet."

TRADITIONAL FLUSH MECHANISM

REPLACEMENT FLUSH MECHANISM

improvements:
kitchen sinks

These days, the materials, styles, and colors available for kitchen sinks are so varied that picking one requires as much research as choosing a computer.

Despite the variety, Richard remains a traditionalist: "I prefer good old stainless steel," he says. It's resilient and resists dings, can be scoured with abandon using cleanser, and doesn't show dirt. "By contrast, I also have a small white porcelain sink in my kitchen, near the coffee maker, and I can never keep it clean," he says. "Every little drip of coffee catches my attention; it seems like I'm constantly rinsing it."

Another decision involves the way a sink is mounted on the counter. Self-rimming sinks are easy to install; they just plunk into a hole cut into the countertop. Flush-mount sinks fit in the same way, but the lip between the sink and the counter is not as pronounced. Undermount and apron sinks fit beneath the countertop and are more difficult to install correctly. "These are easy to keep clean, however," says Tom. "Just wipe crumbs and water right into the sink." Integral sinks, made of the same material as the countertop, are easy to install as well as easy to clean.

Don't forget the sink part that every drop of water must pass. The basket strainer can be a hefty metal casting *(below right)* or a light-duty assembly of plastic *(below left)*. "I'll take chrome-plated metal any day," says Richard.

too much slack, the seal won't lift high enough and the toilet won't flush well. If the chain is too tight, it could leave the flap partially open, resulting in a toilet that runs constantly. Another part that frequently needs adjustment is the float ball. "If it rides too high, water will just keeping running and pouring off through the overflow tube," says Richard. "People come to me and complain, 'My toilet runs and runs.'" The solution is quite simple: Richard simply bends the metal arm slightly until the toilet stops running.

troubleshooting sump pumps In some houses, water that accumulates beneath the basement floor is channeled into a small pit in one corner of the basement. The pit is formed by a perforated shell, and sitting at the bottom of the shell is a sump pump. The pump switches on when it senses that water has reached a certain level in the pit, then pumps it outdoors.

Submersible sump pumps sit inside the sump pit and have a motor that is entirely covered by water. Pedestal sump pumps have a motor that sits atop a pipe that lifts it above the basement floor. Richard doesn't prefer one over the other. What's important is that there's a check valve on the outgoing piping: It looks like a bulged fitting where the discharge pipe comes out of the pump. The check valve contains a rubber flap that prevents water from flowing back into the pit once it's been pumped out. "Without a check valve, the pump will switch off when the water's out of the pit, then switch right back on again when water in the discharge pipe flows back in," says Richard. "The pump will labor like crazy, and could even burn out."

Richard suggests checking a pump occasionally to make sure it's operating properly, by pouring a bucket of water into the pit until the pump switches on. "I'd do this two or three times a year, and right before I go on a long vacation," he advises.

replacing a toilet seat A toilet seat can often be replaced in a matter of minutes. A screwdriver and an open-end wrench are generally all that's needed to remove the plastic bolts holding the seat in place. The bolt heads are often concealed beneath a plastic flap, for aesthetic and sanitary reasons. When attaching the

To remove a submersible sump pump, unplug its power cord. Then disconnect the discharge pipe (shown here in Tom's left hand) at any convenient fitting above the sump pit.

new seat, the nuts should be turned by hand until snug, then turned another quarter turn or so with the wrench. "If you tighten them too much, you'll break the toilet," says Richard. Corrosion can make old nuts—particularly brass ones—nearly impossible to remove. That's when Richard pulls out a hacksaw. "Brass bolts are easy to cut," he says. Just protect the porcelain with a bit of tape.

anti-scald valves   The most common valve design for showers and tubs has two handles, with a diverter in the tub spout. "I have to say they're nothing less than primitive," says Richard. "If someone flushes a toilet or turns on a faucet somewhere else in the house, there will be a drop in the cold-water pressure. Then all that's left rushing out of the showerhead—and all over your body—is scalding hot water." Setting the thermostat on the water heater or boiler below 120 degrees lessens the hazard but won't eliminate it. Instead, Richard recommends replacing old valves with an anti-scald valve. It's a job for a professional, he admits. "But if every household had them, especially in families with young children or elderly adults, scalding wouldn't be a problem."

installing a freezeproof faucet   When water in an outdoor faucet freezes, says Richard, it expands, putting enough pressure on the faucet to split it open. "Nobody notices when the faucet freezes," he says, "but on the day it thaws, there'll be a geyser somewhere until someone turns the nearest shutoff valve."

This problem is easy to avoid. When winter starts, cut off the water supply to the outside faucet. "The shutoff valve is usually located 3 to 7 feet inside the house on the pipe leading to the faucet," says Richard. After the valve is off, open the outside spigot to drain any trapped water. "If you don't, water will freeze just as if you had left the supply on," he warns.

Another solution is to install a freezeproof faucet. It works just like an ordinary faucet, but the washer that opens and closes the pipe is located at the end of a long stem inside the house. "The faucet isn't difficult to install if you know how to work with copper pipe," says Richard, or you can turn it over to a plumber. Either way, he adds, "It's better than a flooded basement."

Freeze-proof faucets eliminate the need to drain spigots in advance of freezing weather. Here Richard inserts the faucet; next he'll solder its end to the copper supply piping.

safety: fire sprinklers

The increasingly common use of smoke detectors has drastically reduced the number of people killed in house fires. But there's an even more effective way to combat fires: fire sprinklers. Installed in ceilings and supplied by a network of pipes that can easily be retrofitted into a house, they send a spray of water onto a blaze. "They make a lot of sense," says Richard.

Sprinkler heads *(below)* fit into the ceiling of a room. When exposed to heat, each head can send 8 to 18 gallons of water per minute into the room. "Only the head that feels the heat comes on," notes Richard. "Most people think that they all come on and wreck the house, but that's not the case at all," he explains. And water from a single head is much less destructive than the deluge from a firefighter's hose.

Full sprinkler systems installed by plumbers or sprinkler specialists most often run on separate piping systems. But partial systems can be installed one room at a time by tapping into the nearest cold-water pipe. Flexible tubing can be snaked through ceilings and walls to make the job even easier.

Sprinklers must be supplied with at least 60 psi of water pressure. That's no problem for a municipal water supply. Wells, however, must be fitted with a pressure-boosting tank and supplied by a backup water source.

EXPOSED AND CONCEALED HEADS

spring service air conditioner / start exterior paint prep / inspect roof and siding for damage / caulk seams and gaps summer check gutters / paint fall check gutters—again / tune up heating system / remove screens and install storm windows / replace worn weatherstripping winter replace heating system filter / get bids for upcoming projects / dream

work calendar

january	
february	
march	
april	
may	
june	
july	
august	
september	
october	
november	
december	

floorplan

⅛ inch = 1 foot

contacts

contractor

plumber

electrician

painter

roofer

heating / AC

handyman

tape business cards here

DRILL BITS

A selection of sharp drill bits is essential for many repairs. Start with an index (a metal box that stores bits by size) of 118-degree bits and a selection of spade bits; buy additional bits as needed. Drilling into wood rarely calls for anything harder than chrome-vanadium steel. Metal boring requires high-speed steel, which has more chromium and molybdenum so the tip won't lose its temper in the high heat of drilling. Drilling into plastic or particleboard calls for steel with tungsten carbide for extra hardness.

ANATOMY OF A DRILL BIT

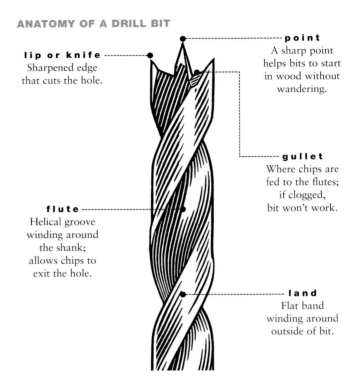

point
A sharp point helps bits to start in wood without wandering.

lip or knife
Sharpened edge that cuts the hole.

gullet
Where chips are fed to the flutes; if clogged, bit won't work.

flute
Helical groove winding around the shank; allows chips to exit the hole.

land
Flat band winding around outside of bit.

SHANKS

round
Standard shank for electric drills. Can slip if not well secured.

reduced round
Allows large bit to fit into a smaller drill chuck.

hex-sided
Facets on shank reduce tendency of bit to slip under power.

tapered square
Suitable only for use in a hand drill called a brace.

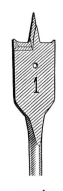

spade
Inexpensive; for holes up to 1½ inch dia.; not for fine work.

brad-point
Point keeps it centered; spurs cut clean, smooth hole.

double-cutter
Auger tip pulls bit into wood; lips cut cleanly.

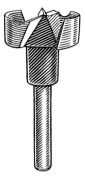

Forstner
Used to make ultra-smooth holes with flat bottoms.

METAL + PLASTIC

multi-spur
Aggressively chews through lumber; the plumber's friend.

118° twist
Good for holes in metal, and for small holes in wood. An all-purpose bit for household use.

60° twist
Designed for use in plastic and plastic laminate.

drill and countersink
Drills a hole for the screw and a countersink for the screwhead in one pass.

SPECIALTY

step
Makes different-size holes in sheet metal and thin materials.

spear-point
Carbide point grinds hole through glass and ceramic tile.

masonry
Carbide tip chews through concrete, brick, and mortar.

hole saw
Best for large through holes in wood; often used when installing door locksets.

SCREWS

Screws fasten materials together, but not like nails. Think of a screw as a miniature clamp and you'll be more likely to use it properly. The threads are one end of the clamp; as they twist through the lower piece of material, they pull the other end—the screwhead—closer.

In general, screws should be long enough so that two-thirds of their length will be threaded into the lower piece of stock. Unless the screw is self-drilling, drill a pilot hole first—the screw will hold better. Pilot holes in hardwood should be slightly larger than those in softwood. The holding power of any screw increases more with length than with diameter.

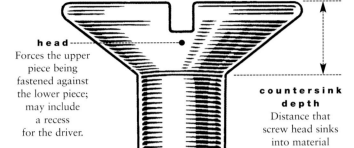

head
Forces the upper piece being fastened against the lower piece; may include a recess for the driver.

countersink depth
Distance that screw head sinks into material being fastened.

shank
Diameter is specified by gauge numbers. A #0 screw has a diameter of $\frac{1}{16}$ inch; each higher number is wider by about $\frac{1}{64}$ inch.

threads
Helical edges draw the head forward and provide withdrawal resistance.

point (tip)
A screw's length specifies how far in it will drive. Countersinking screws are measured from tip to top; others from tip to underside of head.

DRIVER TYPES

slotted
Came first but works worst; screwdriver blade slips easily.

Phillips
Tapered recess has flat-bottomed slots. Slip-resistant.

Frearson
Similar to Phillips, but with less tapered recess.

square
Increasingly common; shape dramatically reduces slippage.

combination
Accepts Phillips or square-drive screwdrivers.

hexagonal
Turned with wrench or socket to increase turning leverage.

HEADS

flat
Can be countersunk so top sits flush.

trim
Countersink; used on thin stock and trim.

bugle
Curved head: screw countersinks itself.

wafer
Like bugle head, but wider and thicker.

hexagonal
Wrench-driven; this one includes washer.

oval
Best where appearance counts.

round
Used where counter-sinking is not practical or desired.

pan
Extra-wide head allows great clamping strength.

truss
Like pan head, but has a lower profile. Used on furniture.

integral washer
Wide head holds even if hole is oversize.

fillister
Thick head allows deeper slot for better turning power.

flat with nibs
Ribs under head cut a countersink hole in hard materials.

THREADS

cut
Shallow threads; typical of wood screws.

rolled
Sharp, close threads; good for hardwoods.

coarse
Deep, wide threads; good for softwoods.

double lead
Two sets of threads; holds well and drives quickly.

hi-lo
Two sets of threads; common on concrete screws.

machine screw
Mostly for prethreaded holes in metal.

POINTS

gimlet
Traditional point for wood screws.

self-driving
Sharp tip starts screw without pilot hole.

auger
Self-drilling; sharp tooth cuts pilot hole, ejects waste.

self-drilling, for metal
Cuts hole and forms threads in metal.

NUTS
AND BOLTS

Nuts and bolts are graded by a variety of characteristics, including strength and thread count. Grade 8 bolts are the strongest among those usually available (they're heat-treated). Grade 2 bolts are cold-forged, and have about half the tensile strength of Grade 8 bolts. If a bolt has radiating hash marks on the head, add two to the number of marks to identify the grade.

When matching bolts to nuts, don't force a fit: the angle and spacing of threads can vary considerably. The two should mate easily.

hex
A general-purpose nut; very common for household use.

locknut
Deformed threads hold nut in place despite vibration.

wing
Allows rapid assembly and can be tightened by hand.

slotted
Used with drilled bolt; locks with a cotter pin or wire.

flange
Enlarged base spreads force and won't gouge surfaces.

acorn
Protects clothing and skin by completely covering bolt end.

TYPES OF DRIVES

slotted
Driver tip tends to slip; turn nut instead of bolt if possible.

socket
Also called an Allen head. Driven with tool called hex key.

Torx
Starlike pattern allows driver to hold bolt without help.

tri-groove
Tamper-resistant; requires special driver to remove.

pin-in-head Phillips
Center pin prevents use of common driver.

pin-in-head Torx
Locks out all but special drivers.

Phillips
Crosspattern reduces driver slippage and provides firm twist.

penta
Five-sided head is easily gripped by wrench or nut driver.

one-way
For security; installed easily but requires special removal tool.

square
Reduces driver slippage; used where no space to drive penta.

BOLTS

carriage
Square neck prevents bolt from turning in wood.

end hanger
Flattened end used for tie-downs.

thumbscrew
Spade head allows quick assembly and disassembly.

thumbscrew
Wing head is easier to turn than spade head.

U-bolt
For attachment to pipes. Requires bearing plate.

shoulder
Secures wheel assemblies on wagons and hand trucks.

stove
A general-purpose bolt with a slotted head.

hex-head
The most common general-purpose bolt.

timber
Low-profile top with flutes resists twisting.

elevator
Fangs dig into surface to eliminate twist.

bucket-tooth
Square fin locks head during tightening.

eye
Used when hanging or lifting things.

BOLT HEADS

square
Older head style, rarely used; socket driver won't work.

self-sealing
Flexible washer prevents liquids from leaking beneath head.

hex
Can drive with wrench, nut driver, or socket set.

flat
Top fits flush with surface of workpiece; primarily for metal.

oval
Used where appearance is important.

round
Domed head provides extra purchase for driver.

button
Low profile and wide; socket drive provides slip resistance.

flange button
Like button, but with greater contact area.

pan
Common head on bolts. Strong; good driving power.

cheese
Like pan head, but deeper slot reduces driver slippage.

fillister
Similar to cheese head, but with rounded top.

truss
Low-profile top; flat bearing surface. Also called oven head.

NAILS

Many problems are solved quickest by a nail. The ones shown here are the types you'll most likely need, but many others are available. Nails are found in various finishes and materials. Uncoated "bright" nails will rust outdoors; use stainless-steel or galvanized nails instead (electrogalvanized nails have a smooth surface and are less durable than rougher, hot-dipped galvanized nails). Nail length (*below*) is typically specified by a system that originated in 15th-century England; the abbreviation "d" stands for "penny." It's not necessarily a logical system anymore—it's just the one we inherited.

diamond
Wedges wood fibers apart; the most common point. Long diamond tips are extra sharp.

blunt
Squared tip of cut nail shears wood fibers to reduce splitting; used for plank flooring.

HEADS

plain
Standard head for common nails; flat on top and bottom.

duplex
Upper head remains accessible; used when removal is likely.

checkered
Holds extra zinc or paint so hammering won't chip it off.

I-head
Sometimes used to install hardwood finish flooring.

finish
Small head can be set below surface of wood and concealed.

countersunk
Curved underside won't dimple wood when driven flush.

THE LENGTH OF NAILS

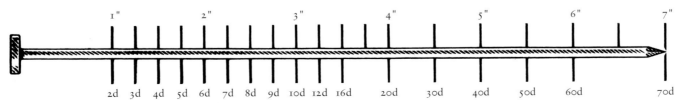

1"   2"   3"   4"   5"   6"   7"

2d 3d 4d 5d 6d 7d 8d 9d 10d 12d 16d 20d 30d 40d 50d 60d 70d

FRAMING

Used for fastening lumber. "Common" types have thick heads and shanks; cement-coated sinkers may hold better.

FINISH

Used mainly on molding and trim. Tiny finish nails are called brads; large ones are called casing nails.

DECK

Spiral flutes twist into the wood as the nail is driven, locking decking down tight. Ring-shank deck nails are also available.

ROOFING

Short and stout; large head holds asphalt and fiberglass shingles without tearing. Not for wood shingles.

SIDING

Typically slender and blunt to minimize splitting. Ring shank holds clapboards tightly to sheathing.

MASONRY

Made of hardened steel; brittle (wear safety glasses). Modest withdrawal resistance, so best on concrete floors.

FLOORING

Ring shank pins down underlayment; holds tight and reduces squeaks. Spiral versions secure finish flooring.

BOX

Thinner head than common nail; slender shank won't split thin wood slats, such as those in fruit crates.

DRYWALL

Extra-sharp point pierces surface; thin, wide head won't tear it. Ring-shank versions hold best.

CREDITS

WRITERS
Steve Thomas, Curtis Rist

PHOTOGRAPHERS
COVER AND INTRODUCTION
Pascal Blancon
CHAPTER OPENERS
Anthony Cotsifas. David Asher, stylist
SITE PHOTOGRAPHY
Keller & Keller
STUDIO PHOTOGRAPHY
Michael Grimm
CONTRIBUTORS
Darrin Haddad, Craig Raine, Thibeault Jeansen, Michael McLaughlin, Michael Myers, David Barry, David Carmack, Quentin Bacon, Noah Greenberg, Mark Lohman, John Kernick

ILLUSTRATORS
CHAPTERS 1 AND 2
Anders Wenngren for Art Department
ANATOMIES
Gregory Nemec
HARDWARE CHOOSER
Clancy Gibson, Gregory Nemec

THIS OLD HOUSE BOOKS®
EDITOR
Mark Feirer
ART DIRECTOR
Delgis Canahuate
PRODUCTION COORDINATOR
Robert Hardin
COPY EDITOR
Kathie Ness
PRODUCTION ASSOCIATE
Duane Stapp
NEW PRODUCT DEVELOPMENT DIRECTOR
Bob Fox

THANKS TO:
Danny Alessandro, Ltd.; Irreplaceable Artifacts/Demolition Depot; Vigilante Plumbing and Heating; Waterworks; Rohm & Haas Paint Quality Institute; Touchstone Woodworks; Stoll Fireplace Equipment; and Andersen Windows & Patio Doors. Special thanks to Anthony Wendling and Anthony Cortazzo at Applied Graphics Technology, and Mary Cahill Farella at WGBH.

Funding for *This Old House* on public television is provided by State Farm Insurance Companies, Ace Hardware Corporation, The Minwax & Krylon Brands, and the Saturn Corporation.